T0385595

THE YEMEN MODEL

THE YEMEN MODEL

Why U.S. Policy Has Failed
in the Middle East

ALEXANDRA STARK

Yale

UNIVERSITY PRESS

New Haven and London

Published with assistance from the foundation established in memory of Amasa Stone Mather of the Class of 1907, Yale College.

Yale University Press books may be purchased in quantity for educational, business, or promotional use. For information, please e-mail sales.press@yale.edu (U.S. office) or sales@yaleup.co.uk (U.K. office).

Set in Janson type by Newgen North America.
Printed in the United States of America.

Library of Congress Control Number: 2023943480
ISBN 978-0-300-25984-1 (hardcover : alk. paper)

A catalogue record for this book is available from the British Library.

This paper meets the requirements of ANSI/NISO Z39.48-1992 (Permanence of Paper).

10 9 8 7 6 5 4 3 2 1

For the survivors and victims of the world's forgotten wars

*For my great-grandmother and her daughter, survivors of
the Armenian genocide, and my grandfather's family
members, survivors of the Holocaust*

Contents

INTRODUCTION   1

1. A Brief History of External Intervention in Yemen's Wars   10

2. The U.S. Counterterrorism War in Yemen   27

3. Arab Spring, Arab Fall: Political Transition and the Failure
    of the National Dialogue Conference, 2011–2014   44

4. Regional Proxy Wars before 2015   59

5. Descent into "Chaos": Yemen's Civil War, 2015–2021   76

6. "Dumb Wars": The Obama Administration's War
    in Yemen   101

7. Maximum Pressure: The Trump Administration's War
    in Yemen   124

8. Congress and the Yemen Advocacy Coalition   139

9. The Biden Administration: Giving Diplomacy a Chance?   169

10. Lessons Learned   178

EPILOGUE   198

Acknowledgments   201
Notes   203
Bibliography   229
Index   257

THE YEMEN MODEL

Introduction

The ongoing flow of arms from the U.S. to Saudi Arabia and the UAE is directly contributing to civilian deaths, injuries, and suffering in Yemen.

—RADHYA AL-MUTAWAKEL, chairperson of Mwatana
for Human Rights

THE MISSILE STRIKE HIT a "legitimate target," Colonel Turki al-Maliki, a spokesman for the Saudi-led coalition, initially claimed.[1] On August 9, 2018, a coalition airstrike hit a bus filled with school-aged children in Saada governorate in northern Yemen. The strike killed at least twenty-nine civilians, including twenty-one children. An investigation by CNN and Mwatana for Human Rights, a prominent Yemeni human rights organization, found that the bomb that struck the bus, a Paveway MK-82, was manufactured by the American company Lockheed Martin.[2] The bomb had been sold to Saudi Arabia with the approval of both the U.S. State Department and Congress.

Ten years after President Barack Obama won an election promising to draw back from the Middle East and stop the United States from getting involved in "dumb wars," how did a U.S.-made bomb end up killing dozens of Yemeni children?

The answer, surprisingly, goes back to that very promise. Prior to March 2015, when the Saudi-led coalition's military intervention in the civil war in Yemen began, U.S. policy makers viewed Yemen through the narrow frame of counterterrorism. U.S. policy makers faced a dilemma: they needed to balance the expansive objective of eradicating al-Qaeda in the Arabian Peninsula (AQAP), while avoiding deploying conventional U.S. forces, which would risk American casualties and a possible quagmire. Instead, U.S. policy makers sought to "split the difference" by providing counterterrorism support to the personalist autocrat President Ali Abdullah Saleh and waging drone and missile strikes against suspected terrorists— strikes that sometimes killed Yemeni civilians—while committing few U.S. forces to the fight on the ground.

The Obama administration dubbed this approach to counterterrorism "the Yemen model" and advertised its success up until the day before the Saudi-led intervention in Yemen's civil war began.[3] Indeed, the Bush, Obama, and later Trump and Biden administrations, despite their policy differences on a wide range of issues, continued to use this approach in many counterterrorism contexts around the world. While this approach goes by many names, such as "by, with, and through" and "remote warfare," the idea is the same: partner with host-nation governments to fight terrorist organizations on the ground while minimizing the risks associated with more direct U.S. involvement.

Although the objectives were different, the U.S. approach to the Saudi-led coalition's intervention in Yemen's war was similar. The Obama administration had more important priorities in the region, namely, getting negotiations for the Iran nuclear agreement, the Joint Comprehensive Plan of Action (JCPOA), across the finish line while maintaining U.S. security partnerships with the Arab Gulf states of the GCC, or Gulf Cooperation Council. The GCC countries opposed the Iran nuclear deal and worried that the United States was withdrawing from the region. When Saudi officials approached the Obama administration to ask for its support for their intervention in Yemen, U.S. officials were not particularly eager to be involved in the war. Nevertheless, they saw supporting the intervention as a necessary exchange to keep GCC security partners onside after the Iran nuclear deal was signed. According to this logic, supporting the intervention would keep the United States from being dragged deeper into regional affairs.

Likewise, candidate Donald Trump ran for president in 2016 on a platform that gestured toward the United States leaving the Middle East. Yet as president, Trump doubled down on the old approach when he came into office. The Trump administration worked to deepen U.S. security partnerships with the GCC via arms sales and gave the coalition a green light to continue its intervention in Yemen.

This approach to managing U.S. security priorities in the Middle East has not worked—a fact that the recent history of U.S. engagement in Yemen has demonstrated time and time again. The narrow lens of counterterrorism did not allow U.S. policy makers to see that their partner, the regime of the corrupt autocrat President Ali Abdullah Saleh, was beginning to wobble even before the Arab Spring erupted in 2011. It meant that U.S. officials felt secure pushing forward Yemen's post–Arab Spring political transition process, the National Dialogue Conference, even as the process failed to resolve the underlying issues that generated the Arab Spring protest movement in the first place. And it allowed U.S. officials to believe that they could ultimately *stay out* of deeper involvement in the war in Yemen by providing logistical support to the intervention.

Instead of staying out, the United States became implicated in the conflict and its humanitarian fallout, including the civilian deaths that resulted from coalition airstrikes, such as the 2018 bus bombing. The intervention failed in its objective of containing the Houthis and Iranian influence. Instead, the war in Yemen created a humanitarian disaster, generated further instability in the region, and gave Iran an opportunity to increase its influence on the Arabian Peninsula on Saudi Arabia's southern border.

This recent history also demonstrates that while Yemen has long been viewed by U.S. officials as peripheral to U.S. security interests, the United States has been continuously pulled back into wars in Yemen. If the humanitarian suffering is not enough to warrant our concern about Yemen's wars (and it ought to be), then U.S. strategic interests should be.

Nor is U.S. engagement in Yemen's war anomalous in how the United States has approached the Middle East more broadly. Rather,

U.S. policy in Yemen is part of a broader pattern of U.S. engagement with U.S. security partners and proxy wars in Syria, Libya, and
elsewhere across the Middle East. The history of the United States'
failures (and occasional successes) in Yemen throughout the war can
therefore provide lessons not just for future U.S. engagement with
Yemen but for the U.S. approach to the Middle East in general.

U.S. engagement in Yemen's war is a case study of how the U.S.
approach to Middle East proxy wars and security partners has failed.
But it can also show us how we can sustainably reform Middle East
policy in a way that makes Americans and Yemenis safer and more
secure.

This book tells the story of U.S. and regional involvement in
the ongoing war in Yemen. It explores how Yemen's seemingly successful post–Arab Spring political transition fell apart, how regional
actors used proxy war strategies to pursue their own interests via
the war in Yemen, and how U.S. logistical and diplomatic support
made the Saudi-led coalition's intervention possible. It also shows
how U.S. diplomacy could help end the war. Instead of proposing
that the United States attempt to impose a peace on Yemen, "lessons
learned" explores how U.S. diplomacy can support a peace process
and political transition designed and led by Yemenis themselves.

The book concludes by drawing on this story to better understand how the United States should reorient its approach to the
Middle East to be more just and humane and to contribute to true
security and stability.

Lessons Learned

There are three major lessons that emerge from the recent history
of U.S. security engagement with Yemen. First, U.S. policy toward
Yemen tells us a great deal about U.S. security objectives in the Middle East—and how we must substantially *revise* the U.S. approach to
achieve our policy objectives there. Historically, U.S. policy makers
have not approached Yemen through the lens of Yemen itself but
rather as a means to achieve some other security end, whether that
was competing with and containing Soviet influence in the Middle
East during the Cold War, pushing back against Iran's proxy part-

nerships across the region while defending U.S. security partners from Iran, or defeating al-Qaeda in the Arabian Peninsula. Instead of achieving these aims, U.S. policy in Yemen has failed to prevent the outbreak of conflict and contributed to local and regional instability. In short, a focus on "security," narrowly defined, leaves all of us less secure.

What would an approach built around helping to give Yemenis the tools to build peace and prosperity look like instead? A stable Yemen that has internal and external support for mediation and conflict prevention, provides economic opportunity for its citizens, and strives to improve governance and stamp out corruption would be less likely to succumb to violent conflict, in turn preventing the potential for external military intervention. A stable Yemen would also make U.S. security partners like Saudi Arabia and the United Arab Emirates (UAE) safer and prevent the regional spillover effects of substate violence. A well-governed, prosperous Yemen would be better not just for Yemenis but also for the wider Middle East and for the United States.

A second lesson is about what U.S. foreign policy can *accomplish*— and what it cannot reasonably be expected to achieve. A major thread running through the U.S. approach to Yemen is the question of U.S. *leverage*. Policy makers and researchers have long debated whether and under what conditions the United States can use leverage with its allies and partners, such as arms sales and other kinds of security assistance, to affect those partners' behavior. This debate became evident in the news, for example, in October 2018, after the Saudi journalist and U.S. resident Jamal Khashoggi was brutally murdered and a United Nations investigation determined that senior Saudi officials were responsible. Some U.S. policy makers, commentators, and activists argued that the United States should substantially revise, if not completely sever, its relationship with Saudi Arabia and its de facto ruler, Crown Prince Mohammed bin Salman, in the wake of the murder. Others countered that to do so would risk losing potential future U.S. leverage with the Kingdom. Congress moved ahead to pass legislation blocking arms sales to the Kingdom and ending U.S. support for the Saudi-led intervention in Yemen, all in an attempt to force Saudi Arabia to pare down the civilian casualties associated with its campaign of airstrikes, open ports and airports to commerce, and eventually withdraw from Yemen altogether. Critics contended that Congress's actions did not matter all that much. Yet both historically and more recently during the current conflict, U.S. policy makers have successfully used U.S. leverage on a number of occasions to affect the behavior of external states that have militarily intervened in Yemen.

During the Obama, Trump, and Biden administrations, U.S. policy makers sometimes used U.S. leverage over the coalition to achieve relatively small but still significant shifts in the coalition's behavior, while at other times, for a variety of reasons, they declined to do so. Evidence in each case shows that U.S. leverage does matter: when the United States chose to exert leverage, it was able to shape how the intervening coalition behaved in Yemen. Understanding what U.S. leverage vis-à-vis its partners in the region can accomplish—and the limits of that leverage—can help us understand what we can expect U.S. policy in the Middle East to actually achieve, so we can calibrate our approach accordingly.

Finally, this book explores how we can *change the U.S. approach* to the Middle East to align U.S. policy goals with the tools we have to achieve them. Even in the absence of elite political will, democratic engagement can change U.S. security policy. The U.S. national security arena has long been dominated by gatekeeping forces who insist that people without a specific expertise are not qualified to weigh in on such existential and complex issues. This has created a resistance to change within the U.S. national security community, as well as a suspicion of anyone deemed an outsider, including activists and even, sometimes, the American people themselves. Yet this is not how we treat domestic U.S. policy issues, and it is not how we ought to approach security policy either. Democratic engagement on any U.S. policy issue, whether in the foreign or domestic policy realm, should be seen as inherently valuable to policy making, not as an impediment to good policy.

The domestic politics of U.S. engagement with Yemen's war provides potent lessons for how we might reform U.S. security policy in the Middle East and the United States' approach to the world more broadly. From 2017 through 2020, U.S. support for the war in Yemen became a surprising rallying cry for Americans to express their discontent with the United States' "endless wars." Stymied by the Trump White House, which prioritized U.S. relationships with Saudi Arabia and other security partners over any other goals, a scrappy group of advocates in Washington, DC, a national network of grassroots activists, and a handful of members of Congress who cared deeply about the issue, working alongside institutions as ideologically diverse as the Charles Koch Institute and the Open Society Foundations, managed to shift the political conversation about the stakes of U.S. involvement in the war in Yemen.

Both of the bills that passed Congress, one that would block arms sales and another that would end U.S. support for the war, were ultimately vetoed by President Trump. Nevertheless, pressure from Congress and advocates still created distinct changes in the U.S. approach to the war. The United States ended its aerial refueling support to the coalition in late 2018, and by engaging the American public and a wider array of policy makers, the legislation created pressure for Saudi Arabia and the UAE to acknowledge that a military victory was out of reach and to engage in cease-fire negotiations. When President Joe Biden came into office in 2021, he announced an end to U.S. offensive support for the coalition. The Yemen advocacy coalition in the United States, and three presidential administrations' responses to pressure from Congress over Yemen, can teach us a great deal about how we can change U.S. Middle East policy.

Two Caveats

There are two important caveats about what the book does not cover. First, it does not provide a comprehensive history of the war in Yemen. As Paul Dresch has written, "All who write on Yemen feel we oversimplify."[4] I have instead chosen to focus on the most relevant events, dynamics, and parties to the conflict, while inevitably leaving things out due to limits in the scope of the book. Chapter 2 in particular, which covers the history of wars and many of the political dynamics in Yemen over the second half of the twentieth and the early twenty-first century, necessarily skims over a lot of important history in a relatively short space, while chapter 6 seeks to provide a short but comprehensive overview of the dynamics of the war itself between 2015 and 2021.

Throughout the book, citations provide the reader with additional resources on other aspects of Yemen's history. There are a number of scholars working today who have produced excellent resources on various aspects of this history as well as the ongoing war, many (but not all) of whom are cited throughout the book. Readers may also consult the bibliography at the end of the book for sources of additional reading.

Second, again because of its scope, the book is focused on U.S. policy in Yemen's war specifically. There is a certain irony in framing a book around the United States when I believe that too much attention has been given to the role of the United States in the Middle East in Western research and media and not enough to local actors, especially Yemenis themselves. The framing of the book is not meant to take away from the agency and autonomy of Yemenis; rather, my aim is to understand how U.S. policy can contribute to better outcomes for Yemenis and for Americans—and where it has gone wrong.

Methods

In the course of my research, I conducted more than sixty interviews, both on and off the record, with current and former officials, advocates, congressional staffers, and other experts on Yemen and U.S. foreign policy. Other primary source material consulted includes public statements from leaders like Saudi Arabia's Crown Prince Mohammed bin Salman (MbS) and the UAE's President Mohamed bin Zayed (MbZ) and other senior officials; U.S. officials' memoirs; newspaper reporting from U.S. and Gulf sources (all translations from Arabic are my own), including statements from officials that I was often able to corroborate and expand on in my interviews; testimony before Congress from policy makers and experts; congressional legislation; and archival research at the John F. Kennedy and Lyndon B. Johnson Presidential Libraries, the Kew National Archives in the United Kingdom, the

CREST archive (the CIA Records Search Tool), and the Foreign Relations of the United States (FRUS) series. I also consulted a wide range of secondary sources, including books by scholars and journalists and reports from key organizations including ACAPS, Amnesty International, the Armed Conflict Location & Event Data Project (ACLED), the Congressional Research Service, Human Rights Watch, the International Crisis Group, Mwatana for Human Rights, RAND, the Sana'a Center for Strategic Studies, the Senate Committee on Foreign Relations, the UN Yemen Panel of Experts, the Yemen Data Project, the Yemen Peace Project, and the Yemen Policy Center. The book draws on the research I conducted for my PhD dissertation at Georgetown University, as well as my subsequent research at New America, a think tank in Washington, DC, where I have had numerous conversations with officials, journalists, experts, advocates, aid workers, artists, academics, and others.

CHAPTER ONE

A Brief History of External
Intervention in Yemen's Wars

This peanut war will be with us a long time yet.

—ROBERT KOMER, senior official in the Kennedy administration, on the civil war in North Yemen

NORTH AND SOUTH YEMEN existed as separate political entities for centuries. Indeed, in recent history, Yemen was a united polity only between 1990 through the Houthi coup in 2014. Even in that brief period of unity, Yemen experienced substantial internal instability, including a secessionist civil war in 1994, six rounds of fighting between the Houthis and the central government throughout the early 2000s, and a southern separatist protest movement beginning in 2004, among other violent and peaceful efforts to contest the legitimacy of the central state.

When both North and South Yemen became independent states in the 1960s, the United States viewed Yemen as largely peripheral to its immediate security interests. While successive U.S. administrations saw their role in the Middle East as increasingly important to U.S. national security, from the perspective of U.S. policy makers, conflicts in Yemen remained proxies for broader regional and global rivalries. This chapter briefly explores the history of conflict and external military intervention in Yemen since the 1960s.

Yemen Divided

In *A History of Modern Yemen*, Paul Dresch writes that the idea of a unified Yemeni state emerged in the twentieth century "in a context shaped by outside powers." Throughout the nineteenth century, political structures across Yemen "were defined by reference to religion or dynasty, not territory," with rulers' claims overlapping "in both time and space."[1] Much of the political history of Yemen in the twentieth century revolves around the idea of a single, central state, although this unified state did not emerge until 1990.[2]

Throughout Yemen's history, "power-hungry outsiders have always lusted after Yemen's strategic location, for whoever controls its western seaboard controls the entrance to the Red Sea," Tim Mackintosh-Smith writes.[3] The British colonized southern Yemen in 1839, when they began to occupy the southern port city of Aden and gradually extended indirect control over Aden's hinterland. The port itself was strategically important to the maritime power, since it served as a stop to refuel steam ships on the journey between Suez and Bombay. As a result, Aden grew into a large cosmopolitan city. The British formed a system of indirect rule via alliances with local sultans that became the Protectorates of South Arabia. By 1958, Aden was one of the world's busiest ports, serving as a point of connection for global commerce and Britain's imperial strategy in the Middle East and beyond. The hinterland outside of Aden, however, primarily served the British colonizers as a buffer between the port city and the Ottoman-occupied north and was largely neglected by its colonizers.

In northern Yemen, Ottoman conquest of territory in Yemen began in the sixteenth century. The territorial scope of Ottoman territory in Yemen expanded and contracted over the ensuing centuries, before the collapse of the Ottoman Empire at the end of World War I. By 1904, most parts of northern Yemen outside of major cities fell under the authority of Imam Yahya, whose family had ruled locally for almost one thousand years. After the Ottoman departure,

Imam Yahya expanded the Imamate's influence southward. By 1934, Imam Yahya had control over much of Yemen's territory outside of British-held Aden.

North Yemen: The Yemen Arab Republic (YAR)

The north-south territorial division persisted through much of the twentieth century. In North Yemen, a 1962 coup by revolutionary military officers, led by Abdullah Sallal and backed by Egypt's President Gamal Abdel Nasser, deposed Imam Yahya's son, Imam al-Badr, and established the Yemen Arab Republic (YAR). Following the coup, Imam al-Badr and a group of supporters were able to flee across the border to Saudi Arabia and conducted an insurgent war, backed by Saudi Arabia and with the support of other monarchies in the region, that lasted until 1970.

The civil war in North Yemen became an arena for regional and global rivalries. While it began as a localized conflict over control of the Yemeni state, the 1962 civil war became a battleground in the competition for regional hegemony between Egypt's President Nasser and his revolutionary socialist, pan-Arab allies, on the one hand, and Saudi Arabia and its coalition of conservative monarchies,

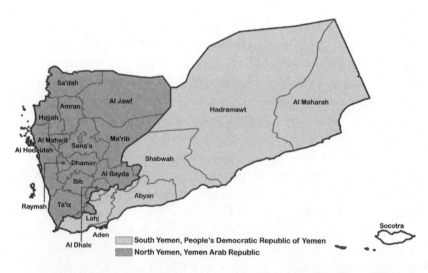

North and South Yemen through 1990. (Credit: Ghaidaa Alrashidy)

on the other, part of a broader ideological conflict that Malcolm Kerr has termed the "Arab Cold War." Dana Schmidt, a journalist who reported from Yemen during the war, wrote that the war in Yemen "has been fought . . . only partly because of Yemen. More of the struggle has been due to the rivalry between Egypt and Saudi Arabia."[4] What otherwise might have remained a localized dispute instead became a regional proxy war that lasted more than seven years and threatened to draw the United States and Soviet Union into a direct confrontation at a time when Cold War tensions were at a peak. Egypt ultimately deployed more than half of its total ground forces, up to seventy thousand troops, to Yemen at points during the conflict. Nasser later referred to the intervention as "my Vietnam," in recognition of its high cost to Egypt and the failure of Nasser's nation-building efforts in the YAR.[5] The conflict also saw one of the first large-scale documented uses of chemical weapons since World War I.[6]

Sallal's forces were inspired by Nasser's revolutionary Free Officers movement, and Sallal's coalition, known as the republicans, was made up of fellow army officers as well as members of the southern Shafi'i tribes, disaffected northern Zaydi tribes, and merchants. Al-Badr's forces, the royalists, included many of the northern Zaydi tribes, as well as Yemenis who opposed Egyptian interference in Yemen.[7] Within a week of the coup, the United Arab Republic (UAR), the official name for Egypt at the time, had deployed troops and supplies to support the new regime, called the Yemen Arab Republic, and its republican forces, while Saudi Arabia and Jordan provided funding and diplomatic support for the royalists. Britain also provided the royalists with covert support.

Saudi Arabia and its fellow Middle Eastern conservative monarchies, on the other hand, provided funding and support to the royalists and the displaced imam. The monarchs feared that if left unchecked, the Arab socialist fervor ignited by Nasser would continue to spread across the Middle East and threaten their own regimes. Saudi and U.S. officials worried that Nasser might use North Yemen as a platform to launch an invasion of Saudi Arabia or support pro-Nasser Saudi dissidents.[8] Nasser's propaganda attacks on the Saudi and Jordanian monarchies and an attempt to drop supplies intended for Saudi dissidents into Saudi Arabia in February

1963 only reinforced this concern.[9] Senior Saudi and Jordanian officials repeatedly registered their concern that the United States was
conceding significant ground by allowing Egyptian forces to remain
in Yemen while pressuring Saudi Arabia and Jordan not to become
further involved.[10]

So commenced a series of negotiations between U.S. and Saudi
officials to try to persuade the Kingdom to end its support for the
royalists. In November 1962, Jordan's King Hussein sent several
Jordanian aircraft to Saudi Arabia at the Kingdom's request to deter
attacks by Egyptian forces. That same day, the State Department
telegrammed the U.S. embassy in Saudi Arabia that the use of the
aircraft, funded by a U.S. military assistance program, "in Saudi Arabia constitutes [a] violation [of the] terms of sale": "You should make
clear to [the government of Jordan] that employment [of] US fi-
nanced weapons for other than defensive purposes would prejudice
future US military sales."[11] The six Jordanian aircraft were summar-
ily returned to Jordan less than two weeks later.[12]

The use of leverage often requires coercion, as it did in the case
of the Jordanian aircraft, when U.S. officials threatened to curtail
future arms sales to Jordan, but it can also involve incentives and
assurances. In July 1963, the United States deployed eight F-100s,
six KB-50 air-to-air refueling tankers, and more than five hundred
U.S. military personnel to Dhahran. Known as Operation Hard
Surface, the aircraft and personnel were provided by U.S. officials
in exchange for Saudi Arabia to cease providing aid to the royalists
in North Yemen and to cooperate with the UN mission to arrange a
cease-fire. U.S. officials agreed to Operation Hard Surface "subject
to the following conditions: (a) it will be wholly contingent on a firm
Saudi undertaking to suspend aid simultaneously to the Yemeni royalists. . . . The squadron will be withdrawn if Saudi Arabia resumes
aid the royalists without U.S. concurrence."[13] According to a memo
recounting a meeting between President John F. Kennedy's personal
envoy to Yemen, Ellsworth Bunker, and Saudi Arabia's King Faisal,
Bunker conveyed that President Kennedy was ready to deploy a
U.S. air force squadron "upon His Highness' agreement to suspend
Saudi aid to the royalists."[14] U.S. officials confirmed in July that the
Saudis had stopped aid to the royalists and that the threat to with-

draw Operation Hard Surface "if they start cheating again acts as a deterrent."[15]

External intervention in the North Yemen civil war ended due to the June 1967 Six-Day War. Heavy casualties and materiel losses inflicted on Egyptian forces meant that Nasser could no longer sustain the intervention in Yemen, and Egypt's withdrawal from Yemen began soon after. At the August 1967 Khartoum Conference, Nasser and Saudi Arabia's King Faisal negotiated Egypt's withdrawal from Yemen. A November 1967 ceremony at Hodeidah port marked the departure of the last Egyptian soldier.

In 1974, another military coup placed a coalition of military officers, tribal leaders, and technocrats at the head of the Yemen Arab Republic through the mid-1970s. In 1978, a junior, relatively unknown military officer, Ali Abdullah Saleh, was appointed president. Like a succession of his short-lived predecessors, he was not expected to last long in office. Yet Saleh served as president of North Yemen until unification in 1990 and remained president of unified Yemen until he was forced to step down in 2011.

South Yemen: The People's Democratic Republic of Yemen (PDRY)

The 1962 coup in the north and the strategic importance of Aden's port spurred the British to deploy more forces to Aden.[16] The presence of British forces, and the sense that imperial Britain's influence was waning as revolutionary movements like Gamal Abdel Nasser's 1952 revolution in Egypt grew, encouraged insurgent forces in Yemen, including the National Liberation Front (NLF) and the Front for the Liberation of Occupied South Yemen (FLOSY), to resist the British colonial occupation. The violence escalated in 1963, leading to the October Revolution, or what the British called the Aden Emergency, a sustained violent insurgency that hastened the British departure from Yemen.

The United Kingdom formally announced its impending withdrawal from the Gulf region in January 1968. But in southern Yemen, after organized opposition led by labor unions and a guerrilla insurgency, Britain hastily withdrew on November 30, 1967, turning the country over to the National Liberation Front. South Yemen officially became the People's Democratic Republic of Yemen (PDRY) in 1970. The PDRY was the only Marxist state in the Gulf region and received substantial backing from the Soviet Union and China.[17]

The new PDRY state had a difficult start: Aden's commerce had been decimated by the closure of the Suez Canal earlier that year, while "the removal of the British military base wiped out thousands of jobs."[18] South Yemen increasingly came to depend on Soviet support and "became almost wholly reliant on [Soviet] arms."[19] The PDRY was the fifth-largest recipient of Soviet aid in the world by 1980, and many of its political leaders had trained in East Germany or the Soviet Union.[20]

The British withdrawal from the Gulf also opened the way for increased U.S. influence in the politics of the Gulf. Acting as successor to the British, "Washington assumed strategic responsibility for the region as a whole," becoming a major source of arms sales to former British clients.[21] The United States established relations with the YAR in 1972, but the PDRY, with its close connection to the Soviet Union, had a rivalrous relationship with the United States.

In contrast to the YAR, where President Ali Abdullah Saleh exploited tribal structures to build up a personal patronage network, the PDRY government worked to eradicate tribal structures and build a large, bureaucratic civil service, engage in national planning, secularize education, and implement land reform. East Germany provided an example for the PDRY's 1968 constitution and subsequent governance structure. Like the YAR, the PDRY also experienced substantial political turbulence, including the assassination of a president in 1978, a proxy conflict with North Yemen that flared up periodically in the 1970s, and a failed coup in 1986 that followed a struggle for leadership of the Yemen Socialist Party (YSP), the PDRY's ruling party.

For three weeks in September and October 1972, fighting broke out in a series of clashes between the YAR and the PDRY. Insurgent groups in the south had been receiving support from the north, and the growing tensions led to clashes along the border and eventually sustained fighting. The YAR was supported by Saudi Arabia, the United States, and the United Kingdom, while the PDRY received support from the Soviet Union. The war ended with a cease-fire brokered by the Arab League and the October 28 Cairo Agreement, in which leadership of both countries agreed to the eventual unification of Yemen—at least in principle.

Despite the agreement around unification, fighting between north and south broke out again in 1979. Hostility between the two countries grew after the president of the YAR, Ahmad al-Ghasmi, was assassinated under mysterious circumstances during a meeting with an envoy from the PDRY in 1978. The president of the PDRY, Salim Rubai Ali, was likewise killed in a coup in 1978. After northern forces crossed the border following border clashes in February 1979, the PDRY, with the support of the Soviet Union, Cuba, and East Germany, retaliated with a three-front invasion of North Yemen. Once again, the Arab League stepped in to negotiate the 1979 Kuwait Agreement, after which Arab League forces deployed along the border to keep the peace.

The Soviet presence in the PDRY worried U.S. policy makers during the Cold War. The Soviets used Aden to support their intervention in Ethiopia and supported the PDRY's efforts to encourage rebellion in North Yemen. During the Carter administration, National Security Advisor Zbigniew Brzezinski saw the Soviet presence in South Yemen as part of a larger "arc of crisis" that extended from the Middle East to Southern Africa via the Horn. The United States supported efforts to "create dissension" in the PDRY and provided arms to the YAR during the war, even dispatching a naval task force to the Red Sea region to deter further incursion into North Yemen from the PDRY.[22] In the 1979 war between North and South Yemen, according to Fred Halliday, the United States saw its role as "'drawing the line' against communism on the border of the PDRY."[23] The United States took the war—and the threat it believed was posed by the PDRY due to Soviet backing—seriously. U.S. intelligence evaluation at the time concluded that the PDRY attacks could "succeed in gaining radical control over the southern parts of the YAR or toppling the government in Sana [sic]."[24] Yet while the conflict in Yemen represented global U.S.-Soviet tensions, it was not itself seen as a security priority for U.S. officials: noting that the conflict is not even mentioned in the memoirs of President Jimmy Carter or his national security advisor Zbigniew Brzezinski, Halliday argues that "the Yemens, even more than other

Third World conflicts, were of symptomatic rather than intrinsic significance" to U.S. foreign policy.[25]

South Yemen experienced its own brief civil war in January 1986. Growing tensions between rival political factions and the Yemen Socialist Party (YSP) led to intraparty conflict and eventually armed violence in Aden and part of the surrounding hinterland. Noel Brehony writes that "the two sides had been arming for months" before January 1986, and "the political situation had deteriorated sharply in the weeks before" the war began.[26] On January 13, over the course of one night, thousands of people were killed in fighting.[27] Official records put the total number of casualties at 4,330, but observer estimates were significantly higher. Casualties included "party officials, ministers and senior government" officials, as well as "officers, NGOs [nongovernmental organizations] and soldiers killed during the ten days of fierce fighting."[28]

While fighting was intense, it was short-lived. The losing faction, led by Ali Nasir Muhammed, who until recently had served as prime minister of South Yemen and general secretary of the YSP from 1980 through 1986, went into exile. Between thirty and forty thousand supporters of Ali Nasir fled, "taking their weapons to North Yemen."[29] A new leadership of South Yemen emerged that included both opponents of Ali Nasir and political leaders who had been neutral during the 1986 civil war in South Yemen. This included Ali Salem al-Beidh, who would go on to serve as vice president of a united Yemen beginning in 1990 and later play a central role in the 1994 civil war.

The Soviet Union played a diplomatic role in resolving the 1986 crisis, seeking to mediate between the two factions. But the conflict also changed Soviet thinking about its attempts to build up its ties to the PDRY and even to communist regimes in the so-called Third World more broadly. "What are we there for?" Mikhail Gorbachev repeatedly asked his advisors in the wake of the 1986 war.[30] From 1986 on, Gorbachev's view of the strategic importance of Soviet engagement in the Third World shifted considerably. Instead, Gorbachev began to believe "that he could use conflicts in Africa, Asia, and Latin America to find common ground with the United States," notes the Cold War historian Odd Arne Westad.[31]

Because the United States did not have strong ties to the PDRY, policy makers believed the United States had little interest in the 1986 crisis. The U.S. response was therefore more muted than it had been in 1979. U.S. officials did, however, make several statements attacking the Soviet Union for its alleged role in the crisis. In late February, for example, CIA director William Casey explained that the conflict began when Ali Nasir "began to draw away a little from the Soviets and seek more help elsewhere . . . [and] hardline pro-Soviet elements in his government initiated a *coup*."[32]

Unification and the 1994 Civil War

The idea of a unified Yemeni polity surfaced repeatedly in Yemeni political discourse in the decades before 1990, with governments of both North and South Yemen pledging their theoretical commitment to unification. Nevertheless, there was substantial disagreement about what a unified Yemen would look like in practice and how political leaders from North and South Yemen would share power in a unified government. The ultimate impetus for unification in 1990 was the end of the Soviet Union, which left South Yemen, until then highly dependent on Soviet aid and support, without a great-power patron. The sudden withdrawal of Soviet aid and the departure of Soviet and East German advisors left the PDRY's economy and government in disarray. The 1986 civil war had been "a catastrophe for the YSP and for the PDRY" since so many government and military leaders had been killed.[33] The war also "undermined [the regime's] legitimacy in the eyes of much of the population," making unification even more pressing.[34] For the YAR, the need for unification was not as critical, but unification did provide an opportunity for President Saleh to consolidate "his dominance in the political arena."[35]

The Sana'a Agreement, signed on April 22, 1990, authorized the unification of North and South Yemen. The two countries officially merged one month later. In comparison with other Gulf states, ruled by monarchies, "the post-unification period saw a dramatic experiment in political liberalization" in Yemen."[36] A new constitution provided for a multiparty political system, voting rights for all adult citizens, an independent judiciary, and other civic rights. April Longley Alley notes that this experiment in democracy, while imperfect, was a first for the Arabian Peninsula and "arguably the most substantive in the Arab world" at the time.[37]

The transitional power-sharing arrangement placed Saleh in the role of interim president and al-Beidh as vice president. In practice, however, the ruling parties of north and south each maintained their own institutions, networks of political support, and some amount of de facto autonomy even in the unified state. There was little trust between the two sides, and each fought to maintain the independence of its own institutions and patronage networks.[38] The details of political power sharing below the level of the allocation of national cabinet positions, including how two militaries would merge into one institution, were not developed in the unification agreement itself, which was rushed through. As a result, "neither side was prepared to relinquish control of its armed forces," according to Victoria Clark.[39] While unification began as a hopeful period, the arrangement began to turn sour as these divisions generated additional mistrust on both sides.

In the 1993 elections, Saleh's General People's Congress party (GPC) won 40 percent of the vote, while al-Beidh's YSP won just 19 percent, reflecting the geographic reality that at eleven million, the population of northern Yemen far outnumbered the two and a half million southerners. The Islamist party Islah, a coalition of Muslim Brotherhood–affiliated Islamists, conservative-minded businessmen, and some highland tribal leaders, received 20 percent of the vote, including parts of the southern highland that the YSP had hoped to win.[40] A campaign of assassinations beginning in 1992 that killed almost one hundred southern politicians further stoked north-south political tensions. The YSP blamed the murders on northern security forces, while Saleh's GPC claimed that mujahideen fighters who had returned from Afghanistan in the 1980s were responsible.

Other factors generated an economic crisis on top of political instability. Yemen happened to hold one of the nonpermanent seats on the UN Security Council when the first Gulf War began. As Yemen was a long-standing friend of Saddam Hussein's government in Iraq, its diplomats cast their vote against the UN Security Council Resolution authorizing the U.S.-led coalition's invasion of Iraq in

November 1990. While the resolution passed, U.S. policy makers saw Yemen's no vote as a diplomatic slight: Secretary of State James Baker declared that the vote would be "the most expensive vote they ever cast."[41] Sure enough, the United States reduced its annual aid to Yemen from $20.5 million to less than $3 million, and the Arab Gulf states followed suit, suspending $200 million in development aid. Saudi Arabia also abruptly expelled about seven hundred thousand Yemeni guest workers from Saudi Arabia in retaliation, severely compounding the economic situation.[42]

By early 1994, "there were signs . . . that the south was preparing for secession and the north for war."[43] In the atmosphere of rising tensions between northern and southern politicians, al-Beidh fled to Aden in August 1993. In April 1994, skirmishing broke out between northern and southern troops stationed near Sana'a that escalated into a full-scale civil war. Al-Beidh formally declared southern independence in May of that year. Northern forces received support in the fighting from the southern Ali Nasir partisans who had fled north in 1986. However, northern military forces, which were both better positioned and prepared than southern forces, quickly gained the advantage.[44] On May 4, northern forces launched an offensive aimed at isolating and eventually taking over Aden. Southern forces were "forced to regroup to defend Aden and the Hadramawt."[45] Saudi Arabia formally called for a cease-fire during the fighting but privately sided with the south. There were even "reports of money and arms reaching Aden" from Saudi Arabia and other GCC countries.[46]

Like the 1986 civil war and the north-south wars in the 1970s, the 1994 civil war was short-lived. On July 7, after two months of fighting, the northern army marched into Aden, forcing al-Beidh and other southern leaders to flee into exile. The war left an estimated five to seven thousand people dead.[47]

The Southern Movement/al-Hirak

The 1994 civil war ended in military victory for northern forces, allowing Saleh to consolidate his regime's control over the unified country. Nevertheless, the civil war did little to resolve the underlying grievances that had generated conflict in the first place. These grievances fueled southern demands for autonomy and eventually the emergence of al-Hirak al-Janoubi, or the Southern Movement.

The Saleh regime's widespread corruption fueled southern perceptions that the central government was "siphoning off revenues" from southern petroleum production for officials' personal gains, writes Stephen Day.[48] Rent-seeking behavior by the central government thereby exacerbated existing regional divisions. Southern grievances were also fueled by the looting and land expropriation in the south at the end of the 1994 civil war. When the war ended, Dresch writes, "Aden was sacked. Not only weapons and money, but electrical and bathroom fittings, window frames, even door knobs were carried off."[49] While the civil war itself was a conflict among political elites, the aftermath of the fighting "was felt by Southerners to be a Northern invasion."[50]

Northern officials responsible for restoring looted property to southerners after the war were instead allowed to profit from corruption and bribe-taking: the office that controlled the land registry in Aden was so corrupt that it became known as the "Office of Plunder and Theft."[51] Many southern Yemenis continued to resent the dominance of northerners in the central government and what they saw as intrusions into southern political life after 1994.

Southern grievances exploded into the Southern Movement, or al-Hirak, in 2007, when southern former military officers began weekly sit-ins to demand better pensions. The protest movement spread across the south. By 2009, protestors were raising the flag of the PDRY and chanting slogans rooted in the anticolonial struggle against the British, like "barra, barra, ista'amaar" (out, out, occupation), framing the northern-dominated regime as occupiers.[52]

Saleh's security forces responded to southern protests with violence. On October 14, 2007, during a protest commemorating the rebellion against British colonial rule, security forces fired on youth protestors, killing four. The killings sparked massive anti-government protests across southern Yemen. In January 2008, state security forces killed two protestors at a rally in Aden.[53] The Southern Movement protestors themselves remained largely peaceful before 2015, but as the movement gained momentum, the authority of the central government in southern Yemen receded. Some southern separatists organized themselves into independent militias in the spring of 2015, eventually becoming part of the Southern Transition Council (STC).

The Houthi Insurgency

The Houthi insurgent movement, which calls itself Ansar Allah (Supporters of God), emerged in 2004 in Saada governorate, in the northwest of Yemen. The Houthi insurgency began as part of a Zaydi revivalist movement to counteract the growing influence of Salafism and other variants of conservative Sunni Islam that were being exported to northern Yemen by Saudi Arabia via Saudi-funded religious leaders and schools.

Yemen's population is 44 percent Zaydi Shia and 56 percent Sunni, with most Sunnis belonging to the Shafi'i school of jurisprudence (there is also a small Ismai'ili minority in the northern highlands).[54] Most Yemenis in the north and northwest of the country are Zaydi, a branch of Shia Islam practiced primarily in Yemen. Zaydis are distinct from mainstream Shias, sometimes called "twelvers" since they recognize twelve imams, while Zaydis only recognize five.[55] There are other "significant Zaydi distinctions from the better-known Iraqi and Iranian version of Shi'ism" as well, "both in doctrine and in practice."[56] Notably, in contrast with Iran's postrevolution approach to exporting the revolution, Zaydis have historically "not been interested in propagating their beliefs or proselytizing."[57] While Zaydis are a minority in the country as a whole, they have historically dominated the northern highlands, with Saada governorate as their center. Yemen has not had a history of sectarian tensions. Indeed, Zaydis and Sunnis tend to live in the same communities, intermarry, and even worship in the same mosques, and Zaydi practices are considered by many observers to be closer to Sunni Islam than to mainstream Shi'ism.[58]

The Houthis emerged out of the broader moderate Zaydi revivalist movement. The Houthi movement was led by Hussein Badaraddin al-Houthi, a charismatic lay preacher, member of parliament, and son of a Zaydi theologian. The Houthi family are *sada* (singular *sayyid*), meaning they trace their lineage back to the Prophet Mohammed. Zaydi doctrine gives the *sada* "a leadership role in both religious and secular affairs," with a requirement that imams come from the ranks of the *sada*.[59] The Houthis "are widely accused of working to bring back the imamate and rule by *sada*."[60]

The Houthi's first leader Hussein Badaraddin al-Houthi came to prominence in the early 2000s, when he criticized President Saleh's alignment with the U.S.-led Global War on Terror and called on his followers to protest the Saleh regime. In 2004, in response to antigovernment demonstrations and occupations of government buildings, Saleh sent in government forces ordered to arrest al-Houthi. Al-Houthi was killed by government forces after ten weeks of fighting and three days of intensive skirmishing. Al-Houthi's father, Badr al-Din al-Houthi, and one of his brothers, Abd al-Malik al-Houthi, took his place as leaders of the movement.

Between 2004 and 2010, Houthi forces engaged in six rounds of fighting with government forces, known as the Saada wars, with each round punctuated by tenuous cease-fires.[61] Saudi Arabia also became engaged in the Saada wars in 2009. In November of that year, while Saleh's military counterinsurgency campaign against the Houthis was at full throttle, Houthi forces moved across the Saudi border, seizing strategic high ground and killing one border guard. In response, Saudi Arabia deployed air and ground forces to create a ten-kilometer "buffer zone" at the border. The Saudi intervention was not a success: estimates suggest that more than one hundred Saudi forces were killed in the fighting, some in friendly fire incidents, by early 2010. A final cease-fire was reached in February 2010, when the Houthis agreed to end their offensive along the Saudi border.[62]

Operation Scorched Earth, launched in August 2009, was a full-scale counterinsurgency military operation against the Houthis that involved forty thousand government troops. Government military forces used harsh tactics, especially in the war's sixth phase, blockading the conflict zone by interdicting humanitarian aid, requisitioning supplies from local markets, billeting military personnel in homes, and interrupting intertribal and intraregional trade routes.[63] The Saada wars displaced up to 130,000 people, with about half of those displaced moving to Saada city. "The lack of reliable information emerging from Saada helped to perpetuate" the conflict, according to the journalist Ginny Hill. Reliable casualty counts were impossible to come by, but estimates of total battlefield and non-combatant deaths numbered in the thousands.[64] The government security forces' counterinsurgency campaign also became increasingly brutal. These government tactics only "perpetuated Houthi resistance" and helped the movement to spread across northern Yemen, as many Yemenis in Saada resented the government violence and its "affront to cultural and religious norms."[65]

The Beginning of Saleh's Unraveling

Over the decades of President Ali Abdullah Saleh's rule, he had built patronage networks around a set of familial, tribal, and regional interests. He used divide-and-rule tactics, playing rival factions off one another and co-opting opposition figures who were ultimately marginalized from the centers of power.[66] After the 1994 civil war, Saleh continued to consolidate his control, governing primarily via personal relationships built with Yemen's military and security forces and with the Hashid tribal confederation and other northern Zaydi tribes.[67] Saleh's personalist method of governing meant that the Yemeni state did not develop the kinds of institutions that could provide stable governance in Saleh's absence, such as a robust civil service bureaucracy.

While Yemen was already the poorest country in the Middle East, by the end of the first decade of this century, the economy was in particularly dire straits. Unemployment was up to 35 percent, with youth unemployment almost doubling between 1999 and 2008. Commodity price shocks in 2007 and 2008 led to a 60 percent rise in food prices, contributing to increased poverty.[68] At the same time, Saleh's patronage networks distributed resources unevenly among Yemeni communities, institutionalizing the access enjoyed by the northern tribes while marginalizing parts of the country that had historically lacked access to power. This meant that southerners were essentially locked out of access to rents derived from oil revenues and from the port in Aden. Yemen's natural resource rents were not large compared to the other Arab Gulf states, but by 2005 they accounted for as much as 40 percent of the country's gross domestic product (GDP).[69]

Saleh's political position was also becoming shakier by the end of the first decade of the century. The Joint Meeting Parties (JMP), an alliance of five opposition parties, formed in 2002 to challenge Saleh's GPC in elections and to push for reform. The opposition alliance brought together Islah, Yemen's Islamist party and with nine hundred thousand members one of the best-organized parties in the country, and the YSP, which continued to enjoy strong support in the south. In the 2006 presidential elections, the JMP candidate, Faisal bin Shimlan, received "a respectable 23 percent of the popular vote, highlighting the [JMP's] combined capacity for electoral mobilization."[70] At the same time, Saleh's victory in 2006 presidential elections left parts of the opposition wondering whether it was worth it to continue playing the game by Saleh's rules.[71] In November 2008, the JMP organized a large demonstration that brought more than one hundred thousand protestors out into the streets of Sana'a to protest fraud in elections.[72]

By 2010, Saleh's regime therefore faced crises on multiple fronts, including "a growing southern secessionist movement, an unresolved rebellion in the north, and a resurgent al-Qaeda," all set against "the daunting background of a festering socioeconomic crisis."[73] Presidential elections scheduled to take place in 2013 meant that a potential succession crisis also loomed.

The Arab Spring protest movement, which swept across the Middle East and North Africa in early 2011, provided the spark that set this dry tinder ablaze. Before we turn to the events of the Arab Spring, however, we need to understand the United States' approach to Yemen in the decade and a half prior to 2015.

CHAPTER TWO

The U.S. Counterterrorism
War in Yemen

I know you're asked this every time something terrible happens in Yemen, but now that we have basically complete chaos in Yemen, does the White House believe that Yemen is the model for counter-terrorism strategy?

—ABC reporter JONATHAN KARL

Jon, the White House does continue to believe that a successful counter-terrorism strategy is one that will build up the capacity of the central government to have local fighters on the ground to take the fight to extremists in their own country.

—White House spokesperson JOSH EARNEST, March 2015

WHILE U.S. COUNTERTERRORISM ENGAGEMENT with Ali Abdullah Saleh's regime dates back to the bombing of the USS *Cole* by al-Qaeda in 2000, Yemen became a high-priority focus of counterterrorism efforts during the Obama administration. President Obama keenly felt that keeping Americans safe was one of his most important—and weighty—responsibilities. At the same time, he campaigned in 2008 on a promise to wind down the Global War on Terror (GWoT).[1] As a *New York Times* editorial following Obama's inauguration address proclaimed, Obama had "swept away eight years of President George Bush's false choices and failed policies and promised to recommit to America's most cherished ideals."[2]

Obama's supporters might therefore have expected him to dial back the United States' counterterrorism approach to Yemen, which under the Bush administration had included partnering with President Ali Abdullah Saleh and the government of Yemen on counterterrorism operations and one drone strike against a terrorist suspect in 2002. Yet a failed terrorist plot on a commercial flight landing on Christmas Day 2009—combined with the Obama administration's insistence that the United States would stay out of wars in the Middle East—led to a renewed counterterrorism focus in Yemen. The failed attack ensured that after 2009, for administration officials, "the threat from Yemen, and the capabilities of AQAP, suddenly loomed much larger, eclipsing even the [threat of the] old core of Al Qaeda in Pakistan."[3]

The "Yemen Model"

The Obama administration viewed Yemen through the lens of counterterrorism from January 2010 until March 2015, when the coalition intervention in Yemen's civil war began. Not only was counterterrorism the administration's overwhelming focus in Yemen, but Yemen also became central to the administration's broader global counterterrorism efforts. U.S. officials were so focused on counterterrorism efforts there that they touted the "Yemen model" of counterterrorism as a model for the fight against the Islamic State in Iraq and Syria in 2014, advancing the approach as an alternative to Bush's more all-encompassing Global War on Terror. Instead of military intervention in conflicts across the region, the Yemen model promised that the United States would take a lighter-footprint approach. Steve Simon, an advisor to the Obama administration, described the Yemen model as "intelligence-driven, dynamic targeting" that uses drone strikes to disrupt terrorist groups.[4] By engaging in airstrikes and partnering with local government forces to carry out counterterrorism missions, the idea went, the United States could disrupt and even destroy terrorist groups like al-Qaeda in the Arabian Peninsula (AQAP), which by this time had become a high-priority threat to the U.S. homeland, U.S. officials thought. At the same time, the Yemen model of counterterrorism allowed President Obama to keep his campaign promises to avoid "dumb wars" like the war in Iraq and to avoid deploying U.S. troops to engage in combat operations, aside from military advisors and U.S. Special Forces.

President Obama and senior administration officials touted the "Yemen model" of counterterrorism on a number of occasions in 2014 and 2015. Obama cited the Yemen model while announcing plans to send U.S. military advisors to Iraq to support the government's fight against ISIS in June 2014. In remarks to the press in June 2014, Obama explained how the Yemen model worked: "We do have a committed partner in President Hadi and his government," Obama noted, "and we have been able to help to develop their capacities without putting large numbers of U.S. troops on the ground at the same time."[5]

The Yemen model allowed President Obama and his administration to draw a bright line between the ongoing wars in Afghanistan and Iraq and his administration's wars in Yemen and Somalia. In a speech announcing U.S. airstrikes against ISIS in September 2014, President Obama noted that the strategy would "be different from the wars in Iraq and Afghanistan. It will not involve American combat troops fighting on foreign soil." Instead, the counter-ISIS approach would mimic the strategy that the United States had "successfully pursued in Yemen and Somalia for years": "[This] is consistent with the approach I outlined earlier this year: to use force against anyone who threatens America's core interests, but to mobilize partners wherever possible to address broader challenges to international order."[6]

In the short term, the Yemen model worked more or less as designed: it allowed the United States to contain AQAP via drone strikes and maintain its partnership with Yemeni government forces, all without deploying a significant number of U.S. troops on the ground. Even at the time, however, critics saw the administration's assessment of the Yemen model's success as overly sanguine. Writing as far back as July 2014, the counterterrorism expert Katherine Zimmerman argued that "the 'Yemen model' has not been as successful as the White House claims; indeed, it is in danger of collapse."[7]

The Yemen model faced two critical problems that ultimately limited its effectiveness. First, local government partners faced perverse incentives. Yemen's President Ali Abdullah Saleh tried to balance the United States' demands with the complexities of Yemen's domestic politics and his own corrupt patronage system. U.S. counterterrorism support and funding created a moral hazard: because the Yemeni government wanted the United States to remain involved in Yemen—and to continue supplying military aid—it was not highly motivated to eradicate AQAP. "Political elites in Yemen used the language of counterterrorism to serve their own political interests," Summer Nasser, CEO of Yemen Aid, said.[8]

Second, by taking such a hands-off approach, the U.S. counterterrorism approach to Yemen ignored fundamental questions about how Yemen was governed and why it became a safe haven for AQAP in the first place. As Summer Nasser put it, "the U.S. only discussed Yemen through a counterterror lens."[9] A narrow focus on terrorism meant that U.S. officials were not asking the right questions about Yemeni politics, blinding them to the realities on the ground as Saleh's regime unraveled. The Yemen model "is all about achieving short-term goals," the journalist Amanda Taub wrote in 2015. The model "focuses on treating the symptoms of terrorism—going after specific militant targets and attempting to disrupt specific plots—but does nothing to address the underlying political problems that allow terrorist organizations to flourish."[10]

When the Yemeni civil war began in 2014, fueled by Saleh's resignation, a rocky political transition, a complex set of grievances that remained unresolved after the Arab Spring and the failed transition process, and the 2014 Houthi coup, it generated a security vacuum in Yemen's south in which AQAP was able to flourish. While counterterrorism operations had limited the military capabilities of terrorist groups in Yemen, the problems that allowed terrorist groups to flourish—including poor governance and corruption—remained unaddressed.[11]

U.S. officials' idea of what constituted "stability" led to a narrow focus on counterterrorism priorities, while largely ignoring or de-prioritizing questions around governance, the allocation of political power, and economic development. In practice, this policy approach meant that the U.S. would never be able to fully eradicate AQAP as long as it followed the Yemen model. As Deputy National Security Advisor Ben Rhodes recalled, Obama saw targeted counterterrorism strikes as "a way of minimizing the chance of getting drawn into a bigger conflict by successful terrorist attacks that create a ground-swell of opinion for more aggressive action."[12] These tensions surfaced repeatedly from 2001 through late 2010.

Counterterrorism in Yemen under the Bush Administration

Prior to 2015, the United States' primary concern in Yemen was pre-venting AQAP, a terrorist group in Yemen formed from the merger of al-Qaeda's Saudi and Yemeni branches, from launching an attack on U.S. soil or U.S. or allied forces in the region.

U.S. counterterrorism interests in Yemen were dramatically heightened following al-Qaeda's bombing of the USS *Cole* in October 2000. The *Cole*, a guided missile destroyer, was in the midst of routine refueling in Aden harbor on the morning of October 12, 2000, when it was hit by a small boat carrying two suicide bomb-ers. The resulting explosion ripped a forty-by-sixty-foot gash in the ship's side, killing seventeen U.S. sailors and injuring another thirty-seven. According to Condoleezza Rice's testimony to the 9/11 Commission, when President George W. Bush took office a few months later, his first national security policy directive "set as a goal the elimination of the al Qaeda network and threat and ordered the leadership of relevant U.S. departments and agencies to make the elimination of al Qaeda a high priority."[13]

Those interests only intensified after the September 11 attacks. According to Gregory Johnsen, an expert on terrorist groups in Ye-men, after 9/11, "intelligence analysts in the CIA worried about al-Qaeda operatives already in Yemen."[14] In exchange for the assistance of Yemen's government, U.S. officials talked about "a package of aid and loans worth around $400 million."[15] For the poorest country in the Arab world, which had not received U.S. economic aid since the First Gulf War—and for a government fueled by patronage politics that required resources to distribute to its supporters—this exchange no doubt presented a tempting offer. And so the United States' counterterrorism partnership with President Ali Abdullah Saleh's regime was born.

But the partnership was troubled from the start. The Yemeni government was ambivalent about what cooperating with the United States on counterterrorism would actually entail. On November 3, 2002, the United States carried out its first drone strike outside of Afghanistan. A Predator drone armed with two Hellfire missiles struck a car traveling through Marib Governorate, where AQAP was active, killing Qaed Salim al-Harethi, aka Abu Ali al-Harithi, a high-level AQ operative suspected of involvement in the USS *Cole* attack. Saleh was willing to allow the United States to conduct such drone strikes as long as they remained secret. But Paul Wolfowitz, then deputy secretary of state, publicly took credit for the strike on CNN. Yemeni officials were furious: "This is why it is so difficult to make deals with the United States," Yaha al-Mutawakkil, deputy secretary general of the GPC, complained.[16]

Shadow War: The Obama Administration's Counterterrorism War in Yemen

While al-Qaeda's organizational structure and capabilities in Yemen were eroded by counterterrorism operations in the early 2000s, by 2006, the organization—and its ambitions—had grown. Using automatic weapons, car bombs, and rocket-propelled grenades, militants conducted an attack on the U.S. embassy in Sana'a in September 2008 that killed twelve people and six of the attackers.[17]

Even at the beginning of the Obama administration, U.S. officials had begun to see AQAP in Yemen as a pressing threat. "There was complete shock when the new team came in and saw what shape Yemen was in," a U.S. counterterrorism official said.[18] Senior Obama administration security officials, including General David Petraeus, the head of CENTCOM, and Deputy CIA Director Steven Kappes, traveled to Sana'a in 2009 to urge President Saleh "to take on AQAP."[19] By the fall of 2009, the government of Yemen had granted the United States "unfettered access to Yemeni airspace, coastal waters and land" for unilateral counterterrorism operations, according to a U.S. diplomatic cable.[20]

On December 17, 2009, the Obama administration carried out its first strike against AQAP targets in Yemen. A U.S. Navy vessel in the Arabian Sea fired cruise missiles at the site of a suspected AQAP training camp in Abyan, in coordination with a ground raid by Yemeni forces. "We'd been wanting to do strikes forever at that point," a U.S. counterterrorism analyst later recalled.[21] A Human Rights Watch investigation found that the strike had killed forty-one civilians in addition to up to thirteen militants.[22] At least one of the U.S. missiles was armed with cluster munitions. Additionally, at least four people were killed and twelve or more were injured by the unexploded bomblets following the strike.[23] The Obama administration's counterterrorism campaign in Yemen had begun with "cruise missiles and cluster bombs utterly unsuited for precise strikes, and collateral damage so extreme that it would permanently poison public opinion."[24]

Then, on Christmas Day 2009, Umar Farouk Abdulmutallab, known as "the underwear bomber" or the "Christmas bomber," unsuccessfully tried to detonate explosives on a flight to Detroit. Abdulmutallab was from Nigeria and had "undergone explosives training at one of the remote Al Qaeda camps" in Yemen.[25] He boarded a flight in Amsterdam to Detroit with a bomb sewn into his underwear. The attack was thwarted when Abdulmutallab tried to detonate the device. Passengers and crew members noticed that Abdulmutallab's trouser leg was on fire and were able to subdue him while putting out the fire. Abdulmutallab was indicted by a federal grand jury in Michigan and later convicted of eight criminal counts in a U.S. federal court, including the attempted use of a weapon of mass destruction and attempted murder.[26]

It was a narrow escape from a potential major terrorist attack. For U.S. counterterrorism officials, the incident "was a nearly catastrophic illustration of a significant new threat from" AQAP, which until then had been seen primarily as a threat to the region but not to the U.S. homeland.[27] Suddenly, AQAP in Yemen, once overshadowed in importance by the original core of al-Qaeda in Pakistan and Afghanistan, now topped the list of U.S. counterterrorism priorities.[28]

The "underwear bomber" vaulted Yemen back into the Obama administration's counterterrorism priorities. Every week beginning in early 2010, John Brennan, a senior counterterrorism advisor, convened a meeting dubbed "terror Tuesdays" in the White House, in which drone targets were selected.[29] In one of these meetings, Obama said, "We're not in Yemen to get involved in some domestic conflict. We're going to continue to stay focused on threats to the homeland—that's where the real priority is."[30]

Yemen remained high on the administration's counterterrorism agenda. In February 2011, Secretary of Homeland Security Janet Napolitano testified to Congress that the terrorism threat was at "its most heightened state" since 9/11. She and other Homeland Security officials cited Yemen as the key "battleground" from which al-Qaeda would be able to launch attacks on the United States. Asked to compare Anwar al-Awlaki to Osama bin Laden, National Counterterrorism Director Michael Leiter told Congress that Awlaki and AQAP were "probably the most significant risk to the U.S. homeland."[31]

Like the Bush administration, the Obama administration also focused on building partner capacity in Yemen to fight al-Qaeda rather than more direct forms of intervention. Press secretary Joshua Earnest summarized the approach this way: the administration's counterterrorism strategy in the Middle East was "predicated on . . . close coordination with central governments and our efforts to try to build up the capacity of central governments to assume security responsibility for their own country."[32]

Well into the Obama administration's second term, officials continued to hold Yemen up as a successful counterterrorism partnership. Earnest told the press in 2014, for example, "What we have seen in Yemen is the effective deployment of a counterterrorism strategy. . . . I don't want to signal to you that this is a mission that has been accomplished, but it has . . . mitigated the threat."[33]

The Obama administration did not initiate the drone war in Yemen but did substantially accelerate it. According to New America data, the 2002 strike that killed al-Harethi was the only drone strike that the Bush administration conducted in Yemen. Under the eight years of the Obama administration, the United States conducted 185 drone strikes in Yemen.[34] The number of annual air and drone strikes conducted in Yemen rose steadily from 2009, peaking in 2012. Since the November 2002 strike, according to data from New America, U.S. counterterrorism operations in Yemen have killed more than one thousand people, including an estimated 125 to 151 civilians.[35]

Drones represented a tool to balance Obama's desire to draw down the United States' boots-on-the-ground presence in the region while remaining vigilant about potential threats. A senior intelligence official in the Obama administration noted that drones were "the keys to a 'light-footprint strategy,' and who wouldn't want a light footprint after the past ten years?"[36] President Obama personally approved strikes in Yemen as well as Somalia. Obama became "the ultimate arbiter of a 'nominations' process to designate terrorists for kill or capture. . . . It was the president who had reserved to himself the final moral calculation."[37] Although Obama intended to add scrutiny to the target-selection process, his close supervision ultimately meant that he was more closely associated with his administration's "kill list" in the public eye.[38]

The administration's approach did not appear to wrestle with the human impacts of the drone and airstrikes, with regard to both

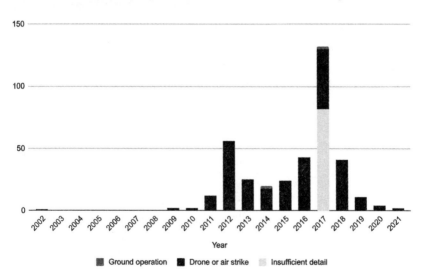

U.S. counterterrorism operations in Yemen. In 2017, U.S. Central Command said it conducted more than 131 airstrikes in Yemen. Strikes listed as "insufficient detail" represent those 131 strikes for which New America was unable to identify specific location and date information. (Source: New America, 2021)

civilian casualties and the ill will that the drone war generated against the United States. "I want to make people understand, actually, drones have not caused a huge number of civilian casualties," Obama said in January 2012, on one of the rare occasions that he spoke about drones publicly.[39] Obama's assertion was met with considerable skepticism from critics. Critics also argued that the targeted killings of U.S. citizens in Yemen and elsewhere violated the Due Process Clause of the U.S. Constitution. The Obama administration conducted a careful internal process to determine whether he had the constitutional and legal authority to direct the killing of al-Awlaki, a U.S. citizen.[40] But the American Civil Liberties Union (ACLU) charged that the targeted killing program was "based on vague legal standards, a closed executive decision-making process, and evidence never presented to the courts, even after the killing."[41] It is difficult to assess the number of civilian casualties associated with drone strikes, and there are often discrepancies between the numbers estimated by the Department of Defense versus NGO monitors, in part because internal military investigations are inconsistent and rarely collect "information from witnesses or survivors of attacks or by visiting the site of strikes."[42]

The drone strikes that killed the U.S. citizens Anwar al-Awlaki and two weeks later his son Abdulrahman al-Awlaki illustrated these problems. Anwar al-Awlaki was a Yemeni American imam who had worked at a mosque in Falls Church, Virginia, before leaving the United States in 2002. In early 2004, al-Awlaki returned to Yemen, where he became a lecturer at al-Iman University, a religious school led by Abdul-Majid al-Zindani, a cleric who was designated as a terrorist by both the United States and the United Nations "for his suspected links with al-Qaeda."[43]

Over the next few years, al-Awlaki became "the leading English-language propagandist for al-Qaeda."[44] Al-Awlaki distributed video and audio recordings in English and Arabic online and oversaw *Inspire*, AQAP's English-language magazine. He also had ties to high-profile terrorist attacks: Nidal Hasan, a U.S. Army officer who killed thirteen people at Fort Hood in November 2009, emailed al-Awlaki for advice (although al-Awlaki does not appear to have responded), and al-Awlaki praised Hasan after the attack, encouraging others in the United States and the West to carry out similar attacks.

Abdulmutallab told FBI agents that Awlaki had helped him plan his attempted Christmas Day attack, putting him in contact with the al-Qaeda bombmaker Ibrahim al-Asiri.[45] Al-Awlaki's propaganda was cited as inspiration for several major attacks after his death in 2011, including the 2013 Boston Marathon bombing and the 2015 *Charlie Hebdo* shootings.[46]

While U.S. officials initially described al-Awlaki as an "inspirational rather than operational" leader, by about 2010, they identified him as a "recruiter" who was "probably the most significant risk to the U.S. homeland," according to former National Counterterrorism Center director Michael Leiter in February 2011.[47] Al-Awlaki was added to the Joint Special Operations Command's list for kill or capture targets by January 2010. April 2010 leaks revealed that he had also been added to the CIA's targeted killing list because he was "believed to have shifted from encouraging attacks to directly participating in them."[48]

Anwar al-Awlaki was killed in a Hellfire-missile strike conducted by a CIA-operated drone, which hit his car while it was traveling through Yemen's Al Jawf governorate on September 30, 2011. His death raised considerable debate about the legal justification for conducting a targeted killing against a U.S. citizen. According to New America, al-Awlaki's was "the first known case of the American government targeting and killing a citizen since the [American] Civil War."[49] Anwar al-Awlaki's son Abdulrahman al-Awlaki, who was just sixteen years old when he died, was "collateral damage" in a strike that targeted Ibrahim al-Banna, an al-Qaeda media operative, two weeks after al-Awlaki's death. The strike killed nine people, including Abdulrahman and his seventeen-year-old cousin.[50]

In addition to the problem of civilian casualties, the Obama administration's drone policy also did not fully reckon with the costs of the drone campaign with regard to the United States' reputation in the region and what that could mean for U.S. strategic aims. As Farea al-Muslimi argued in testimony before Congress in 2013, "Drone strikes are the face of America to many Yemenis. . . . Everyone in Yemen . . . knows about America and its drones." This means that "strikes often cause animosity towards the United States and create a backlash that undermines the national security goals of the United States."[51]

Strikingly, there is little systematic evidence about what Yemenis themselves think about the U.S. drone campaign and how drones affect their perceptions of the United States. Globally, surveys suggest that the U.S. drone campaign is widely unpopular.[52] Researchers have argued that the unpopularity of drone strikes and their record of civilian casualties means that they tend to radicalize populations: "every one of these dead noncombatants represents an alienated family, a new desire for revenge, and more recruits for a militant movement that has grown exponentially even as drone strikes have increased," write the counterinsurgency experts David Kilcullen and Andrew Exum.[53]

The media and analysts had begun to refer to the U.S. counterterrorism wars in Yemen, Pakistan, Somalia, and other countries as a "shadow war." "While the stealth war began in the Bush administration, it has expanded under President Obama," a *New York Times* story noted. "Virtually none of the newly aggressive steps undertaken by the United States government have been publicly acknowledged."[54]

The United States' shadow war in Yemen expanded significantly even before Abdulmutallab's attempted Christmas attack. On September 30, 2009, General David Petraeus, then commander of CENTCOM, signed a secret directive authorizing the deployment of U.S. Special Forces to countries across the Middle East, the Horn of Africa, and Central Asia, to conduct clandestine operations with partner forces and to gather intelligence on the ground. Known as the Joint Unconventional Warfare Task Force Executive Order, the directive "helped lay a foundation for the surge of American military activity in Yemen that began three months later."[55] U.S. Special Forces worked with the Yemeni military, while the Department of Defense carried out cruise-missile strikes targeting suspected AQAP training camps in December 2009.[56] The United States designated $155 million in funding for security assistance to Yemeni military forces and provided military training to more than forty-five hundred members of the Yemeni military and security forces between 2000 and 2014.[57]

U.S. and Yemeni officials both maintained the fiction that the Yemeni government was responsible for the counterterror operations. Yet the *Washington Post*'s Dana Priest reported in late January

2010, "U.S. military teams and intelligence agencies are deeply involved in secret joint operations with Yemeni troops who in the past six weeks have killed scores of people, among them six of 15 top leaders of a regional al-Qaeda affiliate, according to senior administration officials."[58] U.S. Special Forces helped to develop tactics and plan missions, although they did not participate directly in raids. They shared "highly sensitive" intelligence with Yemeni forces, and American advisors staffed a joint operations center to facilitate intelligence sharing. On Christmas Eve 2010, President Obama authorized a strike against the compound where Anwar al-Awlaki was believed to be meeting with other al-Qaeda leaders, although al-Awlaki was not killed in the strike.

During a September 2009 meeting, according to U.S. diplomatic cables, then–Deputy National Security Advisor John Brennan told President Saleh that the United States was planning to expand U.S. counterterrorism operations in Yemen. Saleh offered Brennan "unfettered access to Yemeni airspace, coastal waters and land" but demanded more military equipment and funding in exchange and insisted that the United States take full responsibility for future AQAP attacks. "I have given you an open door on terrorism," Saleh told Brennan. Per the agreement, the Yemeni government continued to claim responsibility for drone strikes executed by the United States. Saleh told U.S. officials, "We'll continue saying the bombs are ours, not yours."[59] In January 2010, U.S. officials promised an increase in U.S. military aid to Yemen, including $45 million in train and equip funding for Yemen's Counter Terrorism Unit (CTU).[60] That same month, President Obama publicly confirmed in his weekly address, "I've made it a priority to strengthen our partnership with the Yemeni government—training and equipping their security forces, sharing intelligence and working with them to strike al Qaeda terrorists."[61]

A Troubled Counterterrorism Partnership

But the U.S.-Yemen counterterrorism partnership presented President Saleh with a dilemma. In exchange for cooperation, Saleh's government received valuable military aid and training. U.S. military assistance to Yemen "more than doubled" in 2010, from $67 million to $150 million, and was slated to rise to $250 million in 2011. This was in addition to the $115 million in counterterrorism assistance the United States had provided to Yemen's security forces from 2002 to 2010.[62]

On the one hand, this funding was important to the survival of Saleh's regime. Since coming to power in 1978, Saleh had deftly used a set of tools that included the distribution of patronage, setting tribes against one another, and repression to keep key domestic constituencies in line, a technique he called "tawazun" (balancing) or, more memorably, "dancing on the heads of snakes."[63] Saleh's "tribal-military complex" had virtually sustained his regime: "As one of the largest employers in Yemen, the military provid[ed] tribal leaders with an ideal opportunity to increase their capacity to bestow patronage," writes Michael Knights.[64] Saleh gave his family members and tribal leaders positions in the military. Saleh's government also diverted some of this counterterrorism assistance toward another effort that was key to the regime's survival: its ongoing counterinsurgency war against the Houthis. According to a report by Human Rights Watch, the Yemeni government "repeatedly diverted US-supported Yemeni counterterrorism forces and possibly US-supplied military vehicles" to the war in 2009.[65] Leaked U.S. diplomatic cables showed that U.S. diplomats' efforts to get the Yemeni government to end this diversion of aid had little effect.[66]

At the same time, cooperating with the United States on its counterterrorism agenda—and taking credit for airstrikes and raids conducted by or in partnership with U.S. forces—undermined the legitimacy of Saleh's government in the eyes of key domestic constituents.[67] As the U.S. drone campaign ramped up under President Obama, Saleh's cooperation "alienated tribal groups from the central government, and strengthened al Qaeda's claim to be fighting on behalf of local people."[68] Cooperating with the United States threatened to upset the delicate balance of domestic constituencies that had kept the Saleh regime afloat for decades.

The partnership also created a principal-agent problem, in which U.S. counterterror interests and Saleh's domestic balancing efforts were misaligned. Saleh faced incentives to cooperate with the United States on counterterrorism in exchange for U.S. funding while at the same time taking measures to balance domestic political considerations. As a result, for example, during the Bush administration, a government-run terrorist rehabilitation program struck deals with prisoners suspected of having ties with al-Qaeda, allowing them to go free if they promised not to conduct attacks inside Yemen.[69]

This moral-hazard dynamic sharpened throughout the early 2000s. U.S. and UK special forces' collaboration with the Yemeni government from 2001 through 2005 was largely successful in shutting down jihadist training camps and capturing al-Qaeda leaders. In fact, the effort was so successful that in 2005, the United States and the United Kingdom began to curtail their military assistance to Yemen, placing the emphasis of their assistance on democracy promotion rather than counterterrorism. Saleh, whose government had come to rely on counterterrorism assistance, was reportedly furious about the shift in funding. Many observers therefore speculated that it was no accident when twenty-three al-Qaeda militants escaped from a Yemeni prison in February 2006, "reportedly with help from Yemeni security officials," a Senate Foreign Relations Committee report later found.[70] In response, U.S. and UK military aid increased again. This "response set the worst possible precedent, write Watling and Shabibi: "It effectively tied millions of dollars in aid—and the corresponding support for President Saleh—not to al Qaeda's elimination, but to its continued presence. From that moment, Yemeni efforts to confront the insurgency lost their previous vigor."[71]

This narrow focus on counterterrorism also led U.S. officials to deprioritize other issues on the bilateral agenda, such as human rights concerns, democracy promotion, anticorruption efforts, and sustainable economic development. "Because American security was given priority over all other concerns, counterterrorism agencies paid no attention to the human rights abuses being committed by their local partners," said Tawakkol Karman, a Yemeni human rights activist.[72]

In fact, in at least one case, development aid intended to bolster responsible governance in Yemen was cut due to counterterrorism concerns. In 2007, the organizer of the USS *Cole* bombing, Jamal al-Badawi, was released from Yemeni prison. In response, the United States cut about $50 million in aid that Yemen was slated to receive via the Millennium Challenge Corporation (MCC), a U.S. aid agency created to encourage good governance. Stephen Seche, who served as U.S. ambassador to Yemen from 2007 through 2010, later noted that the aid was "suspended because people were just looking for a stick to hit [Saleh] with, and that was the closest one. It wasn't a particularly appropriate one given Saleh's lack of real interest in development."[73] The decision made it clear that U.S. officials would sideline all other priorities in favor of counterterrorism engagement.

U.S. officials understood this trade-off. "He was corrupt and autocratic," Secretary of State Hillary Clinton wrote of President Saleh, "but he was also committed to fighting al Qaeda and keeping his fractious country together." As a result, Clinton said, "the Obama Administration decided to hold our noses, increase our military and development aid to Yemen, and expand our counterterrorism cooperation."[74] Still, U.S. officials sought to put a good public face on the partnership with Saleh's regime. An anonymous senior official said in January 2010 that "President Saleh was serious about going after al-Qaeda and wasn't going to resist our encouragement," for example.[75]

Yet it is not clear how much the United States gained from this trade-off. The U.S. officials who dealt with Saleh directly found him to be an infuriating partner. Ambassador Seche put it in blunt terms, calling Saleh "an extraordinary manipulator. He was continuously sounding the alarm, [warning] that al Qaeda was encroaching further into territory that was thought to be secured." Saleh's warnings "captured the imagination of CIA and Department of Defense officials who would go back to Washington with a firm determination to provide more assistance, more training," Seche said.[76]

Likewise, Gerald Feierstein, who served as U.S. ambassador to Yemen from 2010 through 2013, said,

> Fundamentally Ali Abdullah Saleh was a guy who "ran with the hares and hunted with the hounds." He was never a guy who you could rely on. He would respond when the pressure on him became so intense that he had no choice, but left to his own devices, he wasn't going to waste any of his political capital going after these forces. And I can't prove it,

but I'm sympathetic to the view that he was helping AQ [al-Qaeda] as well. There certainly were times that our efforts were undermined because of tip-offs or other things. So I would not say that Ali Abdullah Saleh was ever a committed or honest partner with us in counterterrorism.[77]

Despite Saleh's poor track record as a partner and the increasing fragility of his regime, however, U.S. officials stuck by him until 2011, when the Arab Spring protest movement threatened to upend the Saleh regime altogether.

CHAPTER THREE

Arab Spring, Arab Fall

Political Transition and the Failure of the

National Dialogue Conference, 2011–2014

If you want to know how bad things can go in Syria, study Iraq.

If you want to know how much better things could have gone,

study Yemen.

—*New York Times* columnist THOMAS FRIEDMAN,

writing in 2013

MUCH LIKE THE "YEMEN MODEL," which was a success until it wasn't, U.S. policy makers and analysts saw Yemen's Arab Spring transition as a model—that is, until Yemen descended into civil war in 2014. After widespread Arab Spring protests across Yemen, the United States, with the backing of the Gulf Cooperation Council (GCC), brokered an agreement in 2011 that saw President Ali Abdullah Saleh step down in favor of his vice president, Abdrabbuh Mansur Hadi, who would lead a caretaker government. In the meantime, the GCC, with the backing of the United States, sponsored a political transition process called the National Dialogue Conference (NDC) in Yemen to resolve underlying political issues and write a new constitution, with the goal of paving the way for new elections. At the outset, Yemen's Arab Spring political transition therefore appeared to have avoided the political chaos and violence that had afflicted Libya and Syria in the early days of the Arab Spring.

New York Times columnist Thomas Friedman wrote in April 2013 that Yemen's transition was "maybe the most unique postrevolutionary political process happening in a country experiencing an Arab awakening." Yemen was able to do what many other Arab Spring countries had not, according to Friedman: "have a serious, broad-based national dialogue, where the different political factions, new parties, young people, women, Islamists, tribes, northerners and southerners are literally introducing themselves to one another in six months of talks—before they write a new constitution and hold presidential elections."[1] As late as 2014, the Obama administration continued to hold up the NDC process as a success. President Obama argued in June of that year, for example, that Yemen had held "a wide-ranging national dialogue that took a long time but helped to give people a sense that there is a legitimate political outlet for grievances."[2]

Indeed, the National Dialogue Conference was, on the surface, a model political transition process. Quotas for NDC delegates ensured that women, youths, and southern Yemenis were all represented. With the GCC in the lead, the NDC represented a regional solution to Yemen's political transition. And the conference allowed Yemenis themselves to address long-simmering political problems.

Yet the NDC was also self-evidently a failure. The two-year transition period ended without a new constitution and without setting a date for elections. In short order, the failed transition was followed by a bloody, divisive, and long-lasting civil war. The contradictions of the Arab Gulf monarchies trying to broker a democratic transition also became apparent.

There are several reasons for the National Dialogue Conference's ultimate failure. The NDC's representational inclusivity turned out to be more complex than it appeared at the surface. Additionally, while Saleh was out of power, he was granted immunity and allowed to stay in the country, with his deep political patronage networks intact. The NDC also failed to address long-standing questions about how Yemen would be governed and who would have access to state resources, as well as the very grievances that were at the core of the Arab Spring protest movement, including corruption and unemployment. The NDC did not include either the Houthis or southerners to their satisfaction, nor did it come up with workable solutions to their grievances. This, in combination with President Hadi's failure to implement the NDC's outcomes and to govern effectively, facilitated the Houthi's takeover of Sana'a in September 2014, initially, at least, with the popular support of many Yemenis.

Yemen's Arab Spring and Saleh's Indecision

Inspired by the protest movement across the Middle East and North Africa and the ouster of Tunisia's longtime president, Zine al-Abidine Ben Ali, protestors began organizing Yemen's own Arab Spring protests in January 2011, calling for the end of Saleh's thirty-three-year rule. The Yemeni journalist and activist Tawakkol Karman had organized a number of protests and sit-ins for human rights since 2007, so for her, the Arab Spring protests began in a familiar way. "As I always do when arranging a demonstration I posted a message on Facebook, calling on people to celebrate the Tunisian uprising on 16 January," she wrote.[3] A Yemeni journalist and cofounder of the civil society organization Women Journalists Without Chains, Karman became a leading figure in Yemen's Arab Spring protest movement. She won the 2011 Nobel Peace Prize for her role, becoming only the first Arab woman and the second Muslim woman ever to do so.

By late January, protests spanned the country. On January 27, the Joint Meeting Parties (JMP), an opposition coalition that included Islah and four other political parties, organized protests that brought thousands of people into the streets of Sana'a.[4] The JMP was the loyal opposition to Saleh's regime, and as such, its demands initially addressed reforms Saleh could make while staying in office, including constitutional amendments to limit the number of terms he could serve. "The ruling party can give concessions that will satisfy the demands of the JMP without even threatening its dominant position in parliament and political life," Abdulghani Al-Iryani, an independent Yemeni media analyst, commented at the time.[5]

While linked to the protest movements that swept the region beginning in January 2011, the Yemeni political opposition had already begun mobilizing to protest Saleh's regime toward the end of the previous decade. The previous decade had seen a confluence of movements across the country. In the south, al-Hirak, or the Southern Movement, had formed from a diffuse protest movement calling for greater southern autonomy, while the Houthi insurgency only grew stronger after fighting successive conflicts with Saleh's government in the north. Within the regime itself, tensions between the JMP and Saleh's ruling party, the GPC, had grown in recent years, leading to the repeated postponement of parliamentary elections originally scheduled for 2009. In fact, "there probably would have been significant protests even if the Arab Spring never happened," according to Adam Baron, a European Council for Foreign Relations fellow: "Indeed, establishment opposition actors initially appeared to ground the nascent [Arab Spring] protest movement in preexisting tensions."[6]

Yet, from the beginning, many of Yemen's young activists hoped that the protests would lead to regime change. "We are in the first stage of change in our country, and the feeling among the revolutionaries is that the people of Yemen will find solutions for our problems once the regime has gone, because the regime itself is the cause of most of them," Karman wrote in April. "A new Yemen awaits us, with a better future for all."[7] Baron, who lived in Sana'a at the time, wrote a decade later, "It is difficult to fully capture the mood. . . . Sanaa's Change Square buzzed with excitement and anticipation, faded posters of long-dead Yemeni political figures underlining the feeling among many that it was a moment of historical reckoning."[8] The fall of the regime was a rallying cry that gained momentum over the next several months, even in the face of oppression by government security forces. "The heavy security is evidence that Yemen has no democracy and freedom of expression. This is the last gasp of the regime," Abdulkareem al-Khayati, a Sana'a University student, told reporters during a January protest.[9] February 3 "Day of Rage" protests drew tens of thousands of protestors into the streets.[10]

At first, President Saleh offered minimal political concessions to protestors, promising not to run for another term when his ended in 2013 and not to set up his son as his successor. But these marginal concessions did little to assuage protestors. On February 25, more

than one hundred thousand Yemenis across the country joined protests during a second "Day of Rage" in solidarity with protestors
across the Middle East region. Protestors chanted the infamous slo-
gan of the Arab Spring movement, "The people want the regime
to fall."[11] On March 18, Yemeni government security forces opened
fire on protestors, killing fifty-two and wounding hundreds more.
The violence evoked strong statements from U.S. officials, including President Obama, who "strongly condemn[ed]" the violence and
called "on President Saleh to adhere to his public pledge to allow
demonstrations to take place peacefully."[12] Likewise, Secretary of
State Hillary Clinton said that the United States was "alarmed" by
the violence and "seeking to verify reports that this is the result of
actions by security forces."[13] But the United States had not yet called
for Saleh to step down.

On March 22, General Ali Mohsen al-Ahmar, a military commander and close associate of Saleh who was considered by many
observers to be the second-most-powerful man in the country, defected to the opposition, giving the protest movement a boost in political momentum.[14] That same day, Saleh said he would be willing
to step down by the end of the year as part of a transition process, an
offer rejected by the opposition.

The United States began to call for Saleh to step down as part
of a phased transition process in April, after Yemeni security forces
killed seventeen protestors. Issuing the strongest statement yet on
behalf of the United States, White House spokesman Jay Carney
said, "we urge political dialogue to take place."[15]

As the protest movement continued to grow, over the course
of several months Saleh publicly vacillated about whether he would
step down. On April 23, Saleh agreed to a plan known as the Gulf
Cooperation Council Initiative, nominally brokered by the GCC,
although diplomats from the United States also played a critical role.
The agreement would have Saleh step down within thirty days in exchange for immunity from prosecution. On April 30, however, Saleh
refused at the last minute to sign the deal.[16] After the GCC sent an
envoy to Yemen to try to salvage the deal, Saleh again agreed to
sign it at a ceremony in Sana'a. While opposition groups signed the
deal on May 21, the next day Saleh refused again. Instead, a mob of
armed government supporters surrounded the UAE embassy, where

officials had gathered to witness the signing of the agreement, trapping Ambassador Feierstein and other officials inside for hours.[17]

On June 3, 2011, Saleh and a number of other senior officials were wounded by a bomb placed in a mosque in Saleh's palace compound. Saleh left the country the following day to receive medical treatment in Saudi Arabia, but it was unclear how severe his injuries were and when he would return.[18] Peaceful protests, as well as violent clashes between security forces and armed Saleh supporters, continued in his absence. On September 9, more than one million protestors gathered across the country.[19] On September 23, 2011, after more than three months out of the country even as the protest movement peaked, Saleh returned to Yemen despite earlier reports that he would never return or that Saudi officials would prevent him from leaving Riyadh. Massive antigovernment protests continued, and Saleh finally signed the GCC Initiative on November 23, stepping down from power.[20]

Saleh's vacillations were probably due to his evolving assessment of his political prospects. Saleh had at first initiated the transition process after Ali Mohsen's defection, fearing that Ali Mohsen would bring the military with him. Yet when the Yemeni military did not collapse and members of Saleh's party urged him to stay in office, Saleh's confidence rebounded, and he backed away from the transition process. While he eventually signed the GCC agreement due to a number of factors, especially the pressure he had felt from protestors, the opposition, and the international community since early 2011, the final straw was probably a private call from Saudi King Abdullah to Saleh signaling that it was time for him to step down. This pressure from his most important regional patron, on top of continued pressure from the international community, left Saleh with no alternative but to sign the transition agreement.

The U.S. Response to Yemen's Arab Spring

President Obama did seem to genuinely want to support the nascent pro-democratic movements across the Arab world in 2011. "If I were an Egyptian in my twenties, I'd probably be out there with them," Obama told his advisors after seeing the Tahrir Square protestors in Egypt.[21] Yet his approach to Yemen was cautious and ultimately driven by fears about terrorism and instability as much as support for democracy.

The Arab Spring protests proved "a dramatic real-time test" of the president's ideals.[22] While Obama was personally inclined to support the young pro-democracy protestors, he was also keenly aware that dictators like Saleh were long-standing U.S. partners and seen by many U.S. officials as the lynchpins of regional stability. These positions were staked out by two opposing camps within the administration itself. Obama's younger and more idealistic advisors, including Samantha Power, Ben Rhodes, and Antony Blinken, urged him to get on the right side of history by publicly supporting the ouster of dictators like Egypt's Hosni Mubarak. Others, such as Secretary Clinton, Secretary of Defense Bob Gates, and National Security Advisor Tom Donilon warned that this optimistic view did not account for the potential unforeseen consequences of the Arab Spring. Clinton later described the former camp as having been "swept up in the drama and idealism of the moment."[23] The idealists initially won the day with regard to the U.S. approach to Egypt, where Obama called for Mubarak to step down in February 2011, and in Libya, where the United States spearheaded a NATO-led coalition intervention in March that toppled Libya's dictator Muammar Ghaddafi.

Illustrating the centrality of counterterrorism in the United States' approach to Yemen, John Brennan, who was then serving as homeland security advisor, "became the administration's point person on Yemen" in early 2011.[24] Brennan "was in regular telephone contact with Saleh" until he stepped down, "warning him not to use lethal force against demonstrators."[25] Brennan personally played a role in securing the deal to replace Saleh with his vice president, Hadi, in part to get a Yemeni government that would be more cooperative on counterterrorism issues.[26] Brennan "developed a close relationship with President Hadi," whom he described as "a very good counterterrorism partner. Hadi was very supportive of U.S. missile strikes and broader counterterrorism efforts."[27] Indeed, the Obama administration came to view Hadi as "a vast improvement over his much-disliked predecessor [President Saleh]."[28]

The U.S. position on Yemen's Arab Spring was further complicated by the fact that after Saleh's several decades in office undergirded by a deeply entrenched patronage system, it was difficult to identify a viable successor. Although Saudi officials "viewed Saleh as a 'lying trickster,'" Ginny Hill reports, "not one of the [alternate] contenders was strong enough to assert himself outright, and the Saudis were unwilling to take sides when it was still unclear who would emerge as the eventual winner."[29] With no apparent successor lined up, it was more difficult for U.S. officials to imagine a stable political transition.

In early April 2011, the White House press secretary warned President Saleh, "The United States strongly condemns the use of violence by Yemeni government forces against demonstrators in Sana'a, Taiz, and Hodeida in the past several days. The Yemeni people have a right to demonstrate peacefully."[30] But the United States became more publicly critical of Saleh by May 2011, after he had refused to sign the GCC deal. A subsequent statement from Secretary Clinton called Saleh out directly, noting, "The United States is deeply disappointed by President Saleh's continued refusal to sign the Gulf Cooperation Council (GCC) initiative." "We urge him to immediately follow through on his repeated commitments to peacefully and orderly transfer power. . . . The time for action is now," Clinton said.[31]

According to the terms of the transition deal, Saleh resigned as president, turning over power to Vice President Abdrabbuh Mansur Hadi. Hadi officially became president of Yemen after an uncontested election held in February 2012. Hadi was supposed to act as a caretaker, leading the transition government until new elections in February 2014. In exchange for his acquiescence, Saleh received immunity from prosecution and was able to remain in the country as leader of his party, the GPC. Additionally, there was to be a two-year political transition, including the National Dialogue Conference, which would guide constitutional reforms before the new elections were held.

The National Dialogue Process: Yemen's Failed Post–Arab Spring Transition

The NDC transition process started on a high note: "expectations were high, and the agenda was enormous."[32] The transition process was expected to tackle a wide array of issues that were fundamental to the future governance of the Yemeni state, from creating a transitional justice process to reforming state institutions.

Yet the NDC concluded in January 2014 "without firm plans for a future government beyond general ideas of federalized parliamentary rule."[33] The process produced a set of general principles that were supposed to guide constitutional reform, but there was no agreement on the key issues—namely, the structure of the future state and particularly the status of the south. The subcommittee appointed to work on the southern issue featured strong internal disagreement. Many southern members supported the creation of a federal system with a unitary southern region that could effectively balance against the north, while others called for six federal regions. The subcommittee was never able to reach a formal decision on the issue and punted instead. After the NDC closed in 2014, Hadi extended his own provisional term as president for another year and appointed a committee of experts to work on the southern question. Another committee was appointed to draft a new constitution based on the NDC's recommendations that would then be ratified by vote.[34]

Lessons from Yemen's National Dialogue Conference

While there are several reasons for the NDC's failure—ultimately leading to the onset of Yemen's civil war in 2014—there were three factors that the United States played a role in that led to the NDC's demise: inadequate representation, a lack of transitional justice, and a calculus that favored short-term stability over solving underlying issues. These three factors meant that the old regime was left largely entrenched, even though Saleh was officially removed from his position as president. They also meant that the process left underlying grievances around transitional justice and accountability unaddressed. This, in turn, led directly to the failure of the transition process and the onset of Yemen's civil war in 2014.

Inadequate Representation

In one sense, the NDC process was a notably inclusive process. "With the support of Western diplomats," Yemeni women activists and civil society leaders were successfully able to lobby for a quota for women delegates in the NDC.[35] The quota system influenced the selection of delegates: 30 percent of delegates were required to be women, while 50 percent were of southern origin and 20 percent were youths.[36] These quotas, aimed at boosting the inclusivity of the conference, were due at least in part to the international community's willingness to push for them: according to Ginny Hill, "the international community—notably the EU and the UN—went out on a limb to promote the inclusion of previously marginalized groups," making the process "the most diverse and accessible forum in Yemen's history."[37] Women delegates were able to claim several achievements from the NDC process, including a law passed by Yemen's National Assembly in January 2015 to set the minimum age for marriage at eighteen and a provision in the draft constitution enacting a 30 percent quota for women's political participation.[38]

While the NDC was inclusive on the surface, in practice it functioned as a pact among elites. The main political parties—Saleh's General People's Congress, Islah, and the Yemen Socialist Party (YSP)—controlled a large share of the NDC's 565 seats, while smaller political parties, the Houthis, and al-Hirak controlled fewer.[39]

The dialogue process "failed to recognize and include the demands of major sectors of the population. Instead, it was driven by old tribal and political parties," writes the scholar Noha Aboueldahab.[40] The NDC functioned like an elite pact—a component of many regime transitions.[41] "At every stage in the NDC planning process, inclusivity was scuttled in favor of the embedded interests of established partisan, military, and tribal figures," the scholar Stacey Philbrick Yadav writes.[42]

While the quota system encouraged representation along some dimensions, activists saw it as limiting in others.[43] The NDC did not include significant representation from the cohort of young activists who had led Yemen's Arab Spring protest movement. Hadil al-Mowafak, a Yemeni youth activist who participated in the 2011 protests, wrote, "The high hopes awakened by the protests soon vanished after traditional political elites hijacked the uprising and excluded Yemeni youth from participation in politics."[44] Most of the leadership of al-Hirak, especially the most committed secessionists, boycotted the NDC from the beginning, as did the Houthis. Many ordinary Yemenis saw the NDC process "as disconnected from the needs of the Yemeni people and driven, primarily, by international actors."[45]

At the same time, Hadi's leadership did not inspire much confidence. As the transition proceeded, instead of focusing on providing public goods or alleviating poverty, Hadi's main preoccupation seemed to be "rearranging appointments in the government and military in order to dilute [Saleh]'s support" and limiting the influence of rival elites.[46] The cabinet of the transition government, which was evenly divided between Saleh's GPC and the loyal opposition JMP, was paralyzed by infighting, with ministers "more focused on divvying up state spoils than effectively running the government."[47]

Because the NDC lacked the participation of key groups, it was unable to address fundamental questions that had persisted for decades, notably the Arab Spring protest movement's concerns about economic opportunity and political participation, as well as the role of the Houthis and the Southern Movement in how Yemen would be governed. As the scholar Charles Schmitz notes, while poverty, unemployment, corruption, and deteriorating physical security were some of the key issues driving protestors into the streets in 2011, those issues were largely set aside in favor of securing "the details of the elite's vision for the future of the country."[48] In this atmosphere of dysfunction, the NDC was "increasingly viewed as a sideshow, while the real game involve[d] intra-elite negotiations" that carried on behind closed doors.[49]

The "southern question" was one of the main sticking points in the NDC process. As highlighted in chapter 1, Yemen has a much-longer history of division than it does as a united polity. Neither unification in 1990 nor the 1994 civil war resolved the underlying problem of many southerners' desire to renegotiate the terms of unification. Yemen's future federal structure was therefore a critical question for the national dialogue process.

But delegates appointed to work on the "southern issue" were not in agreement about the solution. Many southern members supported the creation of a federal system with a unitary southern region that could effectively balance against the north, while others called for six federal regions. And all of the NDC's work on the southern issue was marred by the fact that much of al-Hirak's leadership boycotted the NDC. Southern leaders did not have the appropriate grassroot influence to obtain buy-in for NDC outcomes.[50] The "southern question" was never resolved. During the NDC itself, large protests in the south called for secession, demonstrating that the Hirak leaders who boycotted the NDC had at least some grassroots support.[51]

The United States and the international community did not have the final say in who would be included in the national dialogue process—nor should they have. But the international community, including U.S. officials, did play an important role in encouraging representation. Instead of (or in addition to) encouraging a quota system that increased representation from marginalized groups at the surface level, the international community could have pushed for more genuine representation via the inclusion of the leadership of key groups, like Yemeni civil society, as well as the Houthis and the Southern Movement.

Pressure from the international community for even greater inclusion could have helped make the NDC delegates more truly representative of the communities that they came from. As the scholar Maryam Jamshidi writes, while international transitional justice frameworks are typically "viewed as the gold standard, with locally-sourced solutions treated as compromised alternatives," engaging with local conflict resolution mechanisms could have made the NDC process more responsive to the demands of many Yemenis for a transitional justice process. Incorporating local communities and their perspectives in transitional justice mechanisms can generate "popular support for these efforts," while helping to address the problems of corruption, poverty, poor governance, and lack of representation that led to the crisis in the first place.[52]

Lack of Transitional Justice

The diplomats guiding the transition process also had to make an agonizing decision about transitional justice: Should they offer Saleh immunity as an incentive to step down and allow the transition to move forward, or should they support a more robust transitional justice process that addressed the concerns of protestors and the opposition?

At the end of the day, diplomats went with the more expedient option. Under the terms of the GCC agreement, Saleh received immunity from prosecution. A deal with Saleh remaining in the country with immunity appeared to be a better alternative to no transition at all. "The country was divided. As long as Saleh had half the military and a strong base of popular support, we really couldn't force his hand," said Ambassador Feierstein, who was directly involved in transition negotiations. "At the end of the day, . . . it would've been better for Saleh to leave in order to avoid more conflict," Feierstein said. "But this deal was better than no deal at all, and those were the two options."[53]

Immunity laws passed as part of the transition agreement protected Saleh and his aides from prosecution. The transitional justice committee of the national dialogue process was stalled by Saleh supporters, preventing it from putting forward transitional-justice-oriented policies such as prosecuting former regime officials who were responsible for violence against protestors.[54] Farea al-Muslimi, a Yemeni writer and cofounder of the Sana'a Center for Strategic Studies, said that his "biggest concern" about the transition agreement "was always how they gave Saleh unconditional immunity": "That is what ultimately shaped the war after that. They wanted to trade justice for security, and they lost both. We lost both."[55]

While the GCC Initiative succeeded in getting Saleh out of office, it left his support base largely intact. According to the analyst Nadwa Al-Dawsari, the transition failed because "the GCC initiative was by itself deeply flawed. . . . It granted Saleh immunity, and he remained in control of most of the armed forces, but this time without accountability because he was technically out of power."[56] As al-Muslimi said, Saleh was "head of a state and head of a mafia. He suddenly became only head of a mafia, and [he had] international immunity."[57]

Short-Term Calculus

Despite an apparent lack of viable alternative options, some observers later came to regret the decision to grant Saleh immunity for these reasons. Ambassador Feierstein said, "I think that where we fell short was in not pressing harder with the Yemenis to clean away some of the obstacles of the political opponents, and particularly Ali Abdullah Saleh and his efforts to obstruct the transition. We should have pressed harder on that."[58] U.S. officials and international diplomats ultimately decided not to press further on transitional justice issues because they believed there was a zero-sum trade-off between stability, on the one hand, and accountability and justice, on the other. Aboueldahab writes, "For regional and international actors, political stability in Yemen and the containment of non-state actors such as AQAP were vital to prevent a bloody transition that could spill over borders."[59]

In the short term, that was an understandable calculation, since it held off conflict for a couple of years. But in the long run it was a false trade-off because the lack of accountability allowed Saleh and other elite perpetrators to continue to sow chaos.

The NDC's Inglorious End

Even as the NDC and transitional government trudged forward, the military balance of power on the ground began to shift. Saleh and his backers made a tacit alliance with their erstwhile enemies the Houthis. As the Houthis progressed toward Sana'a, Saleh's allies on the ground either put up little resistance or actively fought alongside the Houthis. "In October" 2014, Ginny Hill reports, "Saleh's supporters were found to be manning 'Houthi' checkpoints in Sanaa."[60]

Houthi militias, assisted by members of Saleh's GPC, clashed with Islah-aligned groups in 2013 and early 2014. In September 2014, the Houthis seized Yemen's capital, Sana'a. The Houthis pushed through a Peace and National Partnership Agreement, which left Hadi in place as president and called for the inclusion of representatives from the Houthis, al-Hirak, and other groups to hold cabinet positions and advisory roles in the government. But the Houthis also set up their own shadow government to oversee the work of the ministries and eventually arrested Hadi, prompting his resignation in January 2015. Hadi then fled south to Aden, retracted his resignation, and attempted to reestablish his own government.

In response, the Houthis appointed their own "revolutionary council" to govern and, in February 2015, marched south toward Aden. By March 2015, the Houthis had taken control of Taiz, the country's third-largest city, and encircled Aden.[61]

The NDC left questions about the fundamentals of governance and accountability unresolved, ultimately leading to civil war. Questions about governance, regional autonomy, and access to government resources were left unanswered—and indeed under active dispute—through unification and the 1994 civil war and again through the failure of the NDC process that took place between 2013 and 2014. The 2014 civil war constituted a major new phase in these long-standing conflicts.

Yemen's Arab Spring started as a hopeful moment for the hundreds of thousands of protestors who came out into the streets to oppose Saleh's regime and call for a democratic transition. Instead, they got a flawed transition process followed by civil war and, soon after, an intervention by a coalition of regional countries, driving the conflict into a new and unprecedented phase.

CHAPTER FOUR

Regional Proxy Wars before 2015

W HY DID SAUDI ARABIA and the United Arab Emirates militarily intervene in Yemen's civil war? From an outside perspective, this decision is puzzling: the intervention lasted more than seven years with little to show for it. The Houthis continue to control much of northern Yemen. The Saudi-led coalition has become bogged down in a quagmire, and its members have come to acknowledge that there is no military solution for the conflict. At the same time, the intervention's brutal conduct has significantly dented Saudi Arabia and the UAE's international reputations and damaged their relationships with their most important security partner, the United States. In recognition of all of this, the UAE withdrew most of its forces from Yemen in 2019.

To understand this decision, as well as Iran's support for the Houthis, we must look to Saudi Arabia, the UAE, and Iran's experience of the Arab Spring prior to March 2015. These countries' Arab Spring interventions indelibly shaped how their leadership viewed the conflict in Yemen when it erupted. This perspective helps explain how and why the Saudi-led coalition intervened in March 2015, as well as Iran's escalating support to the Houthis following the coalition intervention. The 2011 through 2015 period of conflict and intervention in the Middle East also shaped how the Obama administration understood the conflict in Yemen and why the United States ended up supporting the Saudi-led intervention.

The war in Yemen began as an internal conflict, with armed groups fighting over access to the power and resources of the central government. But this post–Arab Spring regional history is critical to understanding external intervention in Yemen's war: as the transnational Arab Spring protest movement took off across the Middle East, regional powers including Saudi Arabia, the United Arab Emirates, and Iran saw this new source of instability as both a threat and an opportunity. From the perspective of these Arab Gulf monarchies, the Arab Spring posed a threat to their own countries' domestic stability, since it created examples of democratic revolutions that could inspire similar movements at home. The threat was particularly acute when it affected close allies and bordering states—such as Bahrain's 2011 protest movement. At the same time, when protest movements provoked instability within opponent states, regional powers saw the instability as an opportunity to revise elements of the existing regional balance of power through proxy warfare.

Saudi Arabia's, the UAE's, and Iran's proxy strategies over decade following the Arab Spring can be understood through two strategic lenses: opportunism and status quo maintenance. In the early years of the Arab Spring and its aftermath, Saudi Arabia and the UAE adopted opportunistic and revisionist strategies aimed at assisting regime change in opponent states in order to revise the regional order. By the time the Saudi-led coalition's military intervention in Yemen began in March 2015, however, the Gulf monarchies were taking a more conservative approach to the region's conflicts. The revisionist approach of 2011 through 2014 had been replaced by a status quo orientation.

At the same time, Iran saw its support for the Houthis in Yemen as an opportunity to expand its regional influence and harass Saudi Arabia, Iran's regional opponent, on the Kingdom's southern border. The history of intervention in the Middle East's proxy wars from 2011 through 2014 deeply shaped how both Iran's and the Gulf monarchies' leaders approached the intervention in Yemen's civil war.

Saudi Arabia and the UAE: Opportunism in the Early Post–Arab Spring Period, 2011–2014

From 2011 through about mid-2014, Saudi Arabia and the UAE took a largely opportunistic approach to the Arab Spring. They viewed state weakness and conflict in Libya and later in Syria as an opportunity to revise the regional balance of power by replacing opponents with friendlier regimes. Notably, however, both Saudi Arabia and the UAE took a more conservative approach to instability on the Arabian Peninsula itself, where they deployed forces to quash a nascent protest movement in neighboring Bahrain in 2011.

In the earliest days of the transnational Arab Spring movement, both Saudi Arabia and the UAE saw it as cause for concern. Saudi Arabia experienced some domestic opposition organizing and protest in response to the initial wave of the Arab Spring, including calls for a March 11 "Day of Rage" on Facebook. The Kingdom quickly shut down these nascent organizing efforts with violent repression: the Saudi National Guard was deployed across the country, and protests in Qatif were met with violence from state security services. The Saudi monarchy also sought to discredit protests by depicting the political opposition in a sectarian light, claiming that they were part of an Iranian conspiracy to destabilize the Kingdom.[1] Saudi leaders also announced major new spending packages, state subsidies, and employment benefits designed to reduce tensions.

Like the Kingdom, the UAE also moved quickly to repress any potential source of protest. The de facto head of state, Mohammed bin Zayed (MbZ), then crown prince of Abu Dhabi, viewed the rise of Muslim Brotherhood parties in Egypt and Tunisia as a threat to the Emirates' domestic stability. The UAE did not experience significant domestic mobilization in response to the Arab Spring, in part due to a swift crackdown on any potential dissent.[2] Nevertheless, the regime escalated repression where it perceived even the potential for domestic mobilization, arresting ninety-four people with suspected ties to the Muslim Brotherhood in 2012. Like Saudi Arabia, the UAE government also announced increased public spending in the early months of the Arab Spring.[3]

Saudi and Emirati Arab Spring
Interventions, 2011–2014

In the early years following the Arab Spring protests, Saudi Arabia and the UAE launched interventions in Bahrain, Libya, and Syria. In Bahrain, Saudi Arabia and the UAE intervened to suppress protests and support the ruling regime. In contrast with subsequent interventions in Libya and Syria, the intervention in Bahrain was status quo–oriented, aimed at preserving a fellow Sunni monarchy's rule.

On March 14, 2011, Saudi Arabia, the UAE, and Kuwait sent two thousand security forces to Bahrain, a country with a Shia majority ruled by a Sunni monarchy, under the aegis of the GCC's joint Peninsula Shield Force to suppress protests and shore up the government.[4] Protests that had spread from Bahrain to Saudi Arabia's Eastern Province in mid-February 2011 heightened Arab monarchs' concerns about domestic unrest.[5] The Kingdom had already violently crushed protests in Saudi Arabia's Eastern Province, an area with a significant Shia population. The joint GCC military intervention in Bahrain was intended not just to suppress protests in Manama but also as a message to Saudi Arabia's Eastern Province that the regime would use counterrevolutionary force wherever its interests were threatened.

The Gulf monarchies took a different approach in Libya and Syria, where initially peaceful protest movements were overtaken by violence. In both Libya and Syria, the Gulf monarchies, led by Qatar, played active roles in supporting insurgent groups. The Gulf monarchies saw the March 19, 2011, NATO-led coalition intervention in Libya as an opportunity to replace the erratic Libyan leader Muammar Ghaddafi with a more sympathetic government and thereby increase their regional influence. Qatar and the UAE both played leading roles in persuading the Arab League to vote in favor of the intervention, flew sorties as part of the NATO no-fly-zone mission, and provided arms and training to Libyan opposition militia groups. Nevertheless, Qatar's and the UAE's initial optimism about proxy war in Libya failed to carry into the post-Ghaddafi political landscape. Notably, Al-Watan, an Islamist party preferred by Qatar, only won one seat in 2012 constituent assembly elections.[6]

In Syria, the Gulf monarchies also initially believed that they could replace Bashar al-Assad's regime with a friendlier one. "When the [Syrian] uprising first began," writes the journalist Hassan Hassan, "Gulf leaders felt that the time was ripe to finally pull Syria [away from Iran and] into their orbit."[7] Saudi King Abdullah was the first leader in the Arab world to openly condemn the Assad regime's repression of protestors and first to publicly call for the arming of the Syrian opposition.[8] Saudi Arabia, along with Qatar and Kuwait, provided funding and support to Syria's political and military opposition, while the UAE played a less active role.[9] Saudi Arabia and Qatar cultivated relationships with competing political factions in the Syrian National Council (SNC), the coordinating body for the Syrian opposition. While the largest factions received support from both Saudi Arabia and Qatar, the Gulf states also funded a diverse array of opposition factions, many of which competed with one another for external support, driving the factionalization of the Syrian opposition.[10]

Two axes of competition emerged among state sponsors of proxy forces. Saudi Arabia and the UAE supported proxies that opposed the Muslim Brotherhood affiliates, whereas Qatar tended to support Muslim Brotherhood affiliates and other Islamist groups.[11] As the Free Syrian Army (FSA), a loose coalition of armed Syrian opposition groups, faltered due to internal divisions and increasing factionalization, hope for a rapid opposition victory over Assad's government gave way to quagmire.[12] The faltering of the Gulf monarchies' proxies in both Libya and Syria made them much less sanguine about the possibility of reordering those countries more favorably via proxy war.

This recent history would directly shape regional actors' approaches to Yemen's civil war. It also foreshadowed strategic divisions among the members of the Saudi-led coalition, which in turn would shape the course of the coalition's war in Yemen.

The United States, the Gulf Monarchies, and Proxy Sponsorship through 2014

The United States' approach to the region also shaped the Saudi and Emirati approaches to intervention prior to Yemen's civil war. Hope that the United States might intervene in Syria was dashed in the wake of President Obama's decision not to intervene in August 2013.[13] At the same time, the Obama administration's initial reaction to the Arab Spring had already raised concerns that the United States was stepping back from its traditional role in the Gulf of guaranteeing the Gulf monarchies' security. President Obama's public calls for Egypt's President Hosni Mubarak to step down in February 2011 were not well regarded in Riyadh and Abu Dhabi. As President Obama related in his memoirs, "MBZ told me that U.S. statements on Egypt were being watched closely in the Gulf, with increasing alarm. . . . It shows," MbZ told Obama, "that the United States is not a partner we can rely on in the long term."[14]

The signing of the Iran nuclear deal, or the Joint Comprehensive Plan of Action (JCPOA), caused a further breach in Gulf monarchies' relations with the United States. When the deal was announced, a Saudi diplomat described it as "extremely dangerous," arguing, "if sanctions are lifted, Iran will try even harder to redesign the region."[15] Gulf leaders worried that the Iran deal signaled the United States' acceptance of a de facto Iranian sphere of influence in the region.[16] Driven by their perception that the United States was pulling back from the role of security guarantor, the Gulf monarchies demanded greater reassurance. While this shaped their approach to regional proxy wars, it also gave the Gulf monarchs leverage over the United States. As President Obama later wrote, the Arab Gulf countries were "all aware that when push came to shove, we couldn't afford to risk our strategic position in the Middle East by severing relations with three Gulf countries."[17] Saudi Arabia and the UAE would use this leverage to their advantage in March 2015, when they announced the coalition's military intervention in Yemen.

Saudi and Emirati Approaches to Yemen's War

By late 2014, Saudi Arabia and the UAE had begun to see proxy sponsorship as a means of crisis containment, rather than a way to expand their influence across the Middle East. The coalition's intervention in Yemen in 2015 was a way to shore up border security and contain the crisis of increased Iranian influence on the peninsula. Saudi Arabia has long viewed its southern neighbor as falling within the Kingdom's sphere of influence and as a high security priority. Saudi Arabia also has a history of meddling in Yemeni politics, often by providing tribal leaders and others with cash payments but also occasionally through indirect or direct intervention in Yemen's civil wars, as in the 1960s, when Saudi Arabia provided support for royalist forces, or later during the Saada wars. The Kingdom's typical way of conducting Yemen policy was "slowly, behind the scenes, and in cash," writes the journalist Ben Hubbard.[18]

The loss of Saudi influence in the border region posed a threat to Saudi Arabia's border security strategy, just at a time when a major internal campaign to drive members of al-Qaeda out of Saudi Arabia caused many to flee across the border into Yemen.[19] Border security became increasingly important to Saudi Arabia in the early 2000s with the rise of al-Qaeda in the Arabian Peninsula (AQAP).[20] Saudi Arabia saw trafficking across the border as an acute security threat.[21] Saudi officials traditionally used financial support for tribes in the border region to secure the border. The increasing power of the Houthis in the border region over the course of the Saada wars in the first decade of this century meant that many tribal leaders who had developed long-standing relationships with the Saudis were pushed out of power. "By expelling the most influential shaykhs from their areas along the boundary, the Houthis upset a fragile balance," writes the scholar Marieke Brand. "The Houthi conflict generated a crisis serious enough to destabilize the entire system of bilateral border protection that had evolved since the 1934 Saudi-Yemeni War, which depended heavily on the cooperation and co-optation of the local tribes."[22]

Saudi Arabia also saw Iranian sponsorship of the Houthis as a major threat.[23] In a 2018 interview, Saudi Crown Prince Mohammed bin Salman (MbS) described the threat in existential terms: "I believe the Iranian supreme leader makes Hitler look good," MbS said. "The supreme leader is trying to conquer the world."[24] MbS went on to describe Saudi Arabia's behavior as a defensive reaction to Iran: "We are pushing back on these Iranian moves. We've done this in Africa, Asia, in Malaysia, in Sudan, Iraq, Yemen, Lebanon."[25] In another interview, he clarified his belief that Ayatollah Khamenei, Iran's supreme leader, "wants to create his own project in the Middle East very much like Hitler who wanted to expand at the time."[26]

From this perspective, Iranian support for the Houthis—on Saudi Arabia's own border no less—posed a threat to the Kingdom's security. In an interview with *60 Minutes*, MbS declared, "The Iranian ideology [had] penetrated some part of Yemen. During that time, [the Iranian-supported Houthis were] conducting military maneuvers right next to our borders and positioning missiles at our borders."[27] MbS also likened his security concerns about the Kingdom's southern border to the United States' own southern border, saying, "I can't imagine that the United States will accept one day to have a militia in Mexico launching missiles on Washington D.C."[28] MbS also referred to the Houthis as "a new Hezbollah in the Arabian peninsula."[29] As a commentator wrote in the Saudi-owned daily *Asharq al-Awsat* during the Saudi-led coalition's intervention in Yemen, "this time, Saudi has declared an end to passive neutrality and the end of silence on Iran, and that the time has come to strengthen the central government and a new state of Yemen."[30]

In September 2014, shortly after Houthi forces took over Sana'a, Iranian member of Parliament Ali Reza Zakani said that Sana'a was the fourth Arab capital to fall under Iranian influence, in addition to "the three Arab capitals who are already a subsidiary of the Iranian Islamic revolution," a reference to Beirut, Baghdad, and Damascus.[31] Saudi and Emirati officials saw statements like these as an expression of Iran's direct control over their Houthi proxies. According to Antony Blinken, then deputy secretary of state, when he traveled to Riyadh to meet with Mohammed bin Salman at the beginning of the coalition's intervention in Yemen, MbS told him that "his goal was to eradicate all Iranian influence in Yemen."[32] Likewise, UAE Foreign Minister Sheikh Abdullah bin Zayed Al Nahyan stated in 2015, "Iran is not carrying out this activity only in Yemen, it is conducting the same activity in Lebanon, in Syria, Iraq, Afghanistan and in Pakistan"; he added, "It is not possible to accept any strategic threat to Gulf Arab states."[33] Saudi Arabia thus perceived the Houthis as an Iranian proxy and blamed Iran for the 2014 coup in Yemen.[34]

While Emirati leaders shared Saudi concerns about Iran, they also worried that the war in Yemen could empower Islah, the Yemeni Islamist political party with ties to the Muslim Brotherhood. Islah gained greater prominence in Yemen's politics after 2011.[35] In the eyes of the UAE's Mohammed bin Zayed, Muslim Brotherhood affiliates across the Middle East were a threat to the UAE's domestic security and regime stability. MbZ reportedly told a U.S. diplomatic delegation in 2004, "We are having a culture war with the Muslim Brotherhood in this country."[36] Emirati leadership was also threatened by the Qatar-Turkey axis of support for Islamists and Muslim Brotherhood affiliates across the region and saw sponsorship of opposing groups as a means of balancing against these regional rivals of the UAE.

Saudi Arabia's and the UAE's decision to intervene in Yemen's war was therefore in keeping with a long-standing tradition of both intervening in Yemen's political affairs and sponsoring proxy forces in the wave of substate conflict that had engulfed the Middle East and North Africa (MENA) region post-2011. Additionally, both Saudi Arabia and the UAE had experienced shifts in their regime structures prior to 2015 that enabled both states to engage in more assertive military intervention abroad than they had in the past. The consolidation of foreign-policy-making authority within Saudi Arabia and the UAE created structural conditions that made each more likely to use force abroad: MbS and to a lesser extent MbZ are seen as the architects of the coalition intervention in Yemen.

In Saudi Arabia, multiple power centers, or "veto players," within the monarchy had checked the most aggressive impulses of one another for the past several decades. However, King Salman's consolidation of power within the Saudi royal family beginning in 2015 enabled MbS, who served as minister of defense beginning in late January 2015 and later became crown prince in 2017, to engage in more assertive regional policies. The Saudi royal family governs Saudi Arabia through a system that the scholar Steffen Hertog calls "segmented clientelism," a "pattern of state-building in which rulers have tended to settle conflicts and build alliances within the ruling family by creating new institutions, positions and sources of patronage."[37] This institutional configuration emerged after a power struggle between King Saud and Crown Prince Faisal in the early 1960s. When Faisal prevailed, he rewarded loyal members of the ruling family with the leadership of the Ministry of Defense and Aviation, the Interior Ministry, and the National Guard. Each of these three agencies subsequently served as a position of power for different factions of the ruling family, forming a tripolar balance of power within the regime.[38]

Historically, this dynamic has limited Saudi leaders' ability to engage militarily outside Saudi borders, because factions within the royal family have checked one another's more assertive impulses. However, this institutional setup was altered after Saudi King Abdullah died on January 23, 2015—just two months before the Saudi-led coalition intervention in Yemen began. From the beginning of the reign of his successor, King Salman, "the intricate network of Saudi influence and factional balancing, built up for decades by the King's late brother Sultan, appeared on the verge of collapse."[39] The scholar Gregory Gause writes that prior to King Abdullah's death, "important decisions went through the senior princes, many of whom had veto power. As a result, Saudi politics, both foreign and domestic, usually reflected consensus positions. Change was rare and gradual." But after coming to power in 2015, King Salman took a different path, "sidelining the remaining princes of his own generation and those in the next generation who could rival his favorite son." These changes within the regime, Gause writes, "have removed the constraints that previously rendered Saudi policymaking cautious, predictable, and risk averse."[40] Following King Salman's ascent to the throne, his son Mohammed bin Salman took increasingly assertive steps to consolidate his own authority, pushing out members of the royal family who led rival factions and who therefore might have been able to check MbS's aggressive foreign policy impulses.

Likewise, a major shift in the power centers within the UAE's monarchy made the UAE more likely to use military force outside its borders. The United Arab Emirates is a federal system of seven emirates. While traditionally the leaders of all seven emirates have played a role in foreign policy decisions, Abu Dhabi and Dubai play an outsized role in policy making at the federal level.[41] In 2008, Abu Dhabi provided Dubai with a $20 billion bailout during the global financial crisis. The bailout led to a shift in decision-making authority that heavily favored Abu Dhabi. Since 2009, Abu Dhabi's Crown Prince Mohammed bin Zayed promoted a more assertive role for the UAE in the region and "constructed a security state apparatus characterized by a hardline and zero-tolerance approach to threat prevention."[42] The UAE's active role in the Yemen intervention was facilitated by this consolidation of foreign-policy-making authority in Abu Dhabi. By 2015, MbS and MbZ both shared a drive to reorient the regional balance of power and held similar views on the key security issues facing their countries, building a strong personal relationship based in part around their shared views.[43]

This generational shift in both Saudi Arabia and the UAE also led to the loss of institutional and personal connections with key players in Yemen. In the Saudi royal family in particular, senior leaders had built relationships with key officials and tribal leaders in Yemen over the course of several decades. The shift to a new generation of leadership, and the expulsion of other senior leaders in the royal family who had experience working with Yemeni leaders, meant that many of these personal connections were lost. These lost connections, in turn, hampered the new Saudi leadership's ability to understand what was happening on the ground in Yemen and made them overconfident in their ability to achieve their objectives through the use of force rather than more traditional modes of diplomacy.

It is possible that the Saudi-led coalition's intervention in Yemen in March 2015 would have happened even in the absence of this generational shift in leadership and the consolidation of power within the Saudi and UAE regimes, since other factors were also pushing toward intervention. The Middle East analyst Michael Stephens notes, "there is a tendency to overestimate the impact of [MbS] on foreign policy, attributing almost all of Riyadh's adventurism to him." But Stephens argues that this assumption "misunderstands that Saudi calculations were being recalibrated far in advance of the young prince's rise."[44] Nevertheless, it is notable that these factors pushed in favor of intervention.

2011–2014: Iran in the Early Post–Arab Spring Period

Like Saudi Arabia and the UAE, Iran saw the Arab Spring and the ensuing turmoil across the Middle East through the lens of opportunism and threat.[45] While the early protest movements threatened the stability of some of Iran's regional opponents and empowered potentially friendly Islamist movements, the conflict in Syria threatened Iran's only state ally and a critical geographic link to their proxy Hezbollah.

The previous decade had seen Iran's greatest regional rival, Saddam Hussein, displaced by the 2003 U.S. intervention in Iraq.[46] While Iran was therefore in a strong regional position when the 2009 Green Movement protests began, the protests themselves challenged the regime's internal stability. In 2009, following contested presidential elections, millions of Iranians protested in the streets. The protest movement was the largest Iran had seen since the country mobilized against the Shah during the 1979 revolution, with an estimated three million people taking to the streets of Tehran at the movement's height.[47] While the government repressed the Green Movement, the fact that a large portion of the population had been mobilized prompted introspection among Iran's security apparatus, leading Iranian officials "to grapple with the extent of its internal vulnerability and to take additional measures to suppress internal dissent."[48] When the Arab Spring protests emerged less than two years later, Iranian leaders were concerned that they could inspire the revival of the Green Movement within Iran. According to the scholar Ariane Tabatabai, the Iranian "regime was deeply concerned about the possible domino effect of the [Arab Spring] movement and its implications for its own survival—especially after the 2009 Green Movement."[49]

Iran's leadership tried to frame the Arab Spring as an Islamic awakening that was the logical successor to Iran's 1979 revolution, situating Iran as the inspiration for the protests. Iran's Supreme Leader Ali Khamenei declared in early 2011 that the protests were a "natural continuation of the Iranian revolution of 1979" and were "the same as 'Islamic Awakening,' which [was] the result of the victory of the big revolution of the Iranian nation."[50] Yet the regime's framing of the Arab Spring "was challenged right from the beginning—not least in Iran itself," where the Green Movement organized a series of protests, triggering "a countrywide wave of persecution" in response from the state.[51] Elsewhere in the region, the Arab Spring "toppl[ed] or put at risk [Iran's] political foes," writes the scholar Afshon Ostovar. But at the same time, "seeing the pro-democracy movement spread in the region would have been unsettling for Iran's leaders."[52] Events triggered by the Arab Spring therefore also threatened the Iranian regime's core conceptions of its domestic security.

However, the most serious threat to Iran's security interests posed by the Arab Spring was the revolutionary uprising against the Syrian regime of Bashar al-Assad.[53] Syria quickly became "the most important battlefield of the post–Arab Spring years for Iran," Ostovar notes.[54] Iran's regional strategy of "forward defense" entailed cultivating asymmetric military capabilities by providing support to like-minded actors in the region to counter opponents' conventional military capabilities. Since the 1979 revolution, Iran had been at a military disadvantage due to its international isolation, while at the same time its regional competitors developed increasingly robust security relationships with the United States and other Western countries.[55] To compensate for this disadvantage, Iran's security services had developed a military doctrine "designed to deter state and non-state adversaries by raising the costs of targeting the nation through mostly unconventional means," primarily through its missile system and by developing a network of state and nonstate partners across the region.[56]

This network of security partners—known as the "axis of resistance"—consisted primarily of nonstate actors, including Hezbollah and Hamas. Iran's regional clients allowed it to "export its worldview; reduce the costs of intervention; and overcome its lack of alliances with state actors," while "lowering the cost of defeat for Iran" with deniability and relatively low costs of assisting regional clients.[57] As Qassim Soleimani, commander of the Islamic Revolutionary Guard Corps (IRGC)–Quds Force, who is credited with building many of these relations, explained, "Iran's defeat or victory does not occur in Mehran or Khorramshahr. Our borders have gone further. We must witness victory in Egypt, Iraq, Lebanon, and Syria."[58]

Syria's Assad regime was Iran's only state ally. This partnership with the Syrian state had particular geographic significance, since Syria provided a "land bridge" to Iran's most important client, Hezbollah. Iran helped to create Hezbollah in the early 1980s and "armed, trained and otherwise nurtured it" since, writes the scholar Daniel Byman.[59] As an IRGC officer who served in Syria noted,

Assad "was the one who protected the resistance line in the region and established a connecting bridge between Iran, Hezbollah and Hamas. What Arab country do you know that has provided such a connection for Iran?"[60]

The Arab Spring revolution that threatened the Assad regime therefore posed a major threat to Iran. Writing in 2011, Suzanne Maloney argued that "unrest in Syria must engender deep-seated angst among Iranian decisionmakers. Should the Assad regime collapse, Tehran would lose its most trusted regional partner and its most reliable mechanism for resupplying Hezbollah."[61] Because Syria was an important conduit to Hezbollah, the fall of the regime also threatened Iran's ability to project influence in the region through its nonstate-actor proxies, thereby threatening the core of the axis of resistance. Iran saw the conflict in Syria "as a zero-sum game, fearing that the ouster of the Assad regime could pave the way for the emergence of a new regime and regional order intrinsically hostile towards Tehran."[62] A hostile Syria would, in turn, mean that Iran faced a Western-oriented Sunni crescent, extending from the Gulf through Turkey, Syria, and Jordan: "Iran now saw Syria as the first line of [defense] against a concerted effort by its . . . foes not only to bring about regime change in Damascus and the end of its alliance with Tehran, but also to isolate and overthrow the Islamic Republic."[63] Iran therefore intervened in Syria from the logic of threat, to save a critical partner.

In the earliest years of the Syrian civil war, Iran provided the Assad regime with advice about neutralizing the opposition, including technical guidance on monitoring social media use. Through 2013, Iran dispatched several hundred personnel to Syria, including IRGC units and specialists, as well as intelligence agents and police.[64] Over time, however, Iran's support expanded considerably, to the point that about five thousand Hezbollah fighters were in Syria, in addition to several thousand regular armed forces and IRGC forces and around twenty-five thousand Shia fighters from Afghanistan, Lebanon, Iraq, and elsewhere who had been trained and equipped by Iran.[65] This "train the trainer" model, which Iran would later deploy in Yemen as well, allowed Iran to cultivate Hezbollah's capabilities and in turn leverage Hezbollah's support to other Iranian clients like the Assad regime.[66]

Iran's role in Syria was unpopular at home among Iran's pop-
ulace, however, and was even controversial within factions of the
Iranian regime itself.[67] Reports of potential war crimes and human rights violations, including the Assad regime's use of chemical
weapons, sparked "memories of Saddam Hussein's use of chemical
weapons" during the Iran-Iraq War.[68] Iran's sectarian approach to
regional security affected Iran's efforts to hold together the axis of
resistance. In February 2012, Hamas, a Sunni organization, left its
headquarters in Damascus in protest of Iran's support for Assad and
its sectarian policies.[69] Iran's relations with other Arab governments
and with Turkey also declined as its intervention in Syria ramped
up. Egypt's President Morsi, whom Iran had first seen as a potential
new friend in the region, was "particularly scathing" in "criticism
of Iran's policy towards Syria."[70] By mid-2013, Tehran's leadership
believed "that Iran [was] a net loser from the Arab Spring, and this
trend [was] likely to intensify."[71]

On the other hand, the U.S. intervention in Iraq and ISIS's dramatic rise in the summer of 2014 provided Iran considerable room
for opportunism in its regional intervention strategy. Iran intervened in Iraq via its partnerships with proxy militias due to the logic
of opportunity. Iran had supported Shia militias in Iraq since the
Iran-Iraq War, and it both drew on and expanded these networks
after the 2003 U.S. invasion of Iraq in order to counter "the presence of US military forces and shap[e] the re-emergence of the Iraqi
state."[72]

The Popular Mobilization Units (PMU), an umbrella organization that included Shia militias, as well as Sunni Arab fighters
and fighters from ethnic and religious minority groups, became
the primary vehicle for Iran's military influence in Iraq. Abu Mahdi
al-Muhandis, who was deputy chair of the PMU, was killed in the
same airstrike that killed Qassim Soleimani in January 2020. Al-
Muhandis had coordinated the various PMU factions while serving
as a leading figure in one of the PMU militias, Kataib Hizbullah
(KH). The fact that al-Muhandis was traveling with Soleimani in
Iraq demonstrates the closeness of the relationship between the
PMU and IRGC-Quds Force.[73]

Iran's post–Arab Spring intervention in Syria was therefore
more costly with regard to both resources invested and its regional

reputation. In other arenas, however, such as Iraq, Iran's strategy of partnering with proxies ensured that, according to Ostovar, "the costs associated with Iran's regional policies remained low relative to what the country's defense budget would require if Tehran were to pursue the same objectives by different means. Indeed, Iran was now able to project power across its region without deploying its own troops and suffering too many casualties."[74] In short, "Iran's network of non-state actors [had] become an indispensable, and, indeed, fruitful component of its grand strategy."[75] In Yemen, Iran saw an opportunity to continue to build this network and expand the axis of resistance.

Iran's War in Yemen: Iran's Relationship with the Houthis through 2015

Iran's approach to the Houthis in Yemen was informed by this post–Arab Spring experience. In contrast with its involvement in Syria and Iraq, "Yemen [was] not a priority for Iran," write Dina Esfandiary and Ariane Tabatabai.[76] Instead, Iranian involvement with the Houthis built on Iran's regional asymmetric security strategy. In Yemen, Iran partnered with the Houthis in order to antagonize Saudi Arabia from its southern border and remind the Kingdom that Iran was capable of pushing back.

The Houthis are a Yemeni movement driven by their own particular grievances against the Yemeni government, but the Saudi-led coalition sought to portray them as an Iranian proxy under the direct command and control of Iran or the IRGC. Ironically, this portrayal may have made the Houthis more open to accepting Iranian assistance: "by branding the Houthis as . . . agents of Iran," note Esfandiary and Tabatabai, "President Saleh and Saudi Arabia contributed to a self-fulfilling prophecy, pushing the group into Tehran's all-too-willing hands."[77] Indeed, the Houthis welcomed Iranian assistance, although Iran's support to the Houthis was modest compared to the resources and enduring partnership it provided to Hezbollah. This is in part because the Houthis did not rely on Iranian small arms, since they allied with former Yemeni army units, giving the Houthis "access to local arms, including armor, artillery, and ballistic missiles."[78] At the same time, the Houthis did not necessarily respond to orders from Iran or the IRGC. For example, in 2014, IRGC-Quds Force leadership advised the Houthis not to topple Hadi's government in Sana'a and later advised them not to march south toward Aden—advice that the Houthis self-evidently declined to take.[79]

Iranian officials have also, at times, played into this narrative, since the idea of Iranian control over the Houthis "makes Tehran look like a master puppeteer, further enabling it to project power and dominance over the region."[80] Still, Iranian support for the Houthis, especially before 2014, was not determinative of the Houthis' military capabilities. U.S. Ambassador Stephen Seche wrote in a December 2009 cable that "contrary to . . . claims that Iran is arming the Houthis, [they] obtain their weapons from the Yemeni black market," and he quoted a Yemeni official saying that the "Houthis easily obtain weapons inside Yemen. . . . The military 'covers up its failure' by saying the weapons come from Iran."[81]

Instead of providing a large amount of material support directly to the Houthis, Tehran's approach through 2015 was to build the Houthis' military as well as their administrative capacity. As a Hezbollah fighter said, "we are the guerilla experts, so we give advice about the best timings to strike back, when to hold back."[82] Through at least 2017, IRGC-Quds Force's and Hezbollah's "presence in Yemen [was] likely limited to advice and coordination efforts," in contrast with both organizations' more direct involvement on the ground in Syria.[83]

Iran's engagement with the Houthis deepened, however, following the Saudi-led coalition's intervention in the war in March 2015. External intervention was soon to transform Yemen's war from a local crisis to a regional humanitarian and political catastrophe.

CHAPTER FIVE

Descent into "Chaos"

Yemen's Civil War, 2015–2021

Although Yemen indeed appears to be chaotic from the outside, in the sense that general disorder visibly prevails, it contains its own internal logic, economies and political ecosystems.

—PETER SALISBURY

LESS THAN THREE YEARS after the Saudi-led coalition's intervention began, Yemen had become what the Yemen expert Peter Salisbury calls a "chaos state."[1] As a unified country, Yemen existed only in the international community's collective imagination, as "lines on a map and as a concept in newspaper reports."[2] The internationally recognized government led by President Hadi—who had last faced elections in 2012, when he ran unopposed—was based in Saudi Arabia and had only nominal sovereignty over parts of southern Yemen. On the ground, Yemen was governed by a patchwork of armed groups that collaborated or fought with each other in ever-shifting kaleidoscopic patterns.

Western coverage of the war in Yemen typically framed it as a conflict between the Houthis on one side and the Saudi-led coalition and the internationally recognized government of Yemen on the other. This is true on the surface, but the reality of the conflict is both more complicated and more difficult to summarize. At the same time, although the conflict appears complex and disordered, it also "contains its own internal logical, economies and political ecosystems," Salisbury notes.[3]

While the war formally began in September 2014 when the Houthis took over Sana'a, external intervention on both sides had a transformative effect on the conflict. The Saudi-led coalition's military intervention and Iran's support for the Houthis contributed to the transformation of what began as a localized conflict in an already-impoverished country into a destabilizing regional conflict that spilled across borders. The coalition intervention almost certainly meant that the war lasted longer, generated more deaths—both of soldiers on the battlefield and of civilians from violence and the second-order effects of war—and created the worst humanitarian crisis in the world, including the largest cholera outbreak in recorded history.

In 2021, UNICEF estimated that twenty-one million Yemenis, including eleven million children, constituting more than 60 percent of Yemen's total population, were in need of humanitarian assistance. Only half of Yemen's health facilities were functioning in the midst of a global pandemic, while 2.3 million children under the age of five suffered from acute malnutrition.[4] There were more than fifty active front lines of fighting ongoing in 2021, leaving four million Yemenis internally displaced, 76 percent of them women and children. The national economy had largely collapsed, driven in part by the dramatic devaluation of the Yemeni riyal, which drove up prices and made it increasingly difficult for people to buy necessary goods. Eighty percent of the country lived under the poverty line.[5] In February 2021, the UN Office for the Coordination of Humanitarian Affairs (OCHA) warned that the risk of widespread famine had "never been more acute."[6]

This is the story of Yemen's civil war from the beginning of the Saudi-led coalition's intervention in March 2015 through 2021. The chapter begins with an exploration of the Saudi-led coalition's intervention in March 2015 and Iran's support for the Houthis. It then turns to the dynamics of Yemen's humanitarian crisis as a result of the war and looks at how corruption has hindered the delivery of aid in response to the crisis. The chapter concludes by demonstrating how the dynamics of the conflict have driven factionalization on all sides of the war. Divergence between Saudi Arabia and the UAE over their strategic objectives in Yemen has driven divisions among the militias and political parties supporting the internationally recognized government of Yemen, while fault lines have also emerged among the Houthis.

The Saudi-Led Coalition's Intervention: Operations Decisive Storm and Restoring Hope

On March 26, 2015, Saudi Arabia and a coalition of Arab states launched Operation Decisive Storm at the request of President Hadi's internationally recognized government. The intervention included a sustained campaign of airstrikes, the blockade of air and sea routes into Yemen, and the deployment of forces on the ground.[7] While the intervening coalition is often described as Saudi-led, in practice there was a de facto division of labor between Saudi Arabia and the UAE, with Saudi Arabia taking the lead on the air campaign in the north while the UAE led the southern campaign, primarily through the use of its Special Forces, to both fight alongside and train local Yemeni militias.[8] About thirty-five hundred Emirati troops were deployed to Yemen, supported by approximately three thousand additional UAE forces operating offshore and from bases in the region, according to the defense analyst Michael Knights. This amounted to approximately one-sixth of the UAE's armed forces fighting in Yemen at any given time.[9]

Emirati forces fought alongside southern resistance militias to push the Houthis back from southern Yemen. Building on these gains, the UAE strengthened its "influence in the south and the west coast of Yemen," where the forces it supported "operate[d] entirely outside the Yemeni government chain of command."[10] The coalition's intervention was supported by operational assistance from the United States, France, and the United Kingdom. Several countries in the Horn of Africa—Djibouti, Eritrea, and Somalia—made military bases, airspace, and territorial waters available to the coalition.[11]

The coalition also employed mercenary forces in Yemen. Up to fourteen thousand militants from Sudan fought alongside the local militias aligned with the coalition at any given time in the early years of the coalition's intervention.[12] Most of these forces were from the Darfur region of Sudan and belonged to a militia previously known as the Janjaweed, which was implicated in sexual violence, indiscriminate killing of civilians, and other war crimes in Darfur. Many of these soldiers were seventeen years old or younger.[13] Under international law, armed groups are banned from recruiting or using in hostilities anyone under the age of eighteen.[14]

Saudi officials declared Operation Decisive Storm over on April 21 and replaced it with a new phase of the intervention, Operation Restoring Hope. Decisive Storm had "achieve[d] its goals, . . . removing the threat to Saudi Arabia and neighboring countries especially in terms of heavy weapons," said a Saudi official.[15] Restoring Hope would protect civilians, fight terrorism, and provide relief to the Yemeni people, according to Saudi officials.

Leading an on-the-ground coalition of forces loyal to Hadi's government and southern resistance militias trained by the Emiratis, the UAE moved quickly to take back Aden and surrounding territory held by Houthi forces in May and June 2015.[16] The UAE continued to train and equip southern militias, many of which are united under the banner of the Southern Transition Council (STC).[17] These militias, which numbered some twelve thousand fighters, alongside Emirati Special Forces, also took the lead in clearing AQAP fighters from areas in the south including Mukalla and the Masila oil fields in 2016.[18] After a missile strike on Marib in September 2015 killed more than fifty Emirati troops, the UAE drew down some of its own troops, replacing them with foreign contractors operating under the UAE flag.[19] The UAE also deployed forces to several bases in East Africa to support training of local forces and facilitate the UAE's operations in Yemen.[20]

Despite these initial successes, the conflict settled into a relative stalemate within its first year, with the Houthis controlling much of Yemen's northern territory along much of the Red Sea coast to the west and the governorates of Taiz and Al-Bayda farther east. While each side made battlefield gains and suffered losses in the subsequent years, the broader contours of the conflict did not change a

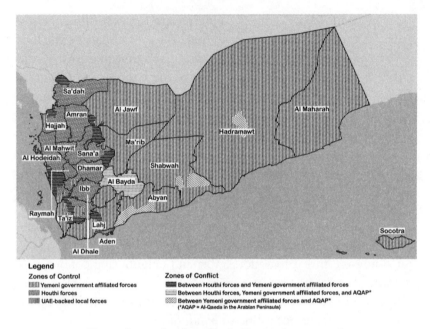

Zones of control and conflict in Yemen, August 2018.
(Credit: Ghaidaa Alrashidy)

great deal. By late 2016, coalition operations had managed to push
the Houthis out of pockets of the northwestern governorates of
al-Jawf and Marib but were unable to advance farther.[21] Blocked
by heavily fortified, mountainous terrain, the coalition had failed
to translate "operational success . . . into strategic victory" and had
made no further progress toward achieving its strategic aims.[22]

Saudi-Led Coalition Airstrikes

On the evening of Friday, November 20, 2017, Abbas Muhammad
Balam and a group of nineteen fishermen were repairing their fishing nets on the shore of Al-Badeaa', an uninhabited island along
Yemen's Red Sea coast. At about 9:30 p.m. that night, according to
witness testimony documented by the Yemeni human rights organization Mwatana for Human Rights, coalition aircraft dropped multiple bombs that struck the site where the fishermen were working

and their four boats moored nearby on the beach. The coalition bombs "killed nine fishermen and wounded five others," according to Mwatana's 2021 report *Starvation Makers*, which documents the use of starvation by both the Saudi-led coalition and the Houthis during the war. "I cannot forget that night. . . . I lost three of my brothers," said Alaallah Abbas, one of Abbas's sons who was also present that night. Research from Bellingcat using open-source data and satellite imagery was unable to identify any nearby military targets that could explain the attack, and none of the survivors knew of any military targets on or near the uninhabited island. The Joint Incidents Assessment Team (JIAT), the coalition's investigative mechanism, later released a statement claiming that their intelligence indicated an imminent weapons-smuggling operation in the area.[23]

The attack was devastating to the fishers, their families, and the larger community because of the lives lost, but it also destroyed the community's main source of livelihood. Abbas and the fishermen typically spent twenty to twenty-five days each month fishing at sea, providing the main source of food and income for 120 people. Salem, another of Abbas's sons, explained, "Fishing is the source of food and livelihood for everyone in the area. . . . Everyone here works in one way or another in fishing." The destruction of the boats and fishing tools meant that Abbas was unable to return to sea until two years later, when he obtained a loan that allowed him to purchase a new boat. This and other attacks on fishermen in the area also left the community with residual trauma, as they worried that they could be attacked again. Abbas's son Salem told Mwatana, "The sea in which we've worked since our childhood became an unsafe place for us. . . . But there is no other way to live."[24]

This airstrike was part of a broader pattern of coalition airstrikes that hit nonmilitary targets and killed civilians, illustrating the ripple effects of each of these attacks on Yemeni communities. According to the Yemen Data Project, between March 2015 and July 2021, the coalition conducted more than twenty-three thousand documented air raids (with each air raid comprising one or multiple strikes) and 453 air raids per month on average, leaving at least 8,773 people dead and 9,843 injured. About 30 percent of all recorded airstrikes targeted nonmilitary sites, with about one-third targeting military sites and an additional one-third targeting sites

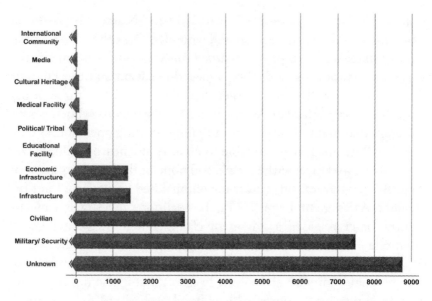

Coalition airstrikes by type. (Credit: Ghaidaa Alrashidy)

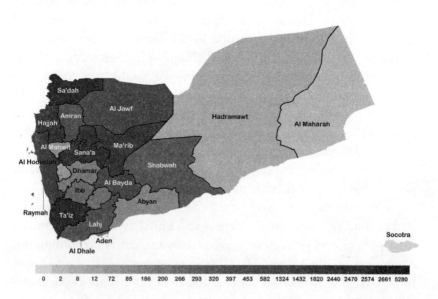

Coalition airstrikes by governorate. (Credit: Ghaidaa Alrashidy)

of an unknown type.[25] Mwatana documented 579 airstrikes from March 2015 through August 2021 that killed or injured thousands of civilians and destroyed nonmilitary infrastructure.[26] It also cited likely violations of international humanitarian law by the Houthis, including "restrictions on humanitarian organizations' operations and the diversion and redirection of humanitarian aid," as well as "the widespread use of landmines in Taiz Governorate."[27]

In the earliest years of the war, when the tempo of airstrikes was highest, several notorious strikes caused large numbers of civilian casualties, drawing international outrage and condemnation. These strikes included the bombing of a funeral hall in 2016, killing at least 140 civilians and wounding an additional 600, and a 2018 airstrike that hit a bus filled with children, killing at least 29 civilians, including 21 children.[28]

Cracks Emerge: Divergence in Saudi and Emirati Strategic Goals in Yemen

Increasing divergence within the coalition also accelerated clashes among armed groups—even those ostensibly on the same side of the war. While Saudi Arabia and the UAE shared leadership of the intervening coalition, in practice their strategic goals diverged over time, with discernable effects with regard to their respective proxy strategies. Saudi Arabia's main goal in the conflict was to push the Houthis out of Yemen entirely; when it became clear that an outright military victory was impossible, the Kingdom's strategy shifted to pushing back Houthi advances and securing the Kingdom's southern border.

The UAE's intervention aims included both defensive and opportunistic elements. The Emirates sought to expand its military and commercial presence in the Horn of Africa and Bab al-Mandeb strait. Control over ports on the Red Sea coast of Yemen and the Aden port would add to the Emirates' growing regional economic presence.[29] The UAE also had defensive security concerns in Yemen: the Emirates' leadership feared the security consequences of an expanded Muslim Brotherhood regional presence and sought to form and back military organizations that excluded, or even clashed with, Islah.

While Saudi Arabia threw its weight behind the internationally recognized government and President Hadi, the UAE also supported militias that were nominally allied with the Hadi government but had their own agendas, including Salafist groups, southern secessionists, and Tareq Saleh's forces. While Islah was one of the strongest factions within the internationally recognized government of Yemen, the UAE has provided staunch support to rival power centers within Hadi's government that oppose Islah, remarkably even hiring mercenaries to carry out targeted assassinations of Islah leaders, as *BuzzFeed News* reported.[30] From January 2016 through November 2018, the Armed Conflict Location & Event Data Project (ACLED) identified fifty-three assassinations and assassination attempts that targeted Islah party leaders and clerics. Although the UAE was only conclusively linked to one of the attempts, many observers suspected that they were responsible for the broader campaign.[31]

From the beginning of the coalition's intervention, the UAE built up, trained, and funded militia groups in southern Yemen. The Security Belt, which consisted of about fifteen thousand fighters and operated throughout most of the south, and the Shabwani Elite Forces, comprising three to four thousand fighters recruited in Shabwah governorate, were armed affiliates of the Southern Transition Council. They operated outside the formal command structure of the internationally recognized government, although they were nominally aligned with Hadi.[32] These UAE-supported militias played an important role in pushing the Houthis out of southern Yemen in 2016 and have since built a network of influence across Yemen's south and west coast.[33]

The coalition aligned with Hadi's government included a dizzying array of military forces, all nominally aligned but in practice with distinct—and sometimes clashing—objectives, values, and chains of command. To make things even more challenging, these armed groups frequently change names, are incorporated into other groups, and even clash with other armed groups that are ostensibly on the same side of the conflict. Tracking the ever-changing kaleidoscope of these forces' allegiances and clashes can be difficult even for close observers of the war. Table 1 lists some of the key factions aligned with the internationally recognized government (although it is not comprehensive).[34] While these armed groups were linked by the overarching goal of preventing Houthi advances in the south, they also had divergent political agendas. The Guardians of the Republic, also known as the Yemeni National Resistance, for example, wanted to take back Yemen's west coast from Houthi control and were loyal to Tareq Saleh, the late president Ali Abdullah Saleh's nephew. Saleh had originally aligned his supporters with the Houthis, but in December 2017, the former president was killed by the Houthis shortly after announcing the end of his alliance with them. The Giants Brigades was one of the larger military groups aligned with the UAE, with twenty to twenty-eight thousand fighters, and also fought to push the Houthis back from Yemen's west coast. The Tihama Resistance Forces are made up of Tihamis from Hodeidah governorate, a historically marginalized region. Many "were drawn from local resistance forces that formed" between 2014 and 2016, while some "came from al-Hirak al-Tihami," a local peaceful resistance movement that emerged during the Arab Spring.[35] The Tihama Resistance Forces were incorporated into the Giants Brigades and Guardians of the Republic, but tensions between Tihami leadership and Tareq Saleh remained.[36]

The Southern Transition Council, a powerful umbrella political organization that favors southern secession, has political roots in the post-1994 Southern Movement. When the Houthis first marched south toward Aden in March 2015, southern fighters from outside the official security services organized the defense of their regions, over the course of several months pushing the Houthi- and Saleh-aligned forces out, with the assistance of the UAE. Southern factions with close relationships with the UAE, led by the Hirak-aligned commanders Aidarous al-Zubaidi and Shelal Shayea, the Salafist leader Hani bin Breik, and other southern forces in favor of southern independence, rose to prominence in the following years, and while some of these leaders served in senior roles in Hadi's government and military forces, tensions between the Hadi government and STC leadership bubbled up repeatedly.

To complicate matters further, still other political and military leaders in the south did not have an allegiance to either the STC

Table 1. Key factions nominally aligned with the internationally recognized government of Yemen

Organization	Key leadership	Relationships
Hadi government	Abdrabbuh Mansur Hadi (president, government of Yemen, until 2022); Ali Mohsen al-Ahmar (vice president, government of Yemen, until 2022)	Nominally the umbrella uniting the internationally recognized government-aligned forces; in practice, clashed with STC
Southern Transition Council (STC) (and allied forces)	Aidarous al-Zubaidi (president, STC); Hani Bin Breik (vice president, STC)	Supported by the UAE; clashed with the Hadi government; clashed with Islah
Islah	Mohammed Abdullah al-Yadoumi (chairperson, Islah Party)	Supported the Hadi government; supported by Saudi Arabia; opposed by the UAE; clashed with STC
Guardians of the Republic/Yemeni National Resistance	Tareq Saleh	Supported by the UAE
Giants Brigades	Abdulrahman Abu Zara'a Al Muharrami (commander)	Supported by the UAE
Support and Backup Brigades (SBB) and Security Belt Forces	—	Supported by the UAE; clashed with the Hadi government; STC-affiliated
Shabwani Elite Forces	—	Supported by the UAE; STC-affiliated
Hadrami Elite Forces	Faraj Salman Al Bahsani	Supported by the UAE

or Hadi, even though they were nominally aligned with (or at least not opposed to) the internationally recognized government. In the Hadramawt, a region that has cultivated a political identity independent from either north or south Yemen, Hadrami leaders have expanded local autonomy. Hadrami leaders also have their own regional political concerns, such as advocating for a greater share of the oil wealth produced in Hadramawt.[37] Likewise, in Shabwa, Saleh Fareed Bin Mohsen al-Awlaki, the paramount sheikh of the Al-Awalak tribe, the largest tribe in Shabwa, joined the STC's leadership in 2017, although most of his tribe chose to remain loyal to Hadi. Al-Awlaki eventually defected from the STC, a decision that proved consequential when STC forces began a 2019 military offensive in Shabwa—while the local Shabwa Elite Forces had supported the UAE's previous anti-AQAP campaign in the region, factions of the forces, including al-Awlaki, declined to join them in 2019.[38]

In addition to Saudi Arabia's and the UAE's allegiance to different external supporters—Saudi Arabia for the Hadi government and the UAE for the STC and affiliated forces—there were two major sources of the latent tension between Saudi and Emirati aims in Yemen. The STC and Islah have been "fierce rivals," writes the analyst Elana DeLozier: Islah has accused the STC "of undermining national unity," while the STC accuses Islah of giving "cover to terrorists."[39] A regional intrasouth political rivalry also saw a split between Hadi and his allies, who were primarily from Shabwa and Abyan, and other political and military leaders from Lahj and al-Dhale, like al-Zubaidi and Shayea.[40]

UAE-supported southern officials in Hadi's cabinet became increasingly critical of his government and openly expressed support for southern independence. Throughout 2017, protests against the Hadi-led government demonstrated the public's frustration with the government's inability to consistently pay government wages and provide public utilities.[41] During the January 2018 Battle of Aden, fighting broke out between pro-STC militias and Hadi's forces when the internationally recognized government's security forces tried to prevent pro-STC protestors from entering Aden. The STC announced that it had won control of Aden by the end of the month.[42] Fighting began again in August 2019 after the STC accused Islah of being behind a Houthi missile attack on a military parade in Aden that killed dozens, including a senior Security Belt commander. Hadi government officials publicly aimed their frustrations at the UAE, accusing the Emirates of supporting a "coup."[43]

Conflicts within the anti-Houthi coalition have also broken out between armed groups supported by the UAE and Islah-affiliated officials. Islah is associated with the Muslim Brotherhood, and as discussed in chapter 5, UAE leaders have cracked down on Muslim Brotherhood affiliates at home in the UAE and supported proxy actors that oppose them across the Middle East, seeing the Muslim Brotherhood as a security threat.[44]

In the summer of 2019, however, the UAE began to draw down the bulk of its forces from Yemen, with remaining Emirati forces primarily assisting its Yemen proxy forces. The drawdown was seen as the result of increasing pressure from the United States, as well as a concession to the reality that the war increasingly did not seem to have a military solution. While the UAE retained its close ties to many southern military and political leaders—some who were actually based in Abu Dhabi—the drawdown marked a transition within the intervening coalition, with the UAE turning over many of its official duties to Saudi Arabia.

As fighting among factions in the south continued, Prince Khaled bin Salman, Saudi Arabia's deputy defense minister (and brother of Crown Prince Mohammed bin Salman) led a mediation effort between the Hadi government and STC. In November 2019, the parties agreed to the Riyadh Agreement, which attempted to address the sources of tension between the Hadi- and STC-aligned factions.[45] The Riyadh Agreement called for the formation of a new government under Hadi that included STC leadership, the integration of STC-aligned militias into the command-and-control structure of Hadi's government forces, the demilitarization of Aden, and the centralization of southern government financial institutions.[46]

The Riyadh Agreement was only partially successful in reducing tensions within the anti-Houthi coalition. The agreement "averted a war within Yemen's civil war" by ending the months-long standoff between forces loyal to Hadi and the STC, but the parties failed to implement many of its terms.[47] Implementation of the agreement's terms was delayed by disagreements between the two sides over sequencing, the STC's deep reluctance to integrate its own forces into the government security forces, and continued sporadic fighting in Abyan. Disagreements about how the agreement should actually be implemented were driven by the vagueness of the agreement's text. This confusion was both a feature and a bug of the Riyadh Agreement: it was "loosely worded, likely because vagueness was required to induce rivals to sign it." Still, the text itself left "a number of questions around implementation unanswered."[48]

In the eyes of the STC, the agreement conferred much-desired international legitimacy to its cause and even was a step toward southern independence.[49] The formation of a government with southern leadership without a parallel step to integrate southern military forces into formal government structures marked a concession to the STC's growing de facto authority: the STC "gained political recognition without having fulfilled its military and security obligations" or abandoning its public aim of secession.[50] By 2021, while still officially part of the internationally recognized government and holding several cabinet positions in Hadi's government, the STC maintained de facto control over Aden and most of the four southern governorates.[51]

The terms of the Riyadh Agreement also, perhaps unsurprisingly, benefited its broker, Saudi Arabia, which had by then taken over many of the UAE's diplomatic and military responsibilities following the UAE's drawdown. The Riyadh Agreement also became a moment for "Saudi Arabia [to] assume ultimate responsibility for southern Yemen politically, militarily and in terms of security."[52]

Iran's Support for the Houthis

Iran's support for the Houthis is often cited as an important source of the Houthis' military effectiveness, but this view overstates the effect of Iran's support. Iranian officials do not have a command-and-control relationship over the Houthis, as is sometimes portrayed. Nevertheless, Iran has provided material support and training to the Houthis via the IRGC and Hezbollah, and that support has escalated since the conflict began in 2014.

Through 2011, Iranian support for the Houthis primarily took the form of advice and capacity building.[53] Iran probably began providing weapons to the Houthis by 2012, with smugglers backed by the IRGC-Quds Force shipping AK-47 rifles, rocket-propelled grenades (RPGs), and other weapons to Yemen.[54] After the Houthis took over significant territory in 2014, Iran began to provide them with more support. As of 2016, according to the International Crisis Group, "the Houthis receive[d] political, moral and, likely, some degree of military support and training from Iran and Hezbollah"; notably, this was "much less than what the GCC funnels to the anti-Houthi block."[55] Likewise, the UN Panel of Experts concluded in January 2017 that they had "not seen sufficient evidence to confirm any direct large-scale supply of arms" from Iran, although there were "indicators that anti-tank guided weapons being supplied to the Houthi or Saleh forces are of Iranian manufacture."[56] The report also noted that the Houthis possessed weapons such as antitank guided missiles "that were not in the pre-conflict Yemeni stockpile," indicating that they had been provided by land via the border with Oman.[57]

Iran provided the Houthis with the technical assistance necessary for the Houthis to develop their own "small but effective military industry," while Hezbollah also provided training and assistance.[58] The development of these weapons systems has been well documented by the UN Panel of Experts. Before 2015, the Houthis were lightly armed and received minimal external support. When they captured state institutions and allied with Saleh's forces, the Houthis acquired many of the weapons that had been held by the Yemeni Armed Forces.[59] Since 2016, the Houthis have used drones, or unmanned aerial vehicles (UAVs), in an increasingly sophisticated manner both on the battlefield and against targets in Saudi Arabia and the UAE. Arms experts believe that earlier generations of UAVs were probably smuggled into the country but that more recently, they have been manufactured in Yemen with some civilian parts, like electronics and engines, brought in from abroad. The UN Panel of Experts determined that these missiles were manufactured in Iran and shipped in parts to Yemen, where they were assembled.[60]

The Houthis received military supplies via routes that circumvent the UN Verification & Inspection Mechanism for Yemen (UNVIM), which oversees the inspection of cargo arriving at Yemen's

Red Sea ports.[61] In 2021, the UN Panel of Experts "documented several supply routes" overland and by sea. The sea routes used traditional vessels known as "dhows" in Somali or Omani water. These boats delivered their cargo to ports on Yemen's southern coast, and it was then smuggled into Houthi-held territory. Other overland smuggling routes crossed Yemen's eastern border with Oman.[62] "Iran has developed a multitude of ways to deliver weapons to Yemen," a senior U.S. official said. "Every time we make some new seizures, Iran finds new ways to move weapons."[63]

In September 2019, drone attacks struck two oil-processing facilities in Saudi Arabia at Abqaiq and Khurais. While the Houthis initially claimed responsibility, the attacks were widely attributed to Iran.[64] The attack demonstrated the utility of Iran's relationship with the Houthis: Iran was able to deny responsibility and avoid escalation with Saudi Arabia.

Yemen's Humanitarian Crisis

Yemen has experienced a multitiered humanitarian crisis as a result of the war. One layer of the humanitarian crisis is hunger. By 2017, Yemen had one of the highest rates of malnutrition in the world. The World Food Programme estimated that 65 percent of Yemen's population was food insecure and that four out of ten children under the age of five were malnourished.[65] Almost nineteen million people, or 70 percent of the population, were in need of humanitarian assistance.[66]

Yemen is dependent on imports to meet much of the country's food and fuel needs: Yemen imports 90 percent of its staple foods, for example.[67] The actors who control ports can charge import taxes and customs, a significant source of revenue.[68] Control over Yemen's points of entry therefore has a significant effect on the availability and prices of food and other humanitarian goods. While the Saudi-led coalition claimed that controlling the flow of imports was key to keeping smuggled weapons out of Houthi hands, many activists and humanitarians saw it as a means of imposing collective punishment on the people of Yemen. Just a few months into the intervention in 2015, Oxfam was already warning that the blockade was accelerating widespread hunger. While Yemen already had the second highest malnutrition rate in the world even before the intervention began, the blockade led to scarcity, which in turn pushed food prices out of reach for many people.[69]

Casualties and mass displacement due to the fighting were another layer of the humanitarian crisis. The UN estimated that by February 2017, more than seventy-six hundred people, mostly civilians, had been killed since the fighting started, and another forty-two thousand had been injured.[70] Both the problems of acute malnutrition and injury were compounded by Yemen's collapsing health care system. The World Health Organization estimated in 2017 that more than 14.8 million Yemenis lacked access to basic health care, with only 45 percent of the country's health facilities still fully functioning and accessible.[71] Dr. Khlade Shuail, the director of one hospital in Hodeidah, reported in February 2017 that hospital staff had not received their salaries for five months. "There are acute shortages of certain medicines and we need more fuel to ensure the hospital has electricity," Dr. Suhail said.[72] A cholera outbreak that began in April 2017 became the largest in epidemiologically recorded history.[73]

Hodeidah port played a central role in several aspects of the humanitarian crisis. Hodeidah, one of the country's most densely populated areas, was controlled by the Houthis in 2017.[74] About 70 percent of Yemen's imports, including food, fuel, and other commercial and humanitarian goods, come through Hodeidah and the nearby Saleef port.[75] Prolonged fighting in Hodeidah would therefore probably have a devastating humanitarian impact. In 2016, Emirati officials proposed that the coalition make an amphibious assault on Hodeidah. But U.S. officials and other diplomats pushed back aggressively, fearing the humanitarian consequences of a coalition offensive on Hodeidah. The pressure sent the UAE "back to the drawing board," demonstrating that the United States had significant leverage over the coalition's conduct—when U.S. officials chose to exert that leverage.[76]

Hodeidah became the center of Yemen's humanitarian crisis once again in late 2017. A ballistic-missile strike launched by Houthi forces on November 4 targeted King Khalid International Airport in Riyadh. In response, the coalition announced the closure of all of Yemen's air, sea, and land ports. Saudi officials claimed that this full blockade was necessary "to fill in the gaps in the current inspection procedures, which cause the continuation of smuggling of these missiles and military equipment."[77] While humanitarian flights and deliveries of some relief materials were allowed to resume on November 22, 2017, humanitarian NGOs noted that "major restrictions on the delivery of essential goods to the civilian population" remained.[78]

The blockade of Hodeidah was compounded by the fact that coalition airstrikes had destroyed five cranes used to unload shipments coming into the port. Although the United States Agency for International Development (USAID) had donated $3.9 million to purchase new cranes for the port, the coalition turned the cranes away when they arrived. After a public rebuke from the Trump administration and private pressure from several senior U.S. officials, the coalition announced a temporary end to the blockade on December 20, 2017, and allowed the USAID-sponsored cranes into the port.[79] This pressure on the coalition from U.S. officials and the international community may have averted an even more dire humanitarian crisis.

Hodeidah once again became a contentious international issue in the summer of 2018. This time, the Trump administration was not willing to quash the coalition's renewed offensive, as the Obama administration had in 2016. Instead, the United States gave what many observers saw as a "yellow light" for the offensive.[80] Trump administration officials internally debated whether to offer direct support to the UAE-led offensive after the UAE asked for U.S. assistance but decided not to take part "in an offensive that it does not think the UAE and associated forces can bring off without considerable humanitarian cost on a relatively short timeline."[81]

Since early 2018, the National Resistance Forces, with support from the coalition, had made significant progress in taking back territory from the Houthis along Yemen's Red Sea coast. By late May of that year, UAE-supported military groups had pushed up against the district just south of Hodeidah city.[82] With a reported 21,000 to 26,500 forces in the area, the coalition-backed forces outnumbered an estimated 2,000 to 5,000 Houthi forces.[83] As these forces made progress toward Hodeidah in spring 2018, all indications were that an offensive on Hodeidah would soon begin. UN agencies and NGOs vehemently opposed the incoming offensive. "A battle for Hodeida[h] is likely to be prolonged and leave millions of Yemenis without food, fuel and other vital supplies," the International Crisis Group warned in June 2018.[84] UN Humanitarian Coordinator for Yemen Lise Grande said, "in a prolonged worst case, we fear that as many as 250,000 people may lose everything [in a Hodeidah offensive]—even their lives."[85]

The 2018 Hodeidah offensive, Operation Golden Victory, began in June.[86] The Houthi strategy for defending this urban territory entailed using antipersonnel and antivehicle mines to slow oncoming coalition forces, building hardened positions on the outskirts of cities, and placing highly fortified command-and-control centers within the city, setting the stage for a protracted urban battle.[87] In July, the offensive was temporarily suspended because, UAE officials said, they wanted to give the UN special envoy space to find a political solution to the crisis.[88]

Despite ongoing UN efforts to negotiate, fighting resumed when talks in Geneva collapsed on September 7, 2018. The Houthi delegates refused to travel to Geneva when they had not received guarantees about their safety from the United Nations. As UN Special Envoy Martin Griffiths put it, the Houthi delegation "would have liked to get here, [but] we didn't make conditions sufficiently correct to get them here."[89] The UAE and the Hadi government resumed the offensive in early November 2018, probably in reaction to an October 30 call by senior U.S. officials for a cease-fire and peace talks to be held within thirty days. A Yemeni government minister, Moammar el Eryani, said that the timing of the renewed offensive was aimed at strengthening their position going into negotiations. Their aim was "to take Hodeidah before the 30 days": "If Hodeidah is freed, the Houthis will be forced to come and sit with us at the table," el Eryani said.[90] In turn, Houthi forces dug in, "prompting fears that they [were] using civilians as human shields," even as the coalition continued airstrikes and deployed Apache helicopters to target areas of the city.[91] A surgeon at a military hospital said that many civilians admitted to the hospital had been struck by air-strike shrapnel: "we have been receiving a lot of civilian casualties," he reported.[92]

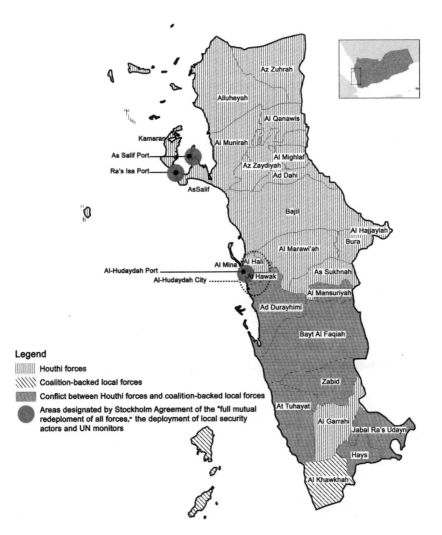

Hodeidah offensive, 2018. (Credit: Ghaidaa Alrashidy)

Against a backdrop of continued warnings about a brewing humanitarian crisis, in December 2018, the conflict parties assembled in Stockholm, Sweden, to negotiate a cease-fire. On December 13, the parties agreed to the Stockholm Agreement, a three-part accord that included an immediate cease-fire in Hodeidah and surrounding areas, with the eventual redeployment of both sides' forces; the establishment of humanitarian corridors to facilitate the movement of aid; and a prisoner exchange.[93]

The Stockholm Agreement met with little success. Within several months, each side had accused the other of failing to execute parts of the agreement. The agreement did end the fighting in Hodeidah and averted a potentially devastating humanitarian crisis. The United Nations estimated that 150,000 people who had been displaced by the fighting returned after the agreement.[94] Nevertheless, the internationally recognized government and the Houthis had both failed to move forward on demilitarization and the redeployment of their forces in Hodeidah, with each side holding to their own interpretation of the text of the agreement. At the same time, fighting had intensified in other parts of the country, and the Stockholm Agreement's unresolved status held back UN talks for a countrywide cease-fire by "undermining [the UN's] credibility as mediator."[95] While the Stockholm Agreement therefore averted some of the worst potential consequences of the Hodeidah offensive, it failed to live up to more optimistic hopes that it could jumpstart a countrywide peace process.

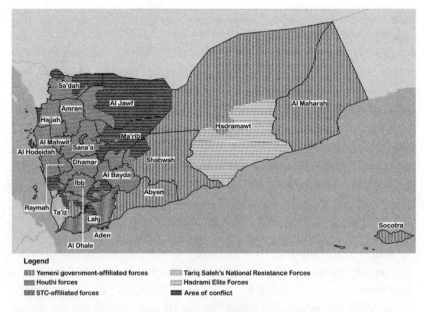

Legend

⦀ Yemeni government-affiliated forces	▨ Tariq Saleh's National Resistance Forces
▧ Houthi forces	▨ Hadrami Elite Forces
▨ STC-affiliated forces	▰ Area of conflict

Zones of control and conflict in Yemen, December 2021.
(Credit: Ghaidaa Alrashidy)

Corruption, Aid, and Yemen's War Economy

Both the internationally recognized government of Yemen and the Houthis drew considerable financial benefits from the war economy and from corruption. The UN Panel of Expert's 2019 report "detail[ed] the rise of a robust, mafia-like war economy that creates disincentives for peace on both sides," Elana DeLozier writes.[96] The Houthis collected taxes and other state revenue but, instead of putting the revenue toward government functions, used much of it to finance their war effort. This included at least $1.8 billion diverted from government funds in 2019, according to the UN Panel of Experts. The Houthis also collected import taxes on several key entry points, including Hodeidah port. The UN Panel of Experts also detailed several investigations into corruption by the Hadi government, including diversion of public funds and the theft of crude oil. The UN Panel of Experts also accused Hadi's internationally recognized government of "money-laundering and corruption practices that adversely affect access to adequate food supplies."[97]

At several points during the war, the Houthis placed increasing restrictions on humanitarian aid for their own gain, diverting aid in several cases. A United Nations World Food Programme (WFP) investigation found evidence that the Houthis were taking food illicitly from distribution centers and selling it for profit, for example.[98] WFP's Executive Director David Beasley called on Houthi authorities "to take immediate action to end the diversion of food assistance and ensure that it reaches those people who rely on it to stay alive."[99]

Houthi diversion of aid reached a crisis point in 2020 when the Houthis moved to block half of the UN's humanitarian aid delivery programs in a push to gain greater leeway over where aid was sent. They also tried to impose a 2 percent import tax on humanitarian aid, although they dropped the tax after significant international pushback.[100] Until that point, UN officials had remained largely silent in public about Houthi demands around humanitarian aid, choosing to negotiate behind the scenes instead. But by 2020, Houthi demands had pushed the conflict into the open. The UN humanitarian coordinator for Yemen Lise Grande sent a letter to Houthi authorities in October of that year pushing back against Houthi demands around

humanitarian aid, the "overwhelming majority" of which would de-
lay or obstruct the delivery of aid.[101]

"When our aid is delivered to the port in Hodeidah, we find that
a portion of it will have been stolen before it leaves the port. There's
also pressure to send aid to areas where [the Houthis] want it to go,"
said Muna Luqman, executive director of Food4Humanity, in September 2020.[102] Likewise, Human Rights Watch found that efforts
to aid the response to COVID-19 and deliver other urgently needed
humanitarian aid were "severely hampered by onerous restrictions
and obstacles that the Houthi and other authorities have imposed on
international aid agencies and humanitarian organizations." From
May through September 2020, for example, the Houthis blocked
containers in Hodeidah port sent by the World Health Organization. Houthi authorities then attempted to use the release of some
of the containers as a bargaining chip in negotiations to lift other
obstacles to aid delivery.[103]

In March 2020, at the beginning of the global COVID-19
pandemic, the Trump administration, Saudi Arabia, and the UAE
slashed their humanitarian assistance to Yemen, citing the imposi-
tion of Houthi restrictions. "While the stakes are very high and we
definitely don't want to cut off lifesaving assistance," a U.S. official
said, "the pressure needs to continue until they fall in line."[104]

Houthi Factionalization

As pro-internationally-recognized-government forces factionalized, factions have also emerged on the Houthi side. When Saleh
attempted to defect from the Houthi alliance and was killed in December 2017, few of his former tribal allies followed him. Yet it was
Saleh who was responsible for maintaining many of these relationships with local and tribal leaders—in some cases for decades. Tribal
opposition to the Houthis therefore increased after Saleh's death.
The Houthis responded to rising tensions with tribes "with severe
repression, resulting in higher levels of violence targeting civilians,"
which in turn drove greater tribal discontent.[105]

Political division also grew among Houthi senior leaders. The
Houthi leaders Mohammed Ali al-Houthi, Ahmed Hamid, and Ab-

dul Karim al-Houthi each "built competing power bases" around their own economic interests, "secured by their separate security and intelligence structures."[106] Dissension within the Houthi ranks also grew. By 2019, as factions among Houthi leadership emerged, so "had their limited ability to control rank-and-file Houthi fighters operating throughout the country."[107] Houthi forces were themselves a "heterogeneous assortment" of regular and special army units and armed militias linked to individual Houthi officials and tribal leaders. While they paid tribute to Houthi ideology, at the local level, "commanders also enjoy[ed] relative autonomy, operating as a network of militias that [were] involved in the extraction of levies," according to the Armed Conflict Location & Event Data Project (ACLED).[108] ACLED documented an increase in fighting in the Houthi ranks from 2018 through 2020, recording "more than 40 distinct battles between opposing Houthi forces" across eleven governorates in 2020.[109]

Chaos into Order

At first glance, Peter Salisbury's invocation of a "chaos state" may seem like a contradiction in terms. Political scientists traditionally conceive of the state as a unified political entity, designed to impose order on chaos. But the dynamics of factionalization in Yemen's polity since 2014, driven by both the intervention of regional actors and the dynamics of the conflict itself, have created a hybrid polity.

At the national level, at the time of writing, Yemen is a "failed state," with ongoing fighting along several battlefronts, but politics and the control of territory are organized by regional and local logics. Military actors, working together with political and tribal leaders, control most of Yemen's territory and government finances. From the outside, Yemen is often depicted as divided between Houthi government in the north and the internationally recognized government in the south, but as we have seen, the reality for local Yemeni communities is far more complicated. Both the internationally recognized government and Houthi "sides" have internal divisions, but each side is held together by its shared opposition to the other side. But if that basic division falls away, these two coalitions are unlikely to continue to cohere.

What this means is that ending Yemen's war requires somehow bringing together this kaleidoscope of warring parties, each with its own objectives, into an agreement. Negotiators face the dilemma of including enough of the conflict parties that they can head off potential spoilers to an agreement without making negotiations too large and unwieldy. At the same time, bringing in the actors who engage in violence while neglecting peaceful parts of civil society has created perverse incentives, as the STC's violent attempts for legitimation and recognition demonstrate. Even striking a durable cease-fire between the internationally recognized government and the Houthis will not be enough to end the war. As the analyst Nadwa Al-Dawsari notes, "A power-sharing agreement between the Hadi government and the Houthis is not going to stitch Yemen back together or give birth to a functional national government."[110]

While external intervention has accelerated factionalization among the conflict parties, it also means that external actors have an opportunity to use their leverage to get the conflict parties to the negotiating table. External actors will not be able to impose a lasting peace in Yemen, but they can shift the stakeholders' incentives to come to an agreement and provide support for its implementation. The United States too can use its leverage with Saudi Arabia and the UAE to get their Yemeni affiliates to engage in negotiations. While Yemenis themselves will need to decide what such an agreement will look like, given the history of Yemen's regional divisions, it will probably involve a federal arrangement that gives the south, Hadramawt, the Houthis, and other groups and regions substantial autonomy.

CHAPTER SIX

"Dumb Wars"

The Obama Administration's War in Yemen

Don't do stupid shit.

—President Obama, quoted by JEFFREY GOLDBERG in the
Atlantic, April 2016

IN OCTOBER 2002, THE same month that Congress voted to authorize the U.S. invasion of Iraq, then–State Senator Barack Obama
gave a speech at an antiwar rally in Chicago. "I know that an invasion
of Iraq without a clear rationale and without strong international
support will only fan the flames of the Middle East," Obama told the
crowd, "and encourage the worst, rather than best, impulses of the
Arab world, and strengthen the recruitment arm of al-Qaida. I am
not opposed to all wars. I'm opposed to dumb wars," Obama said,
highlighting a theme that would come to characterize his administration's policies in the Middle East.[1]

Presidential candidate Obama campaigned on withdrawing
from the war in Iraq and reducing the U.S. military's presence in
the Middle East. One of his first major speeches in office, on June 4,
2009, in Cairo, sought a "new beginning between the United States
and Muslims around the world, one based on mutual interest and

mutual respect."[2] The new president referenced his own roots, describing hearing the call to prayer during his childhood in Indonesia. The warm and open tone of the speech resonated widely with its audience: it was greeted with a thunderous standing ovation.[3]

The Cairo speech was intended to heal breeches between the United States and the Muslim world created by the Bush administration and to mark a fundamental change in U.S. policy toward the Middle East. "President Obama took office with still very heavy echoes of events of the previous decade. . . . The deterioration that happened in Iraq after the war, with the occupation, the Abu Ghraib prison torture photographs and other torture scandals. And what it led to was kind of a serious deterioration of the U.S. reputation in the region," said Daniel Shapiro, an advisor on the speech. "So what [Obama] was trying to do was describe a basis for a new set of relationships . . . while empowering people in the region," Shapiro noted.[4]

Even when Obama did decide to militarily intervene in the Middle East's wars, as in Libya in 2011, the debate within the administration tended to focus on humanitarian protection, guided by values rather than national security interests. In Libya, the NATO-led intervention was designed to prevent what many observers predicted would be a massacre of civilians in Benghazi by Libyan President Muammar Ghaddafi's state forces. Proponents of the intervention, including Secretary of State Hillary Clinton, UN Ambassador Susan Rice, and Special Assistant to the President Samantha Power supported a plan that, in Power's words, would "do what was *actually* required to save Benghazi and other opposition-held areas, . . . going beyond a no-fly zone and striking [Ghaddafi's] forces and the land-based weapons they were using to attack civilians."[5] Within the administration, proponents of the intervention squared off against more cautious figures like Secretary of Defense Bob Gates, who archly asked, "Shouldn't we finish up the two wars we have before we look for another?"[6]

Obama recounted his decision to intervene in Libya, asserting, "If we waited one more day, Benghazi, a city nearly the size of Charlotte, could suffer a massacre that would have reverberated across the region and stained the conscience of the world."[7] In other words, the United States had a responsibility to act. Still, the president was very reluctant to do so. "I was still dealing with a U.S. economy that was barely above water and a Republican Congress that had pledged to undo everything my administration had accomplished in our first two years," Obama later wrote of the decision to intervene in Libya, "and it's fair to say that I found the idea of waging a new war in a distant country with no strategic importance to the United States to be less than prudent."[8]

President Obama reluctantly moved forward with intervention in Libya, but in 2013, he decided not to intervene more directly in Syria's civil war, despite his "red line" comments about the Assad regime's use of chemical weapons, effectively punting the issue by turning it over to Congress. In discussions with his advisors, Obama "expressed strong misgivings about using military force in Syria," according to Power, deeming "the risks too high and the impact too uncertain."[9]

Analysts saw Obama's decision not to intervene more forcefully in Syria in 2013 as a liberating moment for his administration's Middle East policy. The *Atlantic* journalist Jeffrey Goldberg wrote that the day Obama made the decision was "the day he defied not only the foreign-policy establishment and its cruise-missile playbook, but also the demands of America's frustrating, high-maintenance allies in the Middle East—countries, he complains privately to friends and advisers, that seek to exploit American 'muscle' for their own narrow and sectarian ends." In the same article, Goldberg famously quoted Obama summarizing his approach to Middle East policy as "don't do stupid shit."[10]

In short, President Obama wanted to reduce the U.S. military presence in the Middle East and wind down U.S. wars there from the moment he entered office. And when he did decide to use U.S. force in the Middle East, it was intended to prevent the killing of civilians, and the decision was made with great reluctance. It was therefore surprising that in March 2015, the Obama administration chose to back a military intervention in Yemen's civil war.

Yemen would become a sore point in the Obama administration's foreign policy, especially considered alongside signature foreign policy achievements like the Iran nuclear deal. Curiously, although a number of former Obama administration officials have condemned U.S. support for the coalition in Yemen since leaving office, few of them have discussed their administration's own culpability in this decision at length. Both Ambassador Samantha Power, whose book *A Problem from Hell* narrated the United States' failures to avert genocide in places like Rwanda and Bosnia, and Ben Rhodes, who coined the term "the blob" to refer to a foreign policy establishment that he saw as dominated by groupthink, wrote memoirs of their time in office that do not mention the war in Yemen, even though both have subsequently condemned the war's humanitarian toll. While defenders of the decision to intervene in Libya can make a plausible case that the NATO-led intervention averted a humanitarian catastrophe there, the intervention in Yemen did the opposite: it created a humanitarian catastrophe.

In November 2018, a group of more than two dozen former Obama administration officials, including Power and Rhodes, released a statement calling for an end to U.S. support for the war. They acknowledged that while the Obama administration had provided assistance in response to a "legitimate threat," they had not intended for U.S. support to be "a blank check." "Unfortunately," they wrote, "our approach did not succeed in limiting and ultimately ending the war."[11]

How, then, did the Obama administration end up backing the Saudi-led coalition's intervention in Yemen, with all of its disastrous consequences? How did the administration's position on U.S. support for the war change over time? And what were the consequences of these decisions for the war and for Yemenis?

The Saudi-Led Intervention Begins: The Saudi Announcement

Saudi officials announced the launch of the intervention from Washington, DC, an event laden in symbolism because it implied U.S. support for the operation. On March 25, 2015, Adel al-Jubair, Saudi ambassador to the United States, announced that airstrikes had begun at 7:00 p.m., telling reporters in Washington that "the operation is to defend and support the legitimate government of Yemen and prevent the radical Houthi movement from taking over the country."[12]

Behind closed doors, when the Saudis told U.S. officials that they were planning to go ahead with the intervention, they assured their American counterparts that the war would be over within six weeks.[13] As MbS was planning the intervention, he told John Brennan, "we'll finish off the Houthis in a couple of months" (Brennan recalls his response: "I looked at him with a rather blank stare and wondered to myself what he had been smoking").[14]

On the day the intervention began, the National Security Council released a statement expressing support for the intervention, noting that "President Obama has authorized the provision of logistical and intelligence support to GCC-led military operations" and that the intervention came "at the request of Yemeni President Abdrabbuh Mansur Hadi."[15] General Lloyd Austin, then commander of CENTCOM, later testified before Congress that he was first notified of the intervention when he "had a discussion with the Saudi CHOD [chief of defense] the day of the attack, so it was not much before they actually started the attacks."[16]

The Obama administration allowed Saudi Arabia to go ahead with the intervention and provided the coalition with logistical military support, including aerial refueling and intelligence sharing, despite its reservations, "eventually settling into a lukewarm embrace" of the intervention.[17] U.S. officials reported that Saudi Arabia's message "had a 'five minutes to midnight' quality"—Saudi Arabia was determined to act, whether or not it secured U.S. support.[18] Senior National Security Council officials Robert Malley and Stephen Pomper later reported that they "looked on the decision facing the administration with queasiness. . . . U.S. officials thought Saudi Arabia was exaggerating Iran's role, and they had no illusions that the Saudi armed forces, although well supplied with modern U.S. weapons, were a precision instrument. In short, there was plenty that could go wrong. As a former senior official would later tell one of us, 'We knew we might be getting into a car with a drunk driver.'"[19]

When Saudi officials approached senior U.S. national security officials privately and told them they were going ahead with the intervention in Yemen, Obama administration officials felt they had to provide support for the intervention. Despite their concerns, "the decision was not an especially close call. Obama's senior national security team unanimously recommended proceeding with some measure of assistance for the Saudi campaign, and the president concurred."[20] The logic behind this decision was somewhat complicated.

By March 2015, both Saudi and U.S. officials believed—largely at the insistence of the Saudis—that the bilateral relationship between the two security partners had frayed. Obama's comments about "free riders" in the *Atlantic* in 2016 encapsulated these Gulf states' perception that Obama had been dismissive of the importance of their bilateral security relationships with the United States.[21] Obama's assertion in the *Atlantic* interview that "the competition between the Saudis and the Iranians . . . requires us to say to our friends as well as to the Iranians that they need to find an effective way to share the neighborhood" were also seen as indicative of his desire to pull back from the United States' relationships with Gulf countries.[22] All of this followed a series of U.S. policy decisions, namely, Obama's call for Egypt's President Hosni Mubarak to step down and the Iran nuclear deal, that strained the United States' relationship with key Gulf states.

The Obama administration's response to the early Arab Spring protest movement, especially Obama's call for Mubarak to step down, had angered GCC officials. As Obama recounted, after the United States publicly called for Mubarak to step down, "MBZ [the UAE's Mohammed bin Zayed] told me that U.S. statements on Egypt were being watched closely in the Gulf, with increasing alarm. . . . 'The public message does not affect Mubarak, you see, but it affects the region,' MBZ told me. He suggested that if Egypt collapsed and the Muslim Brotherhood took over, there would be eight other Arab leaders who would fall, which is why he was critical of my statement. 'It shows,' he said, 'that the United States is not a partner we can rely on in the long term.'"[23]

Moreover, the administration's willingness to negotiate and sign the Iran nuclear agreement, the Joint Comprehensive Plan of Action (JCPOA), further worried GCC leaders, who thought that the deal had significant negative repercussions for their own regional strategies. Negotiations for the deal that became the JCPOA began in secret, via a series of bilateral talks that took place in Oman, led by Jake Sullivan and William Burns on the U.S. side. Hassan Rouhani, a moderate candidate, was elected president of Iran in June

2013. Soon after his inauguration, Rouhani publicly called for the resumption of multilateral talks on Iran's nuclear program. After the election, Rhodes recounted, "President Obama sent President Rouhani a letter proposing a focus on nuclear negotiations, and for the first time we received a constructive reply."[24] After lengthy, intensive negotiations, the P5+1 (the United States, plus China, France, Germany, Russia, and the United Kingdom) announced agreement on a general framework on April 2, 2015—just days after the coalition intervention in Yemen began—and finalized the agreement on July 14, 2015.[25]

Saudi King Salman signaled his displeasure with the deal—and with the fact that the GCC leadership was not given the opportunity to offer input—by canceling his attendance at a U.S.-GCC summit held at Camp David in May 2015. Ironically, Obama had intended that the summit be a signal to the GCC that the Iran agreement would not lead to the abandonment of its GCC partners.[26] King Salman's cancellation was "widely interpreted as a snub" and represented a rare public breach in the relationship.[27]

As a result, several U.S. officials have subsequently confirmed that when Saudi officials approached them about the coalition intervention in Yemen in March 2015, U.S. officials agreed to support it. They believed that a failure to support the intervention would be a breach too far in the relationship. Supporting the intervention was also implicitly offered in exchange for Saudi Arabia and other Gulf states not publicly opposing the JCPOA.[28] According to Senator Chris Murphy, "The Obama administration was legitimately worried that a major fissure between the United States and Saudi Arabia could weaken the Iran deal."[29] Support for the Yemen intervention as well as increased arms sales during this period was therefore "a way to placate the Saudis."[30] "The truth is, you can dwell on Yemen, or you can recognize that we're one agreement away from a game-changing, legacy-setting nuclear accord on Iran that tackles what every one [sic] agrees is the biggest threat to the region," a State Department official said the day after the Saudi-led intervention began, expressing the White House's regional priorities.[31]

At the same time, U.S. officials wanted to keep Gulf security partners on board with the U.S.-led anti-ISIS coalition, since their participation gave the coalition added legitimacy and allowed the administration to claim that regional partners were sharing the burden. In a May 2015 press briefing immediately following the GCC summit, Rhodes noted, "all of these countries have joined us in the counter-ISIL coalition, and are playing an important role in our efforts to degrade and ultimately defeat ISIL across the region."[32]

U.S. officials also hoped that their engagement could mitigate the worse effects of the coalition's military campaign in Yemen. "Our basic theory was that by being somewhat engaged, we could deal with the inevitable Saudi intervention in Yemen while seeking to impose limits on what they did and to try to broker something diplomatically," Rhodes said.[33] They bargained that if Saudi Arabia was the "drunk driver," U.S. officials "could offer sober guidance and grab the wheel when necessary," according to Malley and Pomper.[34]

Despite President Hadi's failure to lead a successful post-NDC transition process, U.S. officials saw him as a better alternative to Houthi rule of Yemen, as we saw in chapter 4. Hadi was "a vast improvement over his much-disliked predecessor [Saleh]," write Malley and Pomper; "Hadi was also seen as a reliable counterterrorism partner, someone who gave the United States wide berth in its operations against al Qaeda in the Arabian Peninsula."[35] Counterterrorism policy was still a top U.S. priority in Yemen.

U.S. Support for the Saudi-Led Coalition Intervention

From the first days of the intervention, the United States provided military logistical support to the coalition, including aerial refueling for aircraft engaged in airstrikes, as well as intelligence assistance. Up to forty-five U.S. personnel sat in a Joint Combined Planning Cell (JCPC) in Riyadh, presumably providing advice on targeting. Pentagon officials sought to distance U.S. personnel from targeting decisions, stating, "at no point did U.S. military personnel provide direct or implicit approval of target selection or prosecution."[36] In April 2015, a U.S. official said that U.S. personnel at the JCPC "are helping [the Saudis] get a better sense of the battlefield and the state of play with the Houthi forces": "We are also helping identify 'no strike' areas they would avoid."[37] In October 2015, National Security Council (NSC) spokesperson Ned Price affirmed, "The United

States has no role in targeting decisions made by the Coalition in Yemen. Nevertheless, we have consistently reinforced to members of the Coalition the imperative of precise targeting."[38] About one hundred U.S. personnel were involved in advising and assisting the war effort in total, including providing mechanical and technical support for Saudi aircraft.[39]

The United States was also occasionally drawn into the conflict with the Houthis directly. In October 2016, U.S. strikes hit three radar sites in Houthi-controlled territory in response to Houthi missile launches that threatened the USS *Mason*, operating nearby in international waters.[40] U.S. forces were also present in Yemen as part of the ongoing counterterrorism war against AQAP, which U.S. policy makers viewed as distinct from the intervention against the Houthis. Beginning in mid-2016, U.S. Special Forces joined Emirati Special Forces in southern Yemen in an advisory capacity to counterterrorism operations and intelligence gathering against AQAP.[41]

The Saudi Air Force would have been unable to conduct airstrikes in Yemen, at least not at the same operational tempo, without aerial refueling and other logistical support, including the provision of spare parts and maintenance for aircraft, provided by the United States, as well as by France and the United Kingdom. As the defense analyst Becca Wasser said, in the first years of the intervention, the coalition was "really reliant on U.S. aerial refueling," in part due to its decision to fly sorties from bases in central and northern Saudi Arabia rather than from bases farther south, adding to transit time and significantly reducing time on station for targeting in the absence of aerial refueling assistance.[42] The United States "is a partner in this war. . . . If the United States of America and the United Kingdom tonight told King Salman that this war has to end, it would end tomorrow, because the Royal Saudi Air Force cannot operate without American and British support," said Bruce Riedel.[43]

In addition to direct logistical support for operations in Yemen, the United States also continued to supply Saudi Arabia and the UAE with large arms-sale packages. These weapons could have been used in Yemen, although arms sales typically take several years to complete from the start of negotiations to delivery. But more importantly, they demonstrated implicit support for the coalition's Yemen strategy. All told, according to the journalist Nicholas Niarchos, "by the end of Obama's Presidency, the U.S. had offered more than a hundred and fifteen billion dollars' worth of arms to Saudi Arabia, the largest amount under any President."[44]

Supporters of the intervention argued that it aligned with U.S. security interests in the region. To these proponents, the Houthis were closely tied to Iran, and a Houthi victory would give Iran a foothold on the Arabian Peninsula, allowing it to threaten Saudi Arabia's southern border. Summarizing this perspective, a joint statement from Senators John McCain and Lindsey Graham read, "Saudi Arabia and our Arab partners deserve our support as they seek to restore order in Yemen. . . . The prospect of radical groups like Al-Qaeda, as well as Iranian-backed militants, finding safe haven on the border of Saudi Arabia was more than our Arab partners could withstand."[45] Conservatives saw the Obama administration's policies toward Iran, including the JCPOA as well as tacit coordination with Iranian-backed militias in Iraq fighting ISIS, as "giving in" to Iran. Mark Dubowitz, executive director of the conservative Foundation for Defense of Democracies, said that the Obama administration had been unwilling to "push back against aggressive Iranian behavior."[46] From this perspective, a Houthi victory in Yemen would be yet another regional domino falling in Iran's favor. Proponents of the intervention in Yemen also warned that failing to support the Saudi-led coalition would deal yet another blow to the United States' relationship with its Gulf security partners. McCain said about a controversial arms sale to Saudi Arabia, "Blocking this sale of tanks will be interpreted by our Gulf partners, not just Saudi Arabia, as another sign that the United States of America is abandoning our commitment in the region and is an unreliable security partner."[47]

The Obama administration sought to distinguish the threat posed by Iran's destabilizing proxy activities in the region from the negotiations over the JCPOA. In a 2016 speech, Rhodes noted, "From Iraq to Yemen, Iran has continued to engage in destabilizing support for proxy organizations. . . . Some argue that means the [Iran nuclear] deal wasn't worth it. We would argue the exact opposite. Isn't it better when a government with a ballistic missile program that supports terrorism doesn't have a nuclear weapon?"[48] Still, the administration felt the pressure to push back against Iran in other arenas, even as it negotiated and signed the JCPOA. Obama called this a "dual track" approach, in which the United States attempted to reduce tensions with Iran where it could at the same time as it held Iran accountable for other kinds of destabilizing behavior in the region, including Iran's sponsorship of armed proxies and its ballistic missile program.[49]

At the same time, others sounded a prescient warning: "Let's ask ourselves whether we are comfortable with the United States getting slowly, predictably, and all too quietly dragged into yet another war in the Middle East," Senator Chris Murphy said in September 2016 on the Senate floor.[50] Senator Murphy was one of the earliest public critics of the intervention. A handful of members of Congress also became concerned about the humanitarian situation in Yemen, although the level of interest in Congress was still very modest. In October 2015, ten members of Congress signed a letter to Obama urging that the administration "work with our Saudi partners to limit civilian casualties to the fullest extent possible," for example.[51]

As early as a month into the intervention, the White House began to call for "a shift from military operations to the rapid, unconditional resumption of all-party negotiations that allow Yemen to resume an inclusive, political transition process. There's going to be no military solution to this problem."[52] These calls appeared to have little effect.

The Obama Administration Begins to Worry

Despite the Obama administration's public support for the Saudi-led intervention, there was growing concern within the administration about the coalition's conduct almost from the beginning, especially regarding civilian casualties resulting from the coalition's airstrikes. This concern did not emerge publicly, however, until the last months of the Obama administration.

It quickly became clear that the coalition's airstrikes were causing unacceptable civilian death tolls.[53] By April 2015, the coalition had exhausted high-value, fixed military targets and had moved on to "either restriking known targets or hitting suspected gathering places for Houthi and pro-Saleh forces" and trying to limit Houthi forces' forward movement by targeting infrastructure like bridges, roads, and gas stations.[54] By late 2015, although Houthi forces were implicated in the deaths of hundreds of Yemeni civilians, the UN estimated that the majority of civilian casualties in the war—about 60 percent—could be traced back to the Saudi-led coalition's bombing campaign.[55]

Throughout 2015 and most of 2016, Obama administration officials continued to publicly express confidence in Saudi Arabia's willingness to improve its record on killing Yemeni civilians in airstrikes. "I think the Saudis have expressed in the last weeks their desire to make certain that they're acting responsibly and not endangering civilians," Secretary of State John Kerry told MSNBC's Chris Hayes in June 2016.[56] At the same time, Saudi Arabia asserted that it was in compliance with international law. "Coalition forces have a robust process to ensure all targets are genuinely military," the coalition announced, at the same time promising to refer any incidents to an "internal accident investigation team."[57]

Behind the scenes, however, the civilian death toll linked to coalition airstrikes suggested that the United States could be implicated in war crimes. Government lawyers tried to determine whether U.S. support for the coalition made the United States a cobelligerent and therefore culpable for such crimes under international law. U.S. officials privately "worried that the coalition was acting intentionally, perhaps perceiving these strikes [on civilian targets] to have a tactical benefit."[58] The civilian casualties in the air campaign had State Department lawyers' "hair on fire."[59]

Senior officials were divided into two camps. Some officials thought the U.S. ought to stop supporting the coalition, while others thought that additional assistance could improve the coalition's targeting record. Officials in the Office of the Secretary of Defense (OSD) in particular were pessimistic that it was even possible to change the conduct of operations while the conflict was ongoing. Andrew Exum, who was appointed deputy assistant secretary of defense for Middle East policy in May 2015, reported, "When I arrived, I sensed a lot of frustration [about U.S. support for the coalition]. . . . The Administration was unsure about whether it wanted to be involved in the war. Are we supposed to help the Saudis win or not? I don't think we ever made up our minds there."[60]

A key issue was that coalition pilots and air force personnel lacked both the skill and access to intelligence to select targets appropriately. A lack of on-the-ground intelligence often led to a mismatch of targets and the type of weapon used in a strike, "which would sometimes create more civilian casualties or not be as effective in destroying the target, meaning the RSAF has to do another bombing run," Wasser said. The coalition "never built up an intelligence enterprise in the way the U.S. and other militaries have in terms of targeting," according to Wasser. "Being able to do the full targeting cycle, which requires a lot of intelligence if you do it the right way—they never had that."[61] U.S. officials attributed many of the strikes on civilian targets to the Saudi Air Force's lack of capability and experience. Internal State Department documents from this period show that U.S. officials concluded that "the strikes were not intentionally indiscriminate but rather result from a lack of Saudi experience with dropping munitions and firing missiles, . . . compounded by the asymmetric situation on the ground where enemy militants are not wearing uniforms and are mixed with civilian populations. Weak intelligence likely further compounds the problem."[62]

A Technical Fix: The Effort to Mitigate Casualties through Assistance

At first, the Obama administration sought to address these shortcomings by providing assistance to improve the coalition's targeting, thereby hoping to mitigate civilian casualties. The White House held an August 2015 meeting, for example, on how to engage Saudi officials about the alarming number of civilian casualties, while State Department officials met internally about how to track civilian casualties. In January 2016, Deputy Secretary of State Antony Blinken chaired a meeting of State Department officials to talk about "options to limit U.S exposure to LOAC (Law of Armed Conflict) concerns."[63]

The United States provided the coalition with a "no-strike" list of civilian locations such as hospitals and schools and continued to expand the list over time to include more than thirty-three thousand targets. According to the director of USAID's Office of U.S.

Foreign Disaster Assistance Jeremy Konyndyk, "We broadened and broadened and broadened that [no-strike] list over time as the Saudis kept striking things that we would have thought they wouldn't strike."[64] Over the course of 2015, the United States provided lists of critical infrastructure, such as electrical and water facilities, as well as supply routes that were critical to the delivery of humanitarian aid. A talking point that U.S. officials planned to use with Saudi officials read, "We urge you to exercise the utmost diligence in the targeting process and to take all precautions to minimize civilian casualties and damage to civilian infrastructure."[65] Although intelligence support was initially limited to reviewing Saudi targeting information to affirm its accuracy, it gradually expanded in scope to more detailed "vetting."[66]

This increased support did not lead to sustained improvements in Saudi targeting accuracy, however. According to Larry Lewis, an expert on reducing civilian casualties, this was at least in part because the U.S. approach to improving targeting accuracy did not effectively address the underlying operational issues. Lewis's experience highlights the challenge of mitigating civilian casualties through technical assistance. The State Department sent Lewis to Saudi Arabia several times for consultation with coalition forces in 2015 and 2016.[67] Even when Lewis first arrived in Riyadh in October 2015, however, State Department officials were not particularly optimistic that U.S. efforts to reduce civilian casualties could make a significant difference. Lewis described that on his first day in Riyadh, "[The embassy staff and military attaché] basically sat me down and said, 'We think it's great what you're here to do. We think it's really important. So don't be discouraged when they hate you by the end of the week.'"[68]

There were two different processes that the coalition used to select the targets of airstrikes: deliberate and dynamic strikes. Deliberate strikes are preplanned, while for dynamic strikes, pilots work with on-the-ground intelligence sources to select targets in the air without preplanning. Lewis said, "If you look at the problems, all the mistakes—they were during dynamic strikes. But what did the U.S. military do? They sent over advisors to help them during the deliberate targeting process. There was actually a lot of energy and mentoring and so forth, but they weren't working on what was broken."[69] U.S. trainings on the Laws of Armed Conflict and the no-strike list did not address the casualties that were due to targeting errors. A 2018 report by independent experts prepared for the UN High Commissioner for Human Rights concluded, "the failure to ensure that all relevant commanders have access to the no-strike list raises serious concerns about the ability of the coalition to comply with the special protections accorded" to potential targets on the list.[70]

On Lewis's trips to Riyadh, he shared techniques that the Saudi Air Force could use to improve its record during dynamic strikes, such as tactical patience—waiting until a target has moved away from civilian areas—and expanding the use of the no-strike list, which, according to Lewis, was "really well integrated into the deliberate targeting process but was not integrated at all into the dynamic targeting process."[71] A Saudi pilot might target military fighters as they walk into a building, for example, only to learn later that the building was a hospital. "Somebody knew it was a hospital," said Lewis, "but that information is not routinely passed to the pilot."[72] Saudi Air Force pilots' relative inexperience only made the problem worse, since adopting new dynamic targeting processes during operations presented a challenging learning curve.

The Saudi Air Force's approach to risk, combined with Saudi pilots' lack of experience, also led to mistakes. "The Saudi strategic culture has a different risk calculus, that dropping a bomb on a crowded funeral or on a bus that has twenty people, in order to get one bad guy, is acceptable and that's the way you should proceed," a defense analyst told me. "So, yes, there were terrible tactics that the Saudis were doing when flying or when dropping a weapon, due to a lack of skill or a lack of care, but there was also a conscious decision, which is that they approach civilian casualties—and what is an acceptable civilian casualty—very differently from how the U.S. and frankly most of the rest of the world does it."[73]

While Lewis met Saudi airmen who were eager to improve their record on civilian casualties, individual improvements could disappear in the organizational culture of the Saudi Royal Air Force. Lewis's analysis showed that from late 2015 through early 2016, the rate of civilian casualties related to airstrikes did decline due to tactical improvements. The number of airstrikes also declined significantly in April 2016 due to a cease-fire. When strikes resumed after the cease-fire fell apart in August 2016, Lewis found that airmen who had received the tactical training, including the chief of targeting, had rotated out.[74] Saudi Air Force pilots were therefore back to the baseline of tactical mistakes that led to civilian casualties in the first place.

To some analysts, the patterns of civilian casualties and strikes on civilian infrastructure suggested that the Saudi coalition was deliberately waging a war of attrition on Yemeni civilians. In September 2015, the UN reported that about two-thirds of civilian deaths and damaged public buildings were attributable to coalition airstrikes.[75] A 2015 Human Rights Watch report found that the high number of civilian casualties was occurring in part because the coalition chose to use "explosive weapons with wide area effect in populated areas."[76] Yet it was impossible to explain what the intended military target was when bombs fell on weddings or marketplaces. "Did the coalition believe that the large gatherings were Houthi forces or did they carry out attacks on valid military targets using weapons or methods of attack that caused large civilian loss of life?" a Human Rights Watch researcher wrote.[77]

A study from the World Peace Foundation went further, arguing that the pattern of targeting of farms and food processing and storage facilities provided "strong evidence that [the coalition's] strategy has aimed to destroy food production and distribution in the areas under" Houthi control.[78] The pattern of strikes on other types of nonmilitary targets provided additional evidence for this explanation. The International Red Cross reported almost one hundred attacks on health care facilities within the first seven months of the conflict, for example.[79] Human Rights Watch called for a UN investigation after a July 2015 strike in Mokha killed sixty-five civilians, including ten children.[80] A September 2015 strike hit a wedding party in the village of Wahija outside of Mokha, killing as many as 135 people.[81] Instead of taking responsibility or vowing improvement, the Saudi-led coalition stonewalled, denying that it had anything to do with the Wahija strike. "The coalition did not conduct any airstrikes in the area over the past three days," coalition spokesman Brigadier General Ahmed al-Assiri told the press.[82]

When it did acknowledge airstrikes, the coalition claimed that it did not intentionally target civilians.[83]

Even some U.S. officials saw repeated Saudi errors as part of a calculated disregard for civilian casualties. "In the end, we concluded that [the Saudis] were just not willing to listen. They were given specific coordinates of targets that should not be struck and they continued to strike them. That struck me as a willful disregard of advice they were getting," said Tom Malinowski, who was then an assistant secretary of state and in 2019 became a member of Congress.[84]

Ultimately, two factors—operational issues and a lack of high-level political will—are the best explanation for the coalition's track record on civilian casualties. Lax pilot capabilities, the turnover of trained Saudi Royal Air Force officials, and the U.S. military's focus on the wrong kind of training all meant that the coalition continued to make tactical errors that led to large numbers of civilian casualties. At the same time, however, a lack of political will from the top on both the U.S. and Saudi sides meant that there was little concerted effort to address the root of the problems that led to casualties.

On the U.S. side, officials were concerned about civilian casualties and invested in training to minimize them. But legal concerns meant that U.S. officials were barred from giving specific targeting assistance: According to Lewis, when he went back to Riyadh in September 2016, State Department officials told him, "You can't help them with the targeting process. We just don't want you to touch targeting at all."[85] This led to a middle-of-the-road approach that left the United States in the worst of both worlds, continuing to provide operational assistance to the coalition without providing training on targeting and other technical fixes that could have reduced casualties. "That's my overall criticism of what the [Obama] administration did is that they really didn't do much of anything," Lewis said: "If you're going to do something, either stop [providing support] or work with them and make them better. But they really didn't do either."[86]

It is impossible to say conclusively whether the lack of political will from Saudi leadership was due to indifference to the loss of Yemeni lives, a deliberate strategy of degrading Yemeni civilian infrastructure, a concern that the Saudi Air Force's pilots simply did not have the ability to meet the standards that the United States pushed for, or more likely, a combination of these factors. Nevertheless, it is clear that the impetus for change was never passed down from Saudi senior leadership. According to one defense analyst, in Saudi Arabia, "it's such a top-down decision rather than bottom-up, that it would have had to come from MbS or one of his trusted associates to say, 'We will change our ways.' And that was just never going to happen."[87]

Finally, the idea that the United States could limit civilian casualties at scale rested on the premise that it was possible to do so in an active war. The U.S. approach to counterterrorism was based on the same idea, that it was possible to use drone strikes in a surgical manner to kill terrorists with minimal risk to civilians or to U.S. troops. Yet as reporting has demonstrated, the U.S. drone war has incurred significantly more civilian casualties than previously understood. The drone war "has been marked by deeply flawed intelligence, rushed and often imprecise targeting, and the deaths of thousands of civilians, many of them children, a sharp contrast to the American government's image of war waged by all-seeing drones and prevision bombs," Azmat Khan's investigative reporting has found.[88] The Pentagon has rarely gone public with its investigations about civilian casualties, and when it does, "not a single record provided includes a finding of wrongdoing or disciplinary action."[89] These investigations often fail to account for civilian casualties, which has led to systematic undercounting of civilian casualties.[90]

If the U.S. military is unwilling or unable to build transparency into its approach in order to acknowledge mistakes and learn from them, it is optimistic at best to expect that it can successfully teach other countries' militaries to do so.

Civilian Casualties Mount: The 2016 Funeral Hall Strike

By June 2015, coalition airstrikes were already coming under scrutiny for possible war crimes violations.[91] But the situation came to a head for the Obama administration on October 9, 2016, when a coalition "double-tap" airstrike hit the large funeral of a prominent Yemeni family's patriarch, killing at least 140 civilians and wounding an additional 600.[92] A double-tap airstrike consists of two strikes in quick succession, often further injuring or killing the wounded and medical personnel responding to the first strike. Double-tap airstrikes are prohibited under international humanitarian law.[93] UN monitors found that with the second airstrike on that day, "the Saudi Arabia–led coalition violated its obligations in respect of hors de combat and the wounded in this 'double tap' attack. . . . The second air strike, which occurred three to eight minutes after the first air strike, almost certainly resulted in more casualties to the already wounded and the first responders."[94]

The United States did publicly express concerns about civilian casualties in Yemen before the fall of 2016—but these were typically addressed to "all sides of the conflict."[95] U.S. officials had repeatedly pressed their Saudi partners on critical humanitarian access issues, but this engagement was typically presented as positive commitments on the part of the coalition.[96] At a White House visit in September 2015, for example, King Salman had "committed to work with the Coalition and international partners to allow for unfettered access to assistance, including fuel, to the impacted people of Yemen" and to "the reopening of Yemen's Red Sea ports to humanitarian and commercial traffic."[97]

The strike on the funeral hall, where thousands of civilians were gathered, was a dynamic strike, with informants present who were reportedly providing the coalition with information on who was in attendance that day.[98] Still, the logic behind the targeting decision was unclear. "It was such a foolish strike, because even the Saudis recognized that more people who were sympathetic to the Saudi position than the Houthi position were killed," a senior State Department official said.[99] Investigators later discovered the tail fin of one of the bombs that struck the funeral. It was a Mark-82, with a serial number indicating that it was produced by U.S. defense company Raytheon and modified with a Paveway-II laser guidance system produced in factories in Texas and Arizona.[100]

The funeral hall strike "was the last straw" for the Obama White House.[101] While until October 2016 the administration had tried to reduce the humanitarian harm of the intervention by providing additional training and targeting support, after the strike, it publicly rebuked the coalition for the first time and began to place symbolic pressure on the coalition to end the intervention. The funeral strike "so clearly symbolized much of what was wrong" with U.S. support for the coalition, Robert Malley said.[102]

A statement by NSC spokesperson Ned Price immediately following the strike was unusually critical, calling out the coalition directly: "U.S. security cooperation with Saudi Arabia is not a blank check. Even as we assist Saudi Arabia regarding the defense of their territorial integrity, we have and will continue to express our serious concerns about the conflict in Yemen and how it has been waged. In light of this and other recent incidents, we have initiated an immediate review of our already significantly reduced support to the Saudi-led Coalition and are prepared to adjust our support so as to better align with U.S. principles, values and interests."[103] This policy review led the administration to reduce intelligence sharing with the coalition regarding Houthi forces (but not for AQAP targets).[104] The number of U.S. personnel working in the Joint Combined Planning Cell was reduced, and the Obama administration placed a temporary freeze on a planned sale of cluster bombs and precision munitions kits, a deal worth about $350 million.[105] The decision to freeze these weapons sales was "obviously a direct reflection of the concerns that [the administration has] about Saudi strikes that have resulted in civilian casualties," said an administration official. "It's not a matter of how smart or dumb the bombs are, it's that they're not picking the right targets. The case in point . . . is the [strike] on the funeral."[106]

Even as the sale of these munitions was suspended, other sales went forward, including a $3.5 billion deal for forty-eight Chinook helicopters.[107] Jake Sullivan, a senior Obama administration advisor, later testified that the administration's logic behind providing assistance to the Saudi-led coalition "was at least in part that it would give the United States influence in pushing the coalition to (a) abide by international humanitarian law and (b) conduct its military action in a way to maximize the possibility of a diplomatic solution and minimize non-combatant casualties."[108] Yet placing a temporary hold on some arms sales was largely symbolic. These holds were seen by humanitarian advocacy groups as "very limited disciplinary measures."[109]

A Question of Leverage: Did the Obama Administration's Efforts Work?

The "blank check" statement following the funeral hall strike and suspension of some arms sales appear to have temporarily reduced the tempo of airstrikes, which fell off after the October 2016 strike. Nevertheless, because these measures were largely symbolic, they did not have substantial, lasting effects on the coalition's behavior. According to the arms-trade expert William Hartung, the public rebuke, withdrawal of U.S. personnel, and freeze on some weapons sales was "a signal but too weak of a signal. As long as they're refueling aircraft which is central to the bombing campaign, it's hard to see that they're using all the leverage they have."[110]

Administration officials themselves believed that the pressure led to marginal changes but not a fundamental shift in the conduct of the intervention. According to a former senior Defense Department official, the administration became "very frustrated" with the coalition but still believed that U.S. involvement had a net positive effect: "It's always hard to prove a negative, but I think we had some success in improving Saudi efforts to minimize civilian casualties on the margins."[111] While the public rebuke was unusual, the freeze did not fundamentally threaten, let alone cease, the U.S. assistance that was vital to sustaining the intervention.

The decision to scuttle the Hodeidah offensive in late 2016 also suggested that the Obama administration had some leverage over the Saudi-led coalition's decision-making. As recounted in chapter 5, reports emerged in late 2016 that the UAE had developed plans to capture the port of Hodeidah. International humanitarian agencies and the UN warned that an assault on the Hodeidah port could have disastrous humanitarian effects.[112] When Obama administration officials learned of the plans, they reportedly "demanded that planning for the operation be halted," and as a result, the Hodeidah offensive did not go forward.[113]

Thus, the Obama administration was able to use leverage over the Saudi-led coalition with different degrees of success over the course of the first two years of the intervention. Because the coalition intervention was enabled by U.S. operational support—and because of the long-standing U.S. security partnerships with Saudi Arabia and the UAE—U.S. officials were able to temporarily reduce the tempo of airstrikes and cut back on the most egregious targeting of civilians through operational training and symbolic gestures after the October 2016 funeral hall strike. However, because the measures were largely symbolic and because the Obama administration was on its way out, these measures did not have sustained effects on the coalition's behavior that lasted beyond 2016.

Obama administration officials' efforts were probably not as successful as hoped because the pressure was largely symbolic and took the form of a rhetorical rebuke and did not fundamentally threaten assistance that was vital to sustaining the intervention. Additionally, the training that the U.S. Department of Defense did provide to reduce civilian casualties was both inconsistent and not equipped to address the fundamental challenges that the coalition faced with dynamic targeting. The lack of significant pressure meant that there was not sufficient political will in the United States or among coalition leadership to make substantive changes in the conduct of the coalition's air campaign. Combined with continued operational issues, this meant that little had changed by late 2016.

But the Obama administration quickly lost its leverage over the coalition and the chance to change U.S. policy toward Yemen more substantially in November 2016, when Donald Trump was unexpectedly elected the next president of the United States.

Early Peace Talks End in Failure

The international community's first major push to negotiate an end to the war began in April 2016, when the Saudi-led coalition and the Houthis declared a cease-fire. Ismail Ould Cheikh Ahmed had been appointed UN special envoy for Yemen in April 2015, replacing Jamal Benomar, who had served in the role since 2011 with the remit of facilitating Yemen's political transition.[114] While peace talks held in Kuwait beginning in April 2016 were stymied by the intransigence of both the Houthis and Hadi's government, the talks helped sustain the cease-fire, which led to a marked decline in the number of coalition airstrikes.[115]

When talks broke down in late August, Secretary of State John Kerry traveled to Riyadh and met with officials from the "quad"—which also included the United Kingdom, the UAE, and Saudi Arabia—and announced that talks to reach a comprehensive settlement, including simultaneous security and political tracks, would restart.[116] Nevertheless, the coalition airstrikes resumed at their previous tempo, and the war continued unabated. Secretary Kerry attempted to revive the peace talks held in Oman through November 2016 but was ultimately unsuccessful in reengaging the conflict parties.

In the meantime, in the first direct military engagement between the Houthis and U.S. armed forces, in October 2016, Houthi forces launched antiship missiles at U.S. Navy vessels on patrol off Yemen's coast. U.S. forces responded by firing cruise missiles at Houthi radar installations. While the Obama administration labeled the strikes self-defense and indicated that the United States would not escalate against the Houthis, officials publicly marked the Houthis' rejection of the United States' first serious attempts to mediate the conflict.[117]

So why did President Obama get drawn into exactly the kind of war in the Middle East that candidate Obama had pledged to stay out of? Ironically, the United States was drawn into the war in Yemen by the administration's desire to stay out of the Middle East's proxy wars. In an attempt to pivot away from the Middle East to focus on the more strategically important priority of Asia and to avoid getting involved in wars like the U.S. invasion of Iraq, the Obama administration attempted to subcontract some of its interests to regional security partners. The Iran nuclear deal (JCPOA), one of the administration's crowning diplomatic achievements, would prevent more regional instability, therefore facilitating this pivot, in administration officials' view. In exchange for not raising more public disagreement about the JCPOA, and as an attempt to strengthen the United States' fraying security ties with Arab Gulf security partners, the Obama administration agreed to provide logistical military support to the Saudi-led coalition's intervention in Yemen.

CHAPTER SEVEN

Maximum Pressure

The Trump Administration's War in Yemen

T
EN YEARS AFTER PRESIDENT Obama's Cairo speech
that was supposed to presage a new U.S. approach to
the Middle East, President Donald Trump's secretary
of state, Mike Pompeo, declared that "the age of self-
inflicted American shame is over."[1]

Pompeo gave his own speech in Cairo in January 2019, titled "The United States: A Force for Good in the Middle East,"
intended as criticism of the Obama administration. In the 2019
speech, Pompeo criticized Obama's "reluctance to wield our influence," claiming that Obama's administration had mistakenly seen
the United States "as a force for what ails the Middle East." The
Trump administration, however, marked "the real 'new beginning.'
In just 24 months, the United States under President Trump has
reasserted its traditional role as a force for good in this region."[2]
Throughout the speech, Pompeo failed to mention human rights
even once and spoke little about democracy, all while avoiding criticism of the authoritarian regimes that were U.S. security partners
in the region.

Pompeo's speech summarized the Trump administration's approach to the Middle East in contrast to Obama's. Indeed, the
Trump administration's entire approach was consciously designed as

a rebuke to the previous administration. Starting with Trump's contention that the Iran nuclear agreement was a "a horrible one-sided deal that should have never, ever been made" and building on the guidance of the advisors surrounding him, Trump's approach to the Middle East rested on two principles: unbridled, transactional support for the United States' allies and security partners in the region, especially Israel and Saudi Arabia; and ratcheting up coercive pressure on Iran. According to the reporter Michael Wolff, "If Trump had one fixed point of reference in the Middle East, it was—mostly courtesy of Michael Flynn's tutoring—that Iran was the bad guy. Hence everybody opposed to Iran was a pretty good guy."[3] From this perspective, the goal of U.S. policy was to encourage the "good guys," including Saudi Arabia, the UAE, and Egypt, to work with Israel against Iran.

In practice, this meant that U.S. Middle East policy under President Trump was dominated by two themes: arms sales and pressuring Iran. Trump emphasized the importance of bilateral arms deals and counterterrorism cooperation with allies and partners, who in exchange were allowed to do more or less what they liked in the region. The "maximum pressure" campaign against Iran included sweeping sanctions that were supposed to push Iran toward making a better nuclear deal, although the specific contours of such a deal remained unspecified. Following the United States' withdrawal from compliance with the Joint Comprehensive Plan of Action (JCPOA) in May 2018, in mid-2019, Iran also began to break its obligations under the agreement.[4] Escalating tensions also led to a series of tit-for-tat exchanges of missile fire and airstrikes between U.S. forces and the Iranian-supported military group Kataib Hizbullah in Iraq, culminating in a U.S. drone strike that killed the Islamic Revolutionary Guard Corps (IRGC)–Quds Force commander Qassim Soleimani.

The Trump administration's approach to Yemen, like its Middle East policy more broadly, was dominated by its relationships with Saudi Arabia and the UAE, on the one hand, and its Iran strategy on the other. Trump administration officials portrayed Iran as in control of Houthi decision-making and the civil war in Yemen as a proxy war between Saudi Arabia and Iran. "The United States will continue to stand with our partners in the region to counter Iran's malign activity. This includes with Saudi Arabia, which is on the frontlines of Iran's proxy war in Yemen," said Brian Hook, special representative for Iran and senior policy advisor to Secretary of State Mike Pompeo.[5] From this perspective, Yemen was yet another front in the Trump administration's maximum pressure campaign and an arena where the Trump administration could demonstrate its support for Saudi and Emirati strategic goals.

The Trump Administration's Approach to Yemen

Unusually, Trump's first official visit to a foreign country was to Saudi Arabia. A president's first official trip overseas is a carefully or-chestrated series of events designed to signal something important about the president's foreign policy priorities. In recent decades, U.S. presidents have selected Canada and Mexico as their first des-tination abroad, reflecting the importance of these relationships to U.S. trade and security interests. In contrast, in May 2017, President Trump traveled to Riyadh, where he participated in a traditional Ardah sword dance and touched an inexplicably glowing orb for a photo op with Saudi Arabia's King Salman and Egypt's President Abdel Fattah el-Sisi. Trump signed a joint "strategic vision" on the trip that included $110 billion in weapons sales. Timothy Lender-king, who was serving as deputy assistant secretary of state for Ara-bian Gulf affairs, said that the administration felt that it had "truly reset the relationship as a result of this visit."[6]

Saudi Crown Prince Mohammed bin Salman (MbS) returned the visit in March 2018, making stops in five states and Washing-ton, DC, looking for foreign investment to bolster his Vision 2030 economic reforms and to generate support for the upcoming initial public offering of Aramco.[7] MbS's visit sought legitimacy in the eyes of U.S. officials and high-level international investments. The trip "was so sweeping in ambition that Saudi watchers had to go back decades to find another event that came close," writes the journalist Ben Hubbard. "It was a remarkable tour that took him to the White House, Wall Street, Harvard, MIT, Lockheed Martin, Google, and Facebook, and got him sit-downs with three former American pres-idents, Henry Kissinger, and Oprah Winfrey," Hubbard noted.[8]

The Trump administration was also much less concerned than the Obama administration had been about pressuring the Saudi-led coalition to limit the humanitarian effects of intervention and to pursue negotiations to end the war. Trump himself, quite publicly and without subtlety, put arms sales at the center of the U.S.-Saudi relationship. During MbS's White House visit, Trump told him in front of reporters, "Saudi Arabia is a very wealthy nation, and they're going to give the United States some of that wealth hopefully, in the form of jobs, in the form of the purchase of the finest military equipment anywhere in the world."[9] In case anyone missed the point, Trump held up posters during the meeting with images of specific military equipment and captions explaining where it was manufactured in the United States.

The Trump administration therefore intended to reset U.S. relations with Arab Gulf states, in a sharp pivot away from the Obama administration's approach. Both the Trump administration and Saudi leaders saw the change in administration as a chance to strengthen the United States' relationship with Saudi Arabia and its GCC partners. For both Trump and the Arab Gulf monarchies, personal relationships were also at the center of many of their bilateral relationships. Senior White House advisor Jared Kushner, who had been tasked with much of the administration's Middle East policy portfolio, reportedly reached out to key leaders like MbS and the UAE ambassador to the U.S. Yousef Al Otaiba in the earliest weeks of the administration. On a trip to Riyadh in October 2017, Kushner grew close with the Saudi crown prince, staying up until 4:00 a.m. "swapping stories and planning strategy."[10] MbS quickly became "an important reference point" for Kushner; according to a friend of Kushner's, meeting MbS in the midst of Kushner's new political responsibilities felt "like meeting someone nice at your first day of boarding school."[11] Kushner later recounted that he was one of the few administration officials to urge Trump to go to Saudi Arabia on his first overseas trip. In return for supporting the trip, Kushner urged MbS to help make it a success. "Everyone here is telling me I'm a fool for trusting you," Kushner told MbS. "They are saying the trip is a terrible idea. If I get to Saudi Arabia, and it's just a bunch of sand and camels, I'm a dead man."[12] White House officials were even concerned that Kushner's relationship with MbS, alongside his lack of experience in the Middle East policy world, would make him susceptible to manipulation from Saudi officials, and they tried, apparently unsuccessfully, to curtail the two men's private text messages and phone calls.[13]

On the Saudi side, officials identified Kushner as an important source of influence. A slide presentation given to a Saudi delegation that visited Trump officials just after he was elected noted that Trump's "inner circle is predominantly deal makers who lack familiarity with political customs and deep institutions, and they support Jared Kushner."[14] In return, Trump and Kushner provided support for MbS in the intrigues of the Saudi royal family, an area that U.S. officials had long stayed away from for fear of looking like they were meddling in domestic Saudi politics. Kushner reportedly inquired of U.S. officials early during the Trump administration whether the United States could influence the Saudi royal succession.[15] When he learned that MbS had replaced Mohammed bin Nayef, a favored U.S. interlocutor, as crown prince, Trump announced, "we've put our man on top!"[16] Senior Trump officials like Kushner also had close relations with the UAE's long-standing ambassador to the United States, Yousef Al Otaiba.[17] "I am in constant contact with Jared and that has been extremely helpful," Otaiba wrote in an email in the early months of the administration.[18] These personal relationships were bolstered by Saudi and Emirati leaders' eagerness to buy large U.S. arms packages, which the Trump administration welcomed as part of its jobs-creation agenda.

These transactional and personality-driven bilateral relationships, as well as Trump's simplistic view of the region's politics, would overwhelmingly shape the administration's approach to the war in Yemen. This, in turn, led the Trump administration largely uncritically to back the Saudi-led coalition's intervention. As Bruce Riedel noted, it was "more important to [the Trump administration] to have good relations with the Saudis, and the Yemenis got sacrificed on this."[19]

Within the first months of the administration, Defense Secretary Jim Mattis asked the White House to lift restrictions on U.S. military support for the coalition in Yemen. In return, Saudi Arabia made promises to ease U.S. concerns about civilian casualties, according to a private letter from Foreign Minister Adel al-Jubair prior to Trump's visit to Riyadh. The assurances included a promise to engage in a multiyear, $750 million training program provided by the U.S. military and to observe stricter rules of engagement, including an expanded no-strike list.[20] These assurances were pre-conditions for the arms sales officially agreed to during the visit.

However, these assurances did not lead to any change in the conduct of the airstrikes or the intervention more broadly—nor did they reassure critics. Oxfam's Scott Paul argued that "the steps that Saudi Arabia [reportedly agreed] to take are irrelevant because they will not keep seven million people in Yemen from tipping into famine or stem the tide of cholera."[21] Analysts argued that the May 2017 trip and arms agreement "undercut any leverage the administration could have had on limiting the war in Yemen."[22] In June 2017, the Trump administration notified Congress that it would resume sales of precision-guided munitions to Saudi Arabia that had been halted by the Obama administration.

The Trump administration also continued to provide the same logistical military support to the coalition, including aerial refueling and targeting, although Department of Defense (DoD) officials gave conflicting assessments of the precise levels of support that the United States provided. "There are still Americans on the ground providing direct support and logistical help to allied troops. . . . We don't share intelligence, but we will advise and accompany them on some of these missions," an anonymous military official said.[23] U.S. drone and manned airstrikes against AQAP in Yemen more than doubled in 2017, up to ninety from thirty-eight in the previous year.[24]

This license from the U.S. administration, in turn, led the Saudi-led coalition to double down on fighting in Yemen. According to an anonymous Western diplomat, "There was a definite [Saudi] shift after the [U.S.] election from an approach of 'we need a deal' to thinking there might be a military solution after all, and that the Americans might help."[25] Indeed, an anonymous Trump administration official indicated they understood that ending the Obama-era limits to U.S. support for the coalition would be seen by the coalition as "a green light for direct involvement in a major war."[26] This also helps explain why the number of monthly coalition air raids increased in December 2016 and January 2017.[27] An anonymous senior official noted that Trump administration officials had expended little political capital to pressure the coalition: "The Saudis sitting in Riyadh are mostly getting advice from the DoD on targeting. That will always undercut the humanitarian argument anyone is making."[28]

A headline-grabbing counterterrorism raid at the beginning of Trump's term also helped set the tone of the administration's military-led approach to Yemen. The administration increased the tempo of airstrikes and drone strikes against AQAP and affiliates of the Islamic State under Trump, even as officials explored "how to dismantle or bypass Obama-era constraints intended to prevent civilian deaths from drone attacks, commando raids and other counterterrorism missions outside conventional war zones."[29] The president granted a Pentagon request to declare parts of three Yemeni provinces "area[s] of active hostilities," meaning that looser battlefield restrictions would apply to U.S. counterterrorism operations there.[30] This "opened the door" to a Special Operations raid that took place in late January 2017, just a couple of weeks after Trump was inaugurated.[31] The raid was engulfed in mishaps, leading to a fifty-minute firefight that killed several Yemeni civilians, including some children, and an American commando, leaving three other American commandos wounded.[32]

The Trump administration initiated an Iran strategy review, one that would continue to shape the administration's approach to Iran throughout Trump's presidency. The review was finished in September 2017 and publicly announced in an October 2017 speech by the president.[33] The speech is largely remembered for the headline that Trump would not certify to Congress that Iran was complying with the nuclear deal, a requirement that was a remnant of Congress's acquiescence to the 2015 deal. While Trump said that the Iran strategy was "based on a clear-eyed assessment of the Iranian dictatorship," he described Iran and its regional strategy in hyperbolic terms: "Iran is under the control of a fanatical regime that seized power in 1979 and forced a proud people to submit to its extremist rule," Trump claimed. "The regime remains the world's leading state sponsor of terrorism, and provides assistance to al Qaeda, the Taliban, Hezbollah, Hamas, and other terrorist networks." He asserted that Iranian missiles "threaten American troops and our allies" and that Iran "harasses American ships and threatens freedom of navigation."[34]

The administration's approach to Iran was the main guidepost for its Yemen strategy. "Yemen was encompassed within our Iran policy," said Robert Greenway, who served as deputy assistant to the president and senior director for Middle Eastern and North African affairs at the National Security Council under Trump.[35] Likewise, David Schenker, who served as assistant secretary of state for Near Eastern affairs from June 2019 through January 2021, noted, "Yemen, like Iraq and Lebanon, was another priority intersectional issue with Iran."[36] "Iran's support for terrorist proxies in Yemen threatened vital national security interests of the United States," as did AQAP and ISIS, said Greenway.[37] Trump officials saw the capabilities that Iran provided to the Houthis as a direct threat in the maritime domain, including the Bab el-Mandeb strait, and to U.S. security partners. From this perspective, Iran's presence in Yemen could even be a threat to Israel: as Greenway put it, "Iran's increasing ability to threaten Israel, Saudi Arabia, and global trade from Yemen risks U.S. national security interests."[38]

Trump administration officials also perceived a direct command-and-control relationship between Iran and the Houthis—a relationship that most experts would describe as more complicated and certainly less direct. Officials viewed the Houthis as "a wholly owned subsidiary of Iran," according to Greenway: "Yemen has become an extension of Iran's threat to partners and allies of the United States in the region. Iran was using surrogates and proxies to threaten the United States and our partners and allies, for various reasons, and that [includes] Yemen, as they've done in Lebanon, Syria, Iraq, and elsewhere."[39] The administration's public statements also frequently linked Iran to the Houthis, often referring to them as "the Iran-backed Houthis" to drive the point home.[40] Secretary Pompeo described the Houthis as "completely under the boot of the Iranians."[41]

Iran's activities in Yemen also presented the Trump administration with an opportunity of sorts: Yemen became "a place where [the U.S.] can disrupt Iran's terrorist networks in collaboration with partners and degrade the regional threat they represent with lower cost and risk of escalation compared to Lebanon, Syria, or Iraq."[42] From the administration's early days, "it seemed clear ... that Yemen was an area that they could potentially see, incorrectly, as [safe for] containable escalation with Iran," said Matt Duss, foreign policy advisor to Senator Bernie Sanders.[43]

Some senior Trump administration officials pushed against this overly simplified narrative, but they were the exception. In 2018, NSC officials coordinated an interagency process intended to take a longer-term approach to Yemen. The approach was two-pronged, seeking to get buy-in from Yemenis themselves for national-level elections to be held after the war ended and to promote service provision so that a future national government would be seen as legitimate. But by the end of 2018, the stabilization planning had stopped, and Iran again became the administration's most important priority in Yemen.[44]

The Trump administration's "maximum pressure" approach to the Houthis was not, by officials' own account, successful in diminishing Iranian influence in Yemen. In fact, Iran's support for the Houthis "is continuing without any diminution. They might even be stepping it up," an anonymous senior State Department official noted in 2020.[45]

Senior Trump administration officials said they supported the UN-led peace process and believed that they were successful in pressing the Saudis to accept the need for a political solution to the war. According to Schenker, Yemen was one of the "issues that consumed much of [officials'] time at State." "Over time, I believe our engagements with the Saudis . . . had a positive impact. . . . Along the way, the Saudis announced a few unilateral ceasefires," Schenker noted, "and in my view, [Saudi officials] invested in diplomacy and engaged in goodwill negotiations with the Houthis." Yet Trump administration officials' public statements tried to shift blame for the war's continuation away from the coalition: "The problem wasn't the Saudis—it was and remains the Houthis," said Schenker. The main obstacle to peace was that the Houthis "1) lie, 2) don't keep agreements, and 3) are committed to winning this war militarily."[46]

The Exception to the Rule: The Trump Administration Uses U.S. Leverage

The Trump administration's public statements about the blockade on Hodeidah in December 2017 are a telling exception to the administration's support for the coalition and its operations. Here, the Trump administration asserted pressure to rein in the coalition in Yemen, demonstrating that the use of U.S. leverage could successfully change the coalition's behavior.

In August 2015, a Saudi aircraft destroyed five cranes that were used to unload shipments coming into the Hodeidah port. As recounted earlier, the U.S. Agency for International Development (USAID) donated $3.9 million to purchase new cranes for the port, but when they arrived, coalition ships turned them away.[47] A spokesman for the coalition said that the cranes had been blocked because the coalition did not "want to continue to enhance the capabilities of the Houthis to generate money and to smuggle" weapons."[48] In November 2017, the coalition imposed a complete blockade on ports and airports in Yemen in response to a ballistic missile that was fired toward Riyadh. International NGOs and humanitarian organizations issued dire warnings about the effects of the blockade, with the World Food Programme noting that "Hodeidah Port is a humanitarian lifeline for millions who are on the brink of famine."[49]

On December 6, 2017, the Trump administration issued a statement that very unusually publicly rebuked the coalition, calling on it to "completely allow food, fuel, water, and medicine to reach the Yemeni people who desperately need it. This must be done for humanitarian reasons immediately."[50] On December 20, the coalition announced that it would temporarily end the blockade of Hodeidah port and allowed for the delivery of the four new cranes. Saudi Arabia also announced shortly afterward that it would deposit $2 billion in the central bank in Aden to shore up Yemen's currency and pledged an additional $1.5 billion toward the UN humanitarian response plan.[51] Such public statements, in addition to private calls from Trump administration senior officials, was seen by observers as key to getting the coalition to comply. Kushner reportedly called MbS for the explicit purpose of addressing the blockade, and senior Trump administration officials thought that the call helped persuade MbS to open the port.[52] Thus, in an important instance when the Trump administration did decide to use some of its leverage to pressure the coalition, the effort was successful in changing the behavior of the interveners, reopening a vital humanitarian lifeline.[53] By early February 2018, the cranes were at work offloading goods at the port.[54]

In contrast, the Trump administration gave the coalition what amounted to a yellow light for a summer 2018 offensive on Hodeidah. That the coalition went ahead with the intervention this time suggests that the United States had considerable leverage—in 2016, during the Obama administration, U.S. officials had discouraged a similar offensive, as recounted previously. In 2016, National Security Advisor Susan Rice had "personally called UAE Crown Prince Mohammed bin Zayed and told him that the U.S. would not support the offensive."[55] Coalition officials argued in vain "that taking the town would put political pressure on the Houthis and enable the free flow of humanitarian aid through the port," according to Jeremy Konyndyk, director of foreign disaster assistance at the time.[56]

A number of former White House and State Department officials, as well as humanitarian experts, "characterized the [2018] offensive as a major failure by the U.S. to restrain its coalition partners."[57] While senior Trump administration officials had voiced objections to the offensive, they also "tempered their objections," offering the coalition a "blinking yellow light" of caution, according to a U.S. official.[58] The U.S. military reportedly provided the coalition with intelligence on off-limit airstrike targets in the port.[59] Senior officials, including Secretary of Defense Jim Mattis and Secretary of State Mike Pompeo, "offered qualified support for the UAE as the US dropped its appeal for de-escalation."[60]

Pushback to the Trump Administration's Approach and the End of Aerial Refueling

The Trump administration also found itself increasingly embroiled in tussles with members of Congress and Capitol Hill staff who were demanding answers about the United States' role in the war.[61] In response, said Greenway, "[the administration] worked to assure Congress that we were not expanding the scope of U.S. presence and involvement, that we were not in any way enabling the Saudi-led coalition beyond existing constraints."[62] But administration officials were also frustrated by what they felt was an overly simplistic view of U.S. involvement held by some members of Congress and the American public and saw the questions as politically motivated.[63]

Not all advocates and Hill staff saw ending U.S. support for the coalition as a panacea to ending the war. "It may be that the United States lacks the ability to 'solve' the Yemen crisis," Duss said, "but we do have the power to do less harm. And we should do that."[64]

Advocates and members of Congress also had reason to be suspicious of the administration's classification of U.S. involvement with the coalition, most tellingly with regard to aerial refueling of the coalition's aircraft. Dubbed "gas stations in the sky" by activists, air-to-air refueling allowed coalition "aircraft to fly longer combat missions over Yemen, allowing more time to react to changes on the ground and to acquire targets."[65] When aerial refueling assistance began in April 2015, the United States planned to fly one tanker daily, according to the Pentagon. "The planes are refueled outside Yemeni airspace," a Pentagon spokesperson noted.[66]

Yet as the intervention wore on, members of Congress and activists struggled to get answers from the Department of Defense about how much refueling assistance the United States was providing and under which legal authorities. In early 2017, "no one, including DoD, could specifically say how, under what authority, we were providing refueling support or any of the other logistical support that we were offering the coalition," said Kate Kizer, who was the director of policy and advocacy at the Yemen Peace Project in 2017. "And it became a big flashpoint between Congress and the administration, because seemingly basic information that they certainly have the technology to provide," such as the relevant authorities and documentation, was not forthcoming.[67] These activists learned that DoD was using an Acquisition and Cross-Service Agreement, or ACSA, which allows for the transfer of military supplies and logistics support to partner militaries, to authorize the refueling assistance. Under the terms of an ACSA, the recipient country is required to reimburse the United States for the assistance it receives. Yet questioning from members of Congress and from advocates including Kizer revealed in December 2018 that the Pentagon had provided refueling to Saudi aircraft without a formal agreement in place for at least a year and that, due to "errors in accounting," DoD had "failed to charge [the coalition] adequately for fuel and refueling services."[68]

Before late 2018, CENTCOM had given reporters and members of Congress confusing and sometimes even contradictory answers about whether and how it tracked refueling operations for the Saudi-led coalition.[69] In a 2018 congressional hearing, CENTCOM commander General Joseph Votel told Senator Elizabeth Warren that CENTCOM did not track the results of the missions it provided refueling for, such as which targets were struck by aircraft that were refueled by the United States.[70] "How are the Saudis actually abiding by the non-strike list, are they still refueling—those are all things we have no idea about, and the administration isn't exactly forthcoming about it," an anonymous Hill staffer said in 2017.[71] Thus, while Trump administration officials felt that they were being forthcoming about the extent of U.S. involvement in the coalition's intervention, Hill staffers and advocates were frustrated and thought they were not getting the information they were asking for—and that Congress, in its oversight role, had a right to know. Prompted by congressional inquiries, the Pentagon eventually announced in December 2018, right after the Senate passed a resolution that would end aerial refueling, that it would bill the coalition $331 million for the unpaid costs of refueling.[72]

The Trump administration, along with the UK government, also backed the coalition at the UN, providing it with political cover. The United Kingdom is the "penholder" on Yemen-related issues at the UN, the result of an informal division of labor among the United States, the United Kingdom, and France that essentially gives the United Kingdom agenda-setting power over the Yemen portfolio. Under this system, the United Kingdom is charged with drafting relevant resolutions and negotiating text with China and Russia on behalf of the rest of the P5.[73] An alliance of countries led by the Netherlands made a serious push in September 2017 to appoint an international commission of inquiry to investigate human rights abuses in Yemen. After three weeks of intense negotiation, the United States, United Kingdom, and France finally agreed to a compromise text that established an international team of experts to investigate human rights abuses in Yemen. Saudi Arabia engaged in intense lobbying throughout the negotiations, and the compromise outcome "spared Saudi Arabia . . . from a formal panel of inquiry like the one investigating the war in Syria."[74] The United States was therefore able to shield its partners from further investigation and provided the coalition with diplomatic cover.

On October 2, 2018, the journalist and U.S. resident Jamal Khashoggi was murdered by Saudi agents in a Saudi consulate in Turkey, in an operation approved by MbS.[75] As information about the gruesome murder came to light, pressure mounted on the Trump administration to react. Saudi Arabia's intervention in Yemen, a subject that Khashoggi had covered in his newspaper columns, was a prime arena to demonstrate that the administration was doing something in response. At the same time, the Trump administration was not interested in inflicting significant harm on the bilateral relationship with the Kingdom, so "a member of Trump's National Security Council met in Riyadh with Prince Khalid bin Salman, MBS's younger brother, to discuss measures the United States could take against the kingdom," writes the journalist Ben Hubbard.[76] The fact that U.S. officials discussed potential punishments with Saudi officials themselves was indicative of the fact that the Trump administration was keen to maintain the bilateral relationship.

When U.S. officials settled on ending aerial refueling support for the coalition as the measure they would take, they notified Saudi officials of the decision privately before reporting to Congress or making a public announcement. Saudi officials asked in return that they be allowed to make the public announcement first, but the news was leaked to the media before they could release a statement.[77] Still, the Kingdom's statement, released by the Saudi embassy in Washington, DC, claimed that Saudi Arabia had itself requested that the U.S. end refueling because the coalition could now handle its refueling needs on its own. This part of the statement was not wrong: by this time, just one-fifth of the coalition's aircraft required aerial refueling from the United States.[78] Thus, this response had little practical effect on the coalition's capabilities, and U.S. officials' consultations with Saudi officials prior to the announcement seemed designed to take the bite out of the decision.

Parting Shot: Designating the Houthis as a Foreign Terrorist Organization (FTO)

The Trump administration made one last major policy decision about the war in Yemen on its way out the door. Less than two weeks before the transition to the Biden administration was to take place, Secretary Pompeo announced that the United States was officially designating the Houthis as a foreign terrorist organization, or FTO, and placing sanctions on three senior Houthi officials. The designation kicked in on January 19, 2021, the day before President Biden was sworn in. Trump officials said that the move was the culmination of a normal policy decision-making process, but the timing seemed like "an act of sabotage," since it would make it harder for Biden officials to change it.[79]

UN officials and humanitarians decried the decision, pointing out that the designation would "interrupt the humanitarian response in Yemen" and have a "chilling effect" on aid, preventing U.S. organizations and citizens from having "almost any interaction with the Houthis, even though they control a portion of Yemen where 80 percent of the population lives."[80] Schenker argued that the designation's humanitarian impact would be mitigated "through waivers from the Treasury Department's Office of Foreign Assets Control; in any event, the Justice Department would not be prosecuting humanitarian organizations for inadvertent leakage to the Houthis."[81]

While the humanitarian effects of the FTO designation could have been dire, the decision did not stand for long. The Biden administration announced that it was revoking the FTO designation just a couple of weeks into its tenure.[82] In fact, the revocation was one piece of a much-broader policy shift, one that was brought about in large part by pressure from Congress and advocates, as well as growing awareness among the American public about the humanitarian consequences of the war in Yemen.

CHAPTER EIGHT

Congress and the Yemen
Advocacy Coalition

W HEN MEMBERS OF CONGRESS first started asking questions about U.S. support for the Saudi-led coalition, most Americans did not know that the United States was even involved in the war in Yemen.

A coalition of humanitarian organizations and progressive advocacy groups began lobbying Congress to end U.S. support for the war soon after the Saudi-led coalition's intervention began. In meetings with members of Congress and congressional aides over the next two years, this coalition often found that it first had to brief congressional offices on what was happening in Yemen before diving into the details of U.S. policy. Core members of the original Yemen advocacy coalition said that when they first started talking to congressional offices about Yemen, congressional aides would say, "I have no idea where my boss is on this. This has never come up before."[1] As late as 2017, some congressional leaders even denied that the United States was providing aerial refueling support to the coalition, not because they were covering something up but because "it was just not on the radar of leadership," according to a House staffer.[2]

Yet by 2019, many Americans had become concerned about the humanitarian crisis unfolding in Yemen. In October 2018, images of malnourished children were featured on the cover of *New York Times Magazine*. "I understand it's going to make some people turn away," the editor of the magazine said about the cover image, "but hopefully the second response is like: What the hell is going on?"[3] A 2018 poll found that 51 percent of Americans favored ending U.S. support for the war in Yemen, while just 19 percent opposed ending it.[4]

In 2019, Congress passed two pieces of legislation related to Yemen: one bill that would end U.S. logistical support for the coalition and one that would block a tranche of "emergency" arms sales to Saudi Arabia and the UAE. While both bills were ultimately vetoed by President Trump, the passage of these bills in Congress was unprecedented. Supporters had aimed to use congressional consideration of these bills as a tool to raise public awareness of—and to encourage a debate about—U.S. support for the war. The idea that either bill could actually pass, never mind be signed into law, was too far-fetched for supporters to even consider back when this effort began in 2016.[5]

Viewed as an effort to formally constrain the Trump administration through legislation, this legislation was a failure. But as an effort to informally constrain the Trump administration by bringing media and policy-maker attention to the conflict, the legislation was a major and unexpected success. Due largely to these efforts in Congress and the work of advocates, the war in Yemen became a major talking point in the 2020 Democratic presidential primaries. In a November 2019 debate, then-candidate Joe Biden said that his administration would treat Saudi Arabia as "the [international] pariah that they are." Referencing Yemen, Biden said that he would "end the sale of material to the Saudis where they're going in and murdering children."[6] And in February 2021, less than a month after taking office, President Biden made ending U.S. support for Yemen a centerpiece of his first foreign policy speech in office.[7]

These legislative efforts, propelled by Americans' principled reaction to the horrors of the war and its effects on Yemeni civilians, helped shift the domestic politics of U.S. engagement with Gulf security partners. From 2018 through 2020, Yemen became a surprising rallying cry for many Americans to express their discontent with the United States' "endless wars" in the Middle East and its security partnerships with repressive autocracies like Saudi Arabia and the

UAE. Congress's efforts to pass legislation created a positive feedback loop, drawing additional public engagement.

Congressional staffers and advocates deliberately selected specific kinds of legislation because they contained provisions that meant their bills could "force" a vote in Congress.[8] Under the rules of the Arms Export Control Act (AECA), once a joint resolution of disapproval has reached the Senate floor, opponents cannot filibuster it. This means that supporters of the bill can ensure that it gets voted on, unlike other kinds of legislation. It also means that a resolution of disapproval can pass with a simple majority vote.

Nothing about this major shift in U.S. political discourse and policy toward Yemen was inevitable. When this work began in 2015, few who supported it imagined that the Yemen advocacy coalition could be able to take on an issue that was simply unknown to many policy makers and members of Congress, let alone most Americans, and elevate it to national importance.

How did this shift happen? Stymied by the Obama White House and then by a presidential administration that appeared unmoved by anything other than the prospect of increasing arms sales, a small group of progressive advocates in Washington, DC, worked alongside Yemeni American activists, congressional champions, and philanthropic institutions ranging from the Charles Koch Institute to George Soros's Open Society Foundations. This coalition laid the groundwork in Congress to introduce legislation and then organized constituents from across the country to pass it.

While events along the way, notably a coalition airstrike on a bus filled with children in August 2018 and the murder of the Saudi journalist and U.S. resident Jamal Khashoggi that October, propelled the movement forward, Congress's efforts would not have succeeded without the groundwork that the advocacy coalition and its allies in Congress had already laid. Well into the Biden administration, debates around U.S. policy in the Middle East continued to be framed by conversations around whether to end arms sales to Gulf security partners and the conditions under which the United States ought to use force around the world. This framing followed advocates' and Congress's invocation of provisions in the 1976 Arms Export Control Act and the 1973 War Powers Resolution (WPR) in attempts to force successive administrations to end U.S. support for the Saudi-led coalition's intervention in Yemen—provisions that had hardly ever been invoked since the legislation became law in the 1970s and had never before made it to a president's desk.

This advocacy movement has three important implications for how we think about U.S. policy toward Yemen's war—and in the Middle East more broadly. First, when the United States does decide to exert leverage over a security partner, it can change that partner's behavior significantly. Leverage, in other words, does matter—when policy makers choose to use it. As we have already seen, the Obama administration's public statements following the funeral hall airstrikes in 2016 and his administration's decision to pause the sale of some weapons to the coalition appear to have affected the tempo of the coalition's operations in the following weeks. The Trump administration's public statements about the Hodeidah cranes in late 2017—which were, in turn, driven by a months-long quest led by Senator Todd Young to get answers from the administration about the cranes—compelled the coalition to allow the cranes into port. Congressional pressure also resulted in the administration's decision to cut off refueling to the coalition in November 2018, further impacting the coalition's operational tempo. Negative press and pressure from the United States has also been linked to the UAE's decision to draw down its forces from Yemen in 2019 and the declining pace of coalition airstrikes in 2019.[9]

Second, Congress has an important role to play in exerting U.S. leverage over security partners. Congress, advocates, and constituents can "tie an administration's hands" in international negotiations by credibly generating domestic costs that the executive will incur if it does not satisfy domestic constituencies.[10] This, in turn, generates additional pressure on security partners. Saudi and Emirati leaders' decisions over the course of the war show that they understood Congress's role in U.S. foreign policy and that they were responsive to Congress's demands. As a State Department official put it during congressional testimony in 2018, Congress's efforts "have been exceedingly helpful in allowing the Administration to send a message from the whole of government."[11]

Finally, while U.S. security policy is notoriously slow to change, the Yemen advocacy coalition's success demonstrates that it is possible to substantially shift the terms of the debate, even in a short period of time. In 2016, few members of Congress were willing to subvert the status quo of the United States' bilateral relationships with Saudi Arabia and the United Arab Emirates, seen by the U.S. foreign policy establishment as critical security partnerships. Yet by 2020, the Democratic Party Platform stated that Democrats would "end support for the Saudi-led war in Yemen and help bring the war to an end," and legislation to end U.S. support for the coalition had passed with the votes of several prominent Republicans.[12] At the same time, the advocacy coalition also demonstrated that foreign policy views do not shift so rapidly on their own—this shift required a major effort in grassroots organizing, media engagement, and lobbying Congress. This is the story of how that shift happened.

The Yemen Advocacy Coalition's Origins

In some ways, the coalition that became a compelling force for change in U.S. Middle East policy started out of a small windowless office in a law firm in downtown Washington, DC. Layla Picard founded the Yemen Peace Project (YPP), the first Washington, DC, advocacy organization "devoted entirely to Yemeni and Yemeni-American affairs," in 2010.[13] YPP was a scrappy organization: Picard brought on YPP's first salaried employee, Kate Kizer, in early 2017 as director of policy, to establish YPP's Washington advocacy program. Eric Eikenberry, who joined YPP shortly thereafter, called YPP a "very small shop" that was "a real labor of ambition" for its small staff.[14] Their aim was to "empower Yemenis to participate in the US policy-making process."[15] YPP would go on to become a founding member of the Yemen advocacy coalition in 2015.

International humanitarian organizations also began organizing around the intervention in Yemen and raising awareness about its humanitarian implications in the spring of 2015. Oxfam America was one of the first major voices to emerge in this space, calling for a cease-fire and for an end to all international military support for the parties to the conflict. Oxfam was the first to use the word "blockade"—a term that became a rallying cry for the advocacy coalition— in the months following the March 2015 intervention, to describe how the coalition was significantly delaying or blocking consumer and humanitarian goods from entering Yemen's sea- and airports. A July 2015 Oxfam press release warned that thirteen million Yemenis were experiencing food scarcity "as the blockade and fighting restrict food, fuel and other vital supplies."[16]

Oxfam had worked on the ground in Yemen for several decades and periodically brought its Yemen-based advisors to Washington, DC, to share their expertise and explain to U.S. policy makers what was happening on the ground.[17] Drawing on its deep connections to the country and on-the-ground knowledge, Oxfam realized that the humanitarian situation was particularly dire. "The destruction caused by the campaign [was] shocking," even for "seasoned humanitarian responders" who were accustomed to working in difficult conflict contexts, wrote Oxfam's Paul O'Brien.[18]

The earliest U.S.-based advocates quickly drew the conclusion that the United States' approach to the war in Yemen was wrong. In October 2015, Oxfam's O'Brien wrote a *Foreign Policy* piece titled "Yemen Doesn't Need the Obama Administration's 'Deep Concern.'" It was one of the first times that advocates publicly argued that the United States needed to change its approach to the Saudi-led coalition. The op-ed made an argument that even Oxfam itself deemed radical at the time: "To truly stand with Yemenis," O'Brien argued, "the Obama administration must adopt a radically different course" that included withdrawing arms sales and other forms of support for the coalition, openly calling for the free flow of goods into ports, and supporting an unconditional cease-fire.[19]

These two coalitions—progressive foreign policy advocacy organizations, including YPP, the Quaker group the Friends Committee on National Legislation (FCNL), and Win Without War, on the one hand; and humanitarian NGOs including Oxfam, on the other—melded into one, becoming the core of the Yemen advocacy coalition in Washington, DC.

They were joined early on by grassroots activists from around the country, notably members of the Yemeni American community who organized around U.S. participation in the war. Dr. Aisha Jumaan is an epidemiologist who had worked on health projects in Yemen since 2010 and became a leading activist figure. Observing the humanitarian devastation from the earliest months of the war, she said, "was heartbreaking for someone like me, because we worked so hard for so many years to improve public health indicators in Yemen, only for them to be destroyed. What made this even more devastating for me as a Yemeni American was the United States' support for the war."[20] In 2015, Jumaan began giving presentations about the war and humanitarian situation in Yemen "at churches, schools—to anyone who was willing to speak to [her]."[21] Many people wanted to hear her message: a conference that Jumaan organized in February 2018 that also featured Representative Adam Smith, Kate Kizer of Win Without War, and Kate Gould, then of FCNL, overflowed the University of Washington's largest auditorium. Jumaan also coauthored an op-ed in the *Huffington Post* in 2017 urging Americans to contact their members of Congress about U.S. support for the war. "The messages: stop shipping weapons to the Saudis; pressure them to stop the airstrikes and end the blockade; and press for a political solution," they wrote.[22] Jumaan's organization, the Yemen Relief and Reconstruction Organization, which she founded in 2017, along with other groups led by Yemeni Americans, became part of the advocacy coalition's organizing efforts in Washington and across the country.

The fourth set of organizations that made up the coalition comprised conservative and libertarian-minded groups, including the Charles Koch Institute, Defense Priorities, Concerned Veterans for America, and others. While they approached the issue from a different perspective, with a greater emphasis on the constitutionality of the use of U.S. military force abroad without congressional approval, these groups shared progressive advocates' concerns about U.S. military overreach and the humanitarian crisis.[23]

Despite this early mobilization, there was very little appetite on the Hill for changing the U.S. approach in Yemen in these early years of the advocacy coalition's work. When Oxfam first began to argue that the United States should stop supporting the Saudi-led coalition, Oxfam's Scott Paul said, "we sort of got laughed out of the room."[24]

Early Congressional Champions and Arms Sales under the Obama Administration

As civilian casualties from airstrikes mounted, however, the coalition started to draw attention on the Hill. One of the earliest public expressions of concern about the war from Congress came from Representative Ted Lieu, after a strike on a wedding celebration killed more than seventy civilians in September 2015. The wedding attack was the latest in a series of airstrikes that had killed civilians, fueling "accusations that the Saudi-led military coalition is conducting an increasingly reckless offensive as it tries to defeat the Houthis."[25] Congressman Lieu wrote a letter to the Joint Chiefs of Staff in September 2015 asking that the United States "cease aiding coalition airstrikes in Yemen until the coalition demonstrates that they will institute proper safeguards to prevent civilian deaths."[26]

As a former military prosecutor in the JAG Corps and later a colonel in the Air Force Reserves, Congressman Lieu was already closely attuned to issues around the Law of Armed Conflict. By late 2016, he had come to believe that due to U.S. support for the coalition in Yemen, "U.S. personnel are now at legal risk of being investigated and potentially prosecuted for committing war crimes" under international law. "When you're now in it for well over a year, and you've got over seventy of these strikes, then you can't say it's pilot error anymore," Lieu said. "At some point it becomes either international targeting of civilians, or, a coalition that just doesn't care that they're hitting civilians."[27] An expert opinion from the American Bar Association in 2017 came to a similar conclusion: "given the *prima facie* evidence of wrongdoing by Saudi Arabia, continued sale of arms to Saudi Arabia—and specifically of arms used in airstrikes—should not be presumed to be permissible based on the terms of" U.S. law, including the Arms Export Control Act and the Foreign Assistance Act.[28]

From the earliest days of the intervention, Lieu repeatedly raised these concerns by asking pointed questions of senior U.S. officials in hearings and letters, oversight tactics commonly used by members of Congress. Eventually, Congressman Lieu's letters would come to be cosigned by a number of members of Congress from both parties, but some of the letters he wrote in 2015 bore only his own signature.

Representative Debbie Dingell, who had a large Yemeni American constituency in her district, was also an early champion. In October 2015, ten members of Congress, led by Representative Dingell, also wrote a letter asking the administration to "work with our Saudi partners to limit civilian casualties."[29] In addition to leading the October 2015 letter, Representative Dingell sponsored an amendment to a defense-related bill in May 2015 urging the Obama administration to help evacuate Yemeni Americans caught in the war. "Our office has been deluged with calls from Yemeni Americans, most of them my constituents, who are desperate to escape or have family trapped in Yemen," she said.[30]

The idea of using congressional legislation to express concern about the Saudi-led coalition's actions first arose when the Obama administration announced the upcoming sale of precision-guided munitions (PGMs) and other items to Saudi Arabia in November 2015. Congress has played an oversight role in U.S. arms sales since the Arms Export Control Act—then called the Foreign Military Sales Act—was passed in 1976, impelled by increasing concern in Congress about arms sales. But members of Congress have rarely made use of the AECA's provisions. In theory, Congress is able to block an arms sale under the terms of the AECA. To do so, both houses must introduce and pass a bill called a "joint resolution of disapproval." Congress does not otherwise sign off on arms sales: if Congress fails to pass a joint resolution of disapproval within thirty days following notification for sales over a certain monetary threshold, the sale moves ahead.[31] A month, however, is a very short period of time to get a majority of both houses of Congress on board with publicly voting against the president, especially when arms sales are touted as critical to national security and as job creators.[32] In practice, Congress must also overcome practically insurmountable barriers to block a sale, including garnering sixty-seven votes in the Senate to override a presidential veto. This obstacle explains why Congress has never successfully blocked an arms sale.

As of 2015, Congress had never been able to pass a joint resolution of disapproval to block an arms sale. The simple fact that Congress so rarely moved to vote against an arms sale made this an unlikely vehicle for U.S. advocacy around the war in Yemen. However, one aspect of this legislation made it an especially useful tool for advocates: it is "privileged" in the Senate, which in the arcane language of congressional rules means that it takes precedence over a chamber's regular order of business.[33] Nonprivileged legislation can be effectively buried by congressional leadership so that it never comes up for debate or a vote on the floor—but privileged legislation is guaranteed a floor vote.[34] Holding a vote makes it far more likely that legislation will receive additional media and public attention.[35]

In November 2015, after the leaders of the Senate Foreign Relations Committee (SFRC) received notification of the PGM sale, they took the unprecedented step of requesting that the administration notify Congress thirty days before the weapons were actually shipped—the first time Congress had ever issued such a "priori-notification request" for an arms sale.[36] In the spring of 2016, Senator Chris Murphy in the Senate and Congressman Ted Lieu in the House introduced legislation to place conditions on another arms sale to Saudi Arabia.[37] In July, Senator Murphy introduced a bill expressing the sense of the Senate that the "United States–supported Saudi military operations in Yemen should take all feasible precautions to reduce the risk of harm to civilians."[38]

Congress's efforts to block arms sales to Saudi Arabia and the UAE took a major step forward in the fall of 2016. In August of that year, the Obama administration notified Congress of another proposed sale, this time of MiA2S Abrams tanks to Saudi Arabia. Both the House and the Senate introduced joint resolutions of disapproval of the sale in September 2016, a highly unusual step. Even more surprising, the bill won the votes of twenty-seven senators. Democratic and Republican senators who voted against it did so because they did not want to vote against the administration's policies or because they believed that the United States needed to stand firmly behind its Saudi and Emirati partners, linking the war to opposing Iran's military activities in the region. Expressing the sentiment of hawkish senators, Senator Lindsey Graham said, "To those who want to vote today to suspend this aid to Saudi Arabia, people in Iran will cheer you on."[39]

Twenty-seven Senate votes may seem small, but at the time, it represented a major victory. The idea of using arms sales as leverage to affect a security partner's behavior was novel. At the time, even getting that many Senate votes "was a huge victory," said Kate Gould, who led the FCNL advocacy work on Yemen before going to work in Congressman Ro Khanna's office as legislative director and national security and human rights advisor—"especially because it was on human rights grounds." Gould noted, "When you think about how . . . we have this congressional procedure but it's not being used, it's really pretty stunning."[40] CNN noted that the vote "came as the US-Saudi relationship is being carefully examined and managed by restive lawmakers."[41] Members of Congress were publicly questioning U.S.-Saudi security partnership, until then seen by many U.S. foreign policy experts and policy makers as inviolable.

Introducing legislation and holding votes also gave the bills' sponsors a platform to talk about U.S. support for the war in the national media. "There's an American imprint on every civilian life lost in Yemen. Though the Saudis are actually dropping the bombs from their planes, they wouldn't be able to do it without us," Senator Murphy told Jake Tapper on CNN.[42] "America is complicit in the carnage in Yemen," the *New York Times* editorial board charged later that same week.[43] "Why the hell is the US helping Saudi Arabia bomb Yemen?" the headline of a *Vox* news story asked in the weeks following the vote.[44] *Fox News*'s coverage noted that the Saudi-led coalition "is drawing fire from human rights groups, who say the kingdom has been targeting civilians with American-made weapons, and may be responsible for war crimes."[45]

Nevertheless, most members of Congress and their staff still did not know much about the war in Yemen at this stage. "It was just all completely new," Gould said.[46] Members of Congress and their staff had to learn that the coalition's war against the Houthis was separate from U.S. counterterrorism missions against AQAP and the associated drone warfare in Yemen, for example. "What became clear is that we had a lot of work to do to make people feel like this was going to be relevant to them," Gould said.[47] So the advocacy coalition went back to work.

The Yemen Coalition Gains Momentum

The story that is often told about the Yemen advocacy movement points to the murder of the Saudi journalist Jamal Khashoggi in October 2018 as the key turning point. The shocking murder and its political fallout, including the Kingdom's refusal to take responsibility and President Trump's efforts to defend Saudi leadership, horrified many Americans and shed light on a U.S. security partnership that had empowered a repressive regime for decades.

While Yemen advocacy did gain a great deal of momentum following Khashoggi's death, there was nothing inevitable about this trajectory. Although Khashoggi had covered the war in Yemen in his columns, there was no particular reason that the American public and Congress's ire should have settled on Saudi Arabia's conduct in Yemen as the outlet for its anger. The bills that eventually made it to the president's desk were just as much about Yemen as they were about Saudi Arabia, although the U.S.-Saudi relationship was certainly central to the broader debate.

Instead, Khashoggi's death became a transformative event in this story precisely *because* the advocacy coalition and members of Congress had already laid the legislative groundwork. While the bill to block an arms sale gained only twenty-seven senate votes in its favor in September 2016, for example, a vote held less than a year later on similar legislation, in June 2017 (over a year before Khashoggi was murdered), won forty-seven votes in support.[48] Painstaking efforts to enlist congressional champions and sponsors, organize constituents, and hold floor debates about U.S. support for the war in Yemen from 2015 through late 2018 constituted the infrastructure that enabled legislation to advance through Congress.

While advocates had organized around Congress's 2016 efforts to block arms sales to Saudi Arabia, these were ad hoc efforts that were not yet institutionalized as part of a broader effort to end U.S. military support for the Saudi-led coalition. That changed in early 2017, when organizations that had worked on these efforts, including Oxfam, YPP, Win Without War, FCNL, and others, began coordinating their advocacy work together more formally. In January 2017, Kizer, who was already a leader in these earliest organizing efforts at another organization, joined the Yemen Peace Project and began to enlist like-minded progressive, human rights, and humanitarian organizations to work on Yemen in Congress in a more systematic way. Oxfam had also helped to host a Listserv and an advocacy coalition made up primarily of organizations working in the humanitarian space.[49]

Advocacy organizations of all political stripes in Washington often work in coalition. While each organization may have a relatively small grassroots constituency and resource base, coalition organizing allows these groups to have an impact that is greater than the sum

Table 2. Timeline: Key events for Congress and Yemen

Date	Event
March 25, 2015	Saudi-led intervention begins
Sept. and Oct. 2015	Members of Congress write letters to the president and Joint Chiefs of Staff expressing concerns about civilian casualties
Nov. 2015	SFRC requests that the administration provide Congress with notification prior to the shipment of PGMs to Saudi Arabia
Apr. 2016	Legislation introduced to condition transfers of PGMs to Saudi Arabia (S.J.Res.32 and H.J.Res.90)
Apr.–Aug. 2016	Saudi-led coalition's airstrikes decline as part of UN peace talks
Sept. 2016	Joint resolutions of disapproval introduced for proposed sale of M1A2S tanks to Saudi Arabia (S.J.Res.39 and H.J.Res.98); S.J.Res.39 wins twenty-seven votes on the Senate side
Oct. 2016	Funeral hall strike kills 140 civilians in Yemen
	Houthi-Saleh forces launch antiship missiles at U.S. Navy vessels on patrol off Yemen's coast
Mar. 2017	Trump administration notifies Congress that it is moving forward on the proposed sale of PGMs delayed by the Obama administration
June 2017	Senate introduces resolution of disapproval on PGM sale (S.J.Res.42), which gets forty-seven votes; Rep. Ro Khanna introduced a WPR resolution (H.Con.Res.81), compromised with House leadership to postpone after 2018 elections, then adopted a nonbinding alternative (H.Res.599)
Nov. 2017	Houthis fire ballistic missile at Riyadh; coalition retaliates by blockading Yemen's ports
Dec. 20, 2017	Coalition announces it will end the blockade of Hodeidah for thirty days and allow in U.S. cranes

(*continued*)

Table 2. (continued)

Date	Event
Feb. 2018	Sen. Bernie Sanders introduces legislation invoking the WPR and directing the removal of U.S. forces in Yemen not authorized by Congress (S.J.Res.54); Congress votes to table the bill in March after floor debate
Mar. and Apr. 2018	U.S. defense officials testify before Congress that they do not track coalition aircraft after refueling
May 2018	Sen. Todd Young introduces bill to prohibit U.S. funds for refueling without administration certification (S.J. Res. 58); this bill was passed as Section 1290 of the FY2019 National Defense Authorization Act (NDAA)
June–Nov. 2018	Coalition offensive on Hodeidah
June 2018	Sen. Bob Menendez, SFRC ranking member, places a hold on a PGM sale to Saudi Arabia and the UAE
Aug. 2018	FY19 NDAA signed into law; coalition airstrike kills forty children on a school bus
Sept. 2018	Sec. of State Pompeo certifies that funding for refueling can continue; in response, House members introduce a bill directing U.S. forces be removed from Yemen (H.Con.Res.138)
Oct. 2018	Journalist Jamal Khashoggi is murdered
	Sec. of Defense Mattis and Sec. of State Pompeo call for a cease-fire on Oct. 30
Dec. 2018	Stockholm Agreement reached, including a cease-fire in Hodeidah
	Senate passes S.J.Res.54 (with fifty-six voting in favor) and S.J.Res.69, a sense of the Senate that MbS is responsible for the murder of Khashoggi
Jan. 2019	116th Congress begins
Feb. 2019	Sen. Bob Menendez introduces the Saudi Arabia Accountability and Yemen Act of 2019, which would end refueling and suspend certain arms sales
	House passes its version of S.J.Res.54, invoking the WPR (H.J.Res.37)

Table 2. (continued)

Date	Event
Mar. 2019	Senate passes its version (S.J.Res.7), with fifty-four in favor
Apr. 2019	Pres. Trump vetoes the resolution (WPR)
May 2019	Senate fails to override the veto (gets fifty-three in favor, needs sixty-seven); Trump administration notifies Congress of an "emergency" arms sale to Saudi Arabia and the UAE
June 2019	Senate introduces twenty-two joint resolutions of disapproval of the sale; three are also passed by the House
July 2019	Trump vetoes arms sale disapproval; Senate fails to override

of their individual parts. Coalitions are better positioned to design and drive strategy on the Hill, recruit "congressional champions"—members of Congress who not only sponsor a piece of legislation but go out of their way to get other senators and representatives on board—organize grassroots activists, and ultimately aim to deliver outsized impact with limited resources.[50] The formation of these advocacy coalitions therefore helped Yemen advocacy to gain traction within and outside of Congress.

Through lobbying efforts on the Hill and organizing their own constituents, this coalition was able to enlist congressional champions to push forward legislation. The coalition then worked with grassroots supporters to get other members of Congress to sign on. Each member of Congress had their own reasons for supporting or opposing the legislation, and advocates focused on understanding those reasons and providing constituent support and evidence about the situation on the ground to persuade each member of Congress to support the bill.

Advocates had a simple but effective message: the United States can only be a credible actor for peace if it stops arming and aiding one side of the conflict. They were able to point to investigations by the Yemeni human rights organization Mwatana for Human Rights and CNN that traced bombs manufactured by U.S. companies like Raytheon directly to specific incidents of civilian harm. For example, at the scene of an April 2018 strike on a wedding that killed twenty-one civilians, including eleven children, Mwatana documented parts from a Pathway II guided bomb manufactured by Raytheon. Radhya Al-Mutawakel, chairperson of Mwatana, said that the United States bore a "legal and moral responsibility for selling weapons to the Saudi-led coalition."[51]

This message explained the United States' connection to the war and made its impacts tangible to Americans. "Often what turns people away from these issues is when they think, 'Oh, this is too complicated,'" said Gould. "But then what we could explain, what isn't complicated—it isn't contested—is that the U.S. was actively supporting the coalition and the war, was picking a side, and that people were going hungry as a result. There are a lot of other [elements of the war] that are super complicated, but that part was clear," she noted.[52] "We use this very clinical language that distances us from the fact that the American people are implicated in these acts of violence," said Matt Duss, Senator Bernie Sanders's foreign policy advisor. "The level of congressional engagement should reflect that fact. The Yemen effort was a way to get a wedge into that broader debate."[53]

The introduction of legislation then provided a "hook" for advocates to organize and rally their grassroots constituents on the issue. Constituents now had an "ask," in the parlance of lobbying: they could ask their senator or representative to become a cosponsor or vote for a specific bill. Members of Congress started to get calls and emails from their constituents about Yemen-related legislation, sometimes amounting to hundreds per week, in addition to in-person visits in their Washington, DC, and district offices. This lobbying from constituents in turn pushed many congressional offices to look into an issue that may not have been on their radar. Grassroots constituents therefore had a disproportionate impact on Congress's views on U.S. support for the war.[54]

In advocates' lobby visits on the Hill, they used different frames to talk about the issue depending on their audience. In addition to demonstrating the war's humanitarian fallout, advocates used a national security frame to explain how U.S. engagement in the war was detrimental to U.S. security interests. They found that both Democratic and Republican members were willing to come on board with legislation if advocates were able to offer credible answers to their questions about whether ending U.S. support for the war could empower Iran or affect Saudi Arabia's security.[55] When asked about Iran, for example, advocates argued that the coalition's strategy was ineffective and would ultimately alienate Yemenis and empower the Houthis. They noted that while, at the time, the Houthis had "limited ties to Iran and [had] benefitted from small-arms shipments, the Houthis [were] not an Iranian proxy force that follows Iran's marching orders."[56] While the coalition intervention intended to isolate and eradicate the Houthis, it was instead pushing them to search for third-party support—and making the provision of such support more attractive to Iran, which found the Houthis' presence on Saudi Arabia's southern border to be a useful source of leverage against its regional rival. By advancing credible alternative arguments about U.S. national security, advocates and grassroots lobbyists were able to shape the broader conversation.[57] What began as a discussion about choosing a side in a proxy war between Saudi Arabia and Iran became a question of whether the United States should continue to support the coalition in contravention of U.S. security interests.

The coalition was able to build momentum by bringing both congressional Democrats and Republicans on board. The coalition was not bipartisan in the traditional sense of enlisting like-minded centrist politicians. Rather, it became what Heather Hurlburt and Chayenne Palimedio term a "transpartisan" coalition, in which political actors from the right and left become "unlikely allies" that champion the same policies but with "different ideological justifications."[58] Progressive Democrats like Congressman Ro Khanna and Senators Chris Murphy and Bernie Sanders, as well as libertarian-minded conservative Republicans like Senators Rand Paul and Mike Lee, were compelled by the idea of exercising Congress's oversight role to restrain U.S. military action abroad. In a June 2017 op-ed that summarized the basis for this unlikely alliance, Representative Khanna and Senator Paul wrote, "Invading Iraq, toppling Gadhafi in Libya and interfering in Yemen and Syria have been strategic blunders." Instead of achieving U.S. national security objectives, military intervention had "destabilized regions and, in doing so, helped strengthen a new generation of terror groups," they argued. In Yemen, "We have no stake in this fight, and the policy of arming Saudi Arabia has been counterproductive. Yet [the United States is] being blamed by civilians in Yemen, who hold us responsible for the bombs the Saudis are dropping."[59]

Mirroring this transpartisan coalition in Congress, the advocacy coalition also included progressive groups, like Win Without War and the Friends Committee on National Legislation, as well as conservative organizations like the Charles Koch Institute and Defense Priorities, with each able to make persuasive arguments to enlist like-minded members of Congress to the cause. "In addition to getting progressive groups on board, getting libertarian groups on board was critical," Geo Saba, chief of staff to Congressman Khanna, told me.[60] These groups were able to speak to a different audience than progressive groups, writing op-eds in media outlets that appealed to a more conservative audience and talking to Republican congressional offices, even as they worked in coordination with the broader advocacy coalition.

Elections also played a role: 2018 midterm elections gave Democrats control over the House, giving them more leeway to pass legislation. At the same time, progressive primary challengers also pushed Democratic leaders, who had until then been hesitant to support this legislation. Democrat Adam Smith, who became chair of the House Armed Services Committee when Democrats took over the House, was challenged in his primary from the left by Sarah Smith, who received endorsements from Justice Democrats and the Democratic Socialists of America.[61] Sarah Smith frequently referenced Yemen legislation in her campaign: "I went after him about Yemen every time I got an opportunity to and I kept hammering him, . . . and all of a sudden, Adam started to change his tune," she said.[62] Congressman Adam Smith, for his part, rejected this characterization, saying, "I was actually on the Yemen stuff before I even knew she existed."[63] Yet *The Intercept* noted that Adam Smith's "opposition to U.S. involvement in Yemen, however, became decidedly more forceful as Sarah Smith's candidacy became more potent."[64] Once Congressman Adam Smith came on board, other Democratic leaders, including Congressman Steny Hoyer and Congressman

Eliot Engel, who was then chair of the House Foreign Affairs Committee, endorsed the legislation shortly thereafter.

The privileged nature of the legislation meant that sponsors in Congress were able to hold votes on bills that congressional leadership might otherwise have been able to bury. "The way that you create moments [of change] is to force a vote," said Duss. "If members of Congress are going to have to vote 'yes' or 'no' on an issue, that creates an opportunity for education and discussion," Duss noted.[65] In fact, the coalition deliberately selected arms sales and War Powers Resolution votes as vehicles for advocacy because they forced Congress to hold a vote, rather than letting bills languish indefinitely in congressional purgatory. Both types of bills allow their sponsors to bypass congressional committees and the discretion of congressional leadership, both of which can act as choke points in keeping a bill from reaching the floor for debate. Congressional leadership usually decides which bills will come to the floor and which will not, effectively preventing Congress from having to debate or vote on a bill. That power to prevent a vote gives congressional leadership a kind of "negative agenda control," one staffer involved with the effort said.[66] "We were looking for laws we could use to force these debates," Kizer said.[67] Arms sales and the War Powers Resolution provided those tools.

The War Powers Resolution

Alongside arms sales, the War Powers Resolution became another tool for Congress to exert influence over Yemen policy and force debates about U.S. support for the war. The War Powers Resolution has been the most important tool that Congress has to assert its constitutional role in the decision to use force abroad since it passed over President Richard Nixon's veto in 1973. The U.S. Constitution gives Congress the authority to declare war in Article I.[68] Following the United States' disastrous involvement in the Vietnam War, the WPR was the latest entry in a long-running debate over whether the president of the United States has the constitutional authority "to send forces into hostile situations abroad without a declaration of war or other congressional authorization."[69] The WPR did not end this debate, as disputes persist about the WPR's constitution-ality and over exactly what terms in the law, such as "hostilities," mean.[70]

Nevertheless, the War Powers Resolution did provide some transparency around the president's decision to use force and gave Congress a tool to end U.S. involvement in hostilities. The WPR requires that the president notify Congress when armed forces are introduced "into hostilities or into situations where imminent in-volvement in hostilities is clearly indicated."[71] Under specific cir-cumstances, notification triggers a sixty-day clock. When the clock runs out, the president must end the use of armed force if it has not been authorized by Congress. In the 1980s, Congress adopted provisions that allow it to pass a joint resolution of disapproval to remove U.S. forces that, similar to resolutions on arms sales, is con-sidered via expedited procedures.[72]

A serious conversation around introducing legislation related to the War Powers Act first began in Congress in 2017. While sim-ilar legislation did pass in early 2019, in 2017, the idea that this could happen was "a moonshot—the rationale to do it was to force a debate," said Corey Jacobsen, Congressman Ted Lieu's legislative director.[73] While outside advocates had raised the idea of a bill in-voking the WPR on Yemen as early as 2016, it did not feel like a seri-ous proposal to Congress, at least at first. But the idea began to gain traction among congressional members and staffers as a mechanism they could use to force a debate about U.S. involvement in Yemen. Still, all Congress members and aides hardly expected that this kind of bill could pass both houses of Congress. Encouraging a public debate about Yemen and the principles behind Congress asserting its oversight authority on national security were the goals of introduc-ing such legislation. Actually passing it seemed out of reach.[74]

A bipartisan letter signed by fifty-five members of Congress, led by Representatives Mark Pocan and Justin Amash in April 2017, was the first instance in which members of Congress publicly invoked the War Powers Resolution, signaling that they were willing to force a debate and a vote. "At minimum, any decision by the admin-istration to engage in direct U.S. hostilities against Yemen's Houthis must be subject to a congressional debate and vote, as the framers of the Constitution intended and the 1973 War Powers Resolution demands," the letter asserted. "The War Powers Resolution provides a mechanism for individual Members of Congress to force the question of congressional authorization if the administration is not forthcoming in seeking approval for a planned military action."[75]

Then, in September 2017, Congressman Ro Khanna introduced H.Con.Res.81, cosponsored by Democratic Representatives Thomas Massie and Mark Pocan and Republican Representative Walter Jones. The bill directed the president to remove U.S. forces from hostilities in Yemen, except for those engaged in operations against AQAP, "pursuant to section 5 (c) of the War Powers Resolution."[76] The legislation received pushback from Democratic and Republican leaders in the House, who opposed bringing the legislation to the floor. After a series of intensive negotiations with Democratic leadership, Representative Khanna agreed to instead introduce a nonbinding version of the resolution, H.Res.599.[77]

While a small step and a compromise at that, Hill staff still saw the vote on H.Res.599 as a victory. It meant that Congress was going on the record to acknowledge that the United States was involved in the war via its support of the Saudi-led coalition and that this engagement had not been authorized by Congress. It was also the first time that the House held a substantive debate about Yemen and U.S. involvement in the war on the floor. H.Res.599 laid the groundwork for future legislation invoking the War Powers Resolution with regard to Yemen because, as Saba of Congressman Khanna's office said, "Finally Congress had admitted that we were engaged in these hostilities that weren't authorized. So we felt that that gave us really good momentum to continue the effort."[78] "All of that was really laying the groundwork," said Gould. "To work through a problem, you need to first acknowledge that it exists."[79] The passage of this nonbinding resolution was a proof of concept, demonstrating that the WPR approach could work, and on a bipartisan basis at that.

Supporters of the WPR approach also faced pushback from the Trump administration about the definition of "hostilities." While the debate may sound arcane, it is essential to understanding whether or not Congress is required to authorize U.S. forces to provide support for partner military operations. The Trump administration asserted that "the resolution's fundamental premise is flawed. Specifically, the draft resolution incorrectly asserts that U.S. forces have been 'introduced into hostilities.'" The letter went on to say that the "limited military and intelligence support that the United States is providing to the [Saudi]-led coalition does not involve any introduction of U.S. forces into hostilities for the purposes of the War Powers Resolution." Instead, the Trump administration's view was "that 'hostilities' refers to 'a situation in which units of U.S. armed forces are actively engaged in exchanges of fire with opposing units of hostile forces. U.S. personnel providing support to the KSA-led coalition are not engaged in any such exchanges of fire."[80]

It was, to be sure, a novel interpretation of the WPR to assert that providing support for partner forces engaged in combat should be included in the definition of "hostilities."[81] For decades, previous presidential administrations had interpreted the term in a similarly narrow way: the Gerald Ford administration, for example, had defined hostilities as situations in which "U.S. armed forces are actively engaged in exchanges of fire."[82] Yet as Congressmen Khanna, Pocan, and Jones wrote in an October 2017 op-ed in the *New York Times* explaining their position, "There's a good reason that the Constitution reserves for Congress the right to declare war. . . . Clearly, the founders' intent was to prevent precisely the kind of dangerous course we're charting" in Yemen.[83]

In early 2018, Senator Bernie Sanders got involved in the effort to invoke the War Powers Resolution, working with Congressman Khanna and the Congressional Progressive Caucus (CPC) to coordinate the introduction of S.J.Res.54 in February of that year. The bill was bipartisan, with cosponsorship from Senators Chris Murphy and Mike Lee. Like the House version, it invoked the WPR to direct "the removal of United States Armed Forces from hostilities in the Republic of Yemen that have not been authorized by Congress."[84] Senator Sanders had a national platform and was a leader on progressive foreign policy issues. His involvement therefore gave the effort additional momentum. Saba said that working with Senator Sanders's office "breathed new life into the whole effort."[85]

The bill also faced initial skepticism from Democratic leadership on the Senate side. Some Democrats in the Senate were doubtful about the merits of the case, both of the bill's definition of "hostilities" and of taking such a step to challenge the U.S. security relationship with Saudi Arabia. There was also institutional resistance.

Under normal Senate procedure, the relevant committee—either the Foreign Relations or Armed Services Committee, in this case—would be responsible for advancing this kind of bill and bringing it to the floor. Senate leadership looked askance at a senator who was not on the committee using out-of-the-ordinary procedure to jump the legislative queue and use privilege to bring this bill to the floor. "There was resistance in the sense that we were going outside the process," Duss said. "That's what the privilege tool is: you're basically taking this issue out of the hands of the relevant committee, in this case the Senate Foreign Relations Committee," Duss pointed out. "And there is an implicit criticism in there, which is to say, 'This committee has not done its job.'"[86]

After debate, the Senate voted to table the resolution in March 2018. Then, in December 2018, during the "lame duck" session of Congress, after the November 2018 elections but before the newly elected members were sworn in, the Senate voted to pass the Sanders-Murphy-Lee bill, with fifty-six senators voting in favor. But by that time, the House was already in recess, and a new session of Congress would begin in January 2019—meaning that the bill had to start from scratch on both sides.

Then, in late 2018, a move by Secretary Pompeo had a galvanizing effect on Congress. A provision championed by Senators Todd Young and Jeanne Shaheen and supported by the advocacy coalition was added to the fiscal year 2019 National Defense Authorization Act (NDAA) requiring the secretary of state to certify that the coalition was taking such action. Without a certification, congressional appropriations for aerial refueling would automatically be suspended.[87] A number of members of Congress endorsed this approach because it was seen as less radical than invoking the WPR.[88]

This was another piece of legislation that might have sounded toothless but had an outsized impact in practice. In September 2018, Secretary Pompeo formally issued the certification that would allow refueling to continue. The certification stated that Saudi Arabia and the UAE had undertaken "demonstrable actions to reduce the risk of harm to civilians and civilian infrastructure."[89] Coming just over a month after an August 9 coalition airstrike that hit a bus killing at least twenty-nine civilians, including twenty-one children, the certification felt like a slap in the face to members of Congress who had pressed the administration to take good-faith action to reduce civilian harm resulting from the coalition's airstrikes.[90] NYU law professor Ryan Goodman noted that the memo itself cited actions that the coalition was taking on paper, rather than how military strikes were being executed in practice.[91]

In issuing the certification, Pompeo evidently overruled the concerns of State Department officials and legal advisors involved in the policy review, who flagged "a lack of progress on mitigating civilian casualties," according to an internal State Department memo. State Department officials argued that issuing the certification would "provide no incentive for Saudi leadership to take our diplomatic messaging seriously" and in the meantime could "damage the Department's credibility with Congress." The only State Department officials who supported going forward with the certification were from the Bureau of Legislative Affairs, who argued that "lack of certification will negatively impact pending arms transfers."[92]

The egregious nature of the bus bombing in August—and the feeling that they were being lied to by Saudi officials—got more members of Congress interested in what was happening in Yemen.[93] Members of Congress like Senators Todd Young and Jeanne Shaheen, who had sponsored the certification amendment, had at first wanted to take a more measured approach. But the bus bombing and Pompeo's subsequent certification convinced many members of Congress that this was not enough. Advocates found that immediately after the bus bombing, they received meetings with congressional offices that had not responded to previous requests. Members of Congress who had not been closely following the issue wanted to get up to speed, requesting information about what was happening in the war, civilian casualties, and what the United States was doing about it.[94]

As the advocacy coalition built momentum, it got more attention in the media and from Americans across the country. This growing attention, in turn, gave the WPR bill more momentum. The actor Mark Ruffalo filmed an ad on social media in February 2018, for example. "This is a U.S. war in Yemen, yet it's never had any legal justification. It's never been authorized by Congress," Ruffalo said in the video, directing viewers to call their senators. "I believe that when the American people are presented with the facts, we will act to stop our tax dollars from being used to bomb and starve innocent Yemenis," Ruffalo said.[95]

Democrats won control of the House in the 2018 midterm elections, and by early 2019, Democratic House leaders were on board with the WPR effort and indicated to the bill's sponsors that they would push the bill forward in the new year.

Throughout the process of drafting the bill and shepherding it through Congress, Senate aides paid careful attention to the language and timing of the bill in order to ensure it could pass smoothly through intricate and sometimes arcane Senate procedures. Senate staffers consulted with constitutional scholars and attorneys throughout the process.[96] They felt strongly that they had to get it right because this had never been done before. But the legislation hit one more obstacle in early 2019 that underscored the importance of congressional procedure and the role of the parliamentarian. The parliamentarian, sometimes called the referee of the Senate, is the official, nonpartisan advisor who interprets the chamber rules.[97] Because different kinds of legislation follow different procedures to passage, the parliamentarian's ruling can make or break a bill.

A series of votes in early 2019 illustrated the power of the Senate parliamentarian. On February 13, 2019, the House passed a new version of the WPR legislation by a vote of 248 to 177.[98] But House Republicans managed to add an amendment to the resolution before it passed that decried antisemitism and expressed support for Israel. The amendment effectively proved a poison pill when the resolution moved over to the Senate for approval: the Senate parliamentarian deemed the amendment not germane. This meant that the bill was "deprivileged" in the Senate, and Senate Majority Leader Mitch McConnell was able to block it from coming up for a vote.[99] Instead of starting from scratch, Senator Sanders moved to discharge the same bill that had passed the Senate in late 2019—because that version of the bill had previously been ruled as privileged, its Senate sponsors knew it would not encounter the same issue.[100] The Senate passed yet another new version of the WPR bill in March 2019, with fifty-four senators voting in favor; the House followed with its own version of the same bill. President Trump vetoed the resolution in April 2019, and the Senate failed to garner enough votes to override the veto: thirty-three senators voted in favor, short of the sixty-seven needed to override the presidential veto.[101]

Arms Sales, Round 2: 2017–2019

In June 2017, a few months before the WPR legislation was introduced in the House, the Senate narrowly voted down a bill that would have blocked a sale of precision-guided munitions to Saudi Arabia. The bill, introduced by Senator Rand Paul, came unexpectedly close to getting enough support to pass after Senate Minority Leader Senator Chuck Schumer announced that he opposed the sale, giving more Democrats political permission to vote the same way. Trump administration officials were so concerned that the bill could pass that they "spent the hours before the vote frantically making phone calls and holding briefings with lawmakers to stave off defeat."[102] Still, the vote to block the sale garnered forty-seven Senate votes in its favor, compared to the twenty-seven votes to block a similar sale less than a year earlier, in the fall of 2016. The vote reflected rising concerns in Congress about the course of the war and the continued civilian casualties.

In June 2018, Senator Bob Menendez, the most senior Democrat on the Senate Foreign Relations Committee (SFRC), placed a "hold" on the sale of PGMs to the coalition. Explaining the decision, Senator Menendez wrote, "I am concerned that our policies are enabling perpetuation of a conflict that has resulted in the world's worst humanitarian crisis."[103] By a long-standing norm, previous presidential administrations had respected the holds that SFRC leadership placed on arms sales, declining to push sales through, even though these holds are not legally binding. But in May 2019, the Trump administration decided to get around the hold placed by Senator Menendez by invoking an emergency justification for an arms sale to Saudi Arabia and the UAE. In its justification for the emergency measure, the administration cited the "rapidly-evolving security situation in the region" and noted that the Houthis had publicly threatened to increase their operations targeting Saudi Arabia and the UAE.[104]

Much like Pompeo's certification in 2018, the Trump administration's invocation of an emergency to justify this arms sale also an-
tagonized many members of Congress, who believed—rightly—that
the administration was trying to circumvent Congress. In June 2019,
a group of bipartisan senators introduced twenty-two joint resolutions of disapproval of the sales. Senator Lindsey Graham, who had
previously vigorously opposed efforts to block such sales, was a cosponsor this time, expressing his frustration that the administration
would try to "go around legitimate concerns of Congress."[105] Three
of these joint resolutions, blocking the sale of air-to-ground munitions, passed both the House and Senate. Like the bill invoking the
War Powers Resolution, these measures were also vetoed by President Trump, and the Senate was unable to produce a veto-proof
majority.[106]

Even some officials within the Trump administration thought
that the emergency measure had been improperly invoked. Steve
Linick, who was fired as the State Department inspector general,
later testified that senior State Department officials had "pressured
him to act in ways" that he felt were "inappropriate," including telling him not to pursue an investigation into whether the Trump administration's declaration of an emergency in this case was lawful.[107]
The investigation found that Secretary of State Mike Pompeo had
recommended to President Trump that he fire Linick, presumably in
part because of the Saudi arms-sales investigation (although Pompeo
denied that that firing was retaliation for the investigation).[108] "It's
becoming clearer and clearer to me that Secretary Pompeo was so
driven to get these weapons out the door that he not only abused the
law and ignored Congress's concerns about civilian casualties, but he
also ignored the Department's own warnings," Representative Eliot
Engel said.[109]

Congressional Pressure and Yemen: Hodeidah, the Stockholm Agreement, and the Emirati Drawdown

How much did congressional engagement on Yemen matter? There
is substantial evidence that in several instances, pressure from

Congress had an effect both on the Trump administration and on the behavior of the Saudi-led coalition.

Security partners like Saudi Arabia and the UAE understand Congress's role in the United States' bilateral security relationships, especially when it comes to arms sales. Arms sales are important to U.S. security partners not just to enhance their own military capabilities but also because of the symbolic value of these sales, as the scholar Jennifer Spindel shows: advanced weapons sales can serve as a symbol of the strength of the bilateral relationship between the United States and a partner country, as much as a means of transferring actual military capabilities.[110] As a result, Congress's role in arms sales matters to top security partners. As one advocate put it, no U.S. security partner "wants to get on Congress's shit list."[111]

Accordingly, as pressure from Congress intensified, Saudi officials tried to persuade Congress that they were taking the necessary steps to avoid civilian casualties. Saudi Foreign Minister Adel al-Jubair visited Washington, DC, in the spring of 2017 to unveil the coalition's new targeting process and met with members of the Senate Foreign Relations Committee and other members of Congress.[112] A congressional delegation also traveled to Saudi Arabia in February 2018. As part of the trip, the delegation visited the Air Operations Center at King Salman Air Base, where they were briefed by the center's leadership, given a tour of the facility, and allowed to view surveillance feeds.[113] These efforts show that Saudi leaders understood the importance of trying to dampen criticism from Congress.

The blockade of Hodeidah in late 2017 is one specific instance in which pressure from Congress played a role in the Saudi-led coalition's behavior. Senator Todd Young took a particular interest in the blockade and starvation in Yemen: "For him, this was a moral issue," FCNL's Jim Cason said.[114] The Republican senator's engagement, in turn, ratcheted up the pressure on the Trump administration. In late 2017, Senators Young and Murphy placed a hold on the confirmation of State Department legal advisor Jennifer Newstead until the administration took steps to address the blockade.[115] Gould said that Senator Young's effort "to try to get answers on what the administration was doing on the blockade, and particularly whether the administration was pushing for the . . . crane to be allowed in," was a key moment for efforts to lift the port blockade. "It's another example of the power of Congress to push for change."[116]

At around the same time, in late 2017, a group of humanitarian organizations began meeting on a monthly basis with senior officials from the State Department and USAID, including Deputy Secretary of State Sullivan and USAID Deputy Administrator Mark Green.[117] Senior officials from the humanitarian organizations briefed State Department and USAID officials on the situation on the ground in Yemen, including the latest humanitarian developments and obstacles they faced in delivering aid.[118] An attendee of some of these meetings said that the concern from U.S. officials about the potentially catastrophic effects of the blockade "was palpable."[119] U.S. officials asked the humanitarian organizations for information about what was happening on the ground in Yemen. At the December meeting, for example, Deputy Secretary Sullivan "underscored the Administration's deep concern about deteriorating conditions, the recent spike in violence by the Houthis, and the suffering of the Yemeni people."[120] The timing of these meetings, soon before the Trump administration began to publicly pressure Saudi Arabia to let the cranes into Hodeidah, suggests that they played a role in bolstering the concerns of officials within the administration and making their case at the senior level. "There was a ton of pressure" from Congress about the cranes, said a Trump administration official.[121]

Pressure from the Trump administration probably also played a role in getting Saudi Arabia and the UAE to the table in Stockholm. In late October 2018, Secretary Pompeo called "on all parties to support UN Special Envoy Martin Griffiths in finding a peaceful solution to the conflict in Yemen." The statement noted that after Houthi missile and UAV strikes in Saudi Arabia and the UAE stopped, "Coalition air strikes must cease in populated areas in Yemen."[122] That same day, in a talk at the United States Institute of Peace, Defense Secretary Jim Mattis made a similar statement: "30 days from now, we want to see everybody sitting around the table, based on a cease-fire, based on a pullback from the border, and then based on ceasing dropping of bombs," he said.[123] A month later, as the talks in Stockholm moved forward, Secretary Mattis "reportedly made last-minute phone calls to leaders in Saudi Arabia" and the UAE that "apparently clinched the Gulf monarchies' support for the deal."[124] Saudi and Emirati leaders, in turn, pressured Hadi's government to accept the terms.[125]

Additionally, pressure from Congress played an important role in the UAE's decision to draw down its forces from 2019. While the decision was in part a recognition that there was no military solution to the conflict, Emirati leadership was also influenced by international perceptions of the UAE's role in the war. Notably, advocates who pushed for the coalition to withdraw, supporters of the UAE's role, and neutral observers believed that pressure from Congress played an important role in the Emirati decision.[126] One former Trump administration official said that, in their view, congressional pressure was the primary reason for the Emirati withdrawal.[127] Defense Secretary Jim Mattis and Senator Lindsey Graham also reportedly advised the Emiratis to withdraw.[128]

Finally, the number of civilian casualties due to coalition airstrikes had also finally begun to decline by the summer and fall of 2019, an achievement that many observers trace back to pressure from Congress and the advocacy movement.[129] "If nothing else," an advocate said, while violence against civilians still continued in other parts of the conflict, "there are a number of people in Yemen who are alive today who would not be alive" had civilian casualties from airstrikes not declined.[130]

CHAPTER NINE

The Biden Administration

Giving Diplomacy a Chance?

This war has to end.

—President BIDEN, announcing his administration's new
approach to the war in Yemen, February 4, 2021

JOE BIDEN'S FIRST MAJOR foreign policy speech as president included
a major announcement about the U.S. approach to the war in Yemen.
In the February 4, 2021, speech, Biden promised to end offensive
military support for the Saudi-led coalition, "including relevant arms
sales," and to step up "our diplomacy to end the war in Yemen—a
war which has created a humanitarian and strategic catastrophe."[1]
Biden also announced that he would appoint a special envoy for Yemen—Timothy Lenderking, a career Foreign Service member who
had served in State Department posts across the Middle East—to
lead U.S. diplomatic efforts in Yemen.

Yemen had long been at the periphery of U.S. foreign policy
making and strategy. Under both the Obama and Trump administrations, ending the war in Yemen was subsumed under strategic priorities deemed more important, namely, maintaining the U.S-Saudi

relationship, fighting Iranian influence on the Arabian Peninsula, and counterterrorism concerns. Yet in early 2021, despite a number of other pressing foreign policy priorities, including the global COVID-19 pandemic and Biden's efforts to end the long-running U.S. war in Afghanistan, the U.S. approach to Yemen's war was centrally featured in the administration's thinking about "America's place in the world."[2]

The State Department also announced that it would revoke the Trump administration's designation of the Houthis as a foreign terrorist organization (FTO). Reflecting concerns raised by humanitarians, a State Department official clarified that the decision was "due entirely to the humanitarian consequences of this last-minute designation from the prior administration."[3]

Biden's announcement marked a victory for the advocates and policy makers who had fought to end U.S. support for the Saudi-led coalition, and it was greeted with enthusiasm by many U.S. policy makers, experts, and advocates. Representative Ro Khanna called it "a profound and historic shift"; Senator Mike Lee said that he was "thrilled" by the announcement.[4] At the same time, many noted that the details of the actual policy shift needed to be further explicated. What exactly did ending U.S. "offensive support" for the coalition mean? The United States had already ended aerial refueling in late 2018, so the remaining U.S. support consisted primarily of intelligence sharing, as well as U.S. contractors' maintenance and servicing of the Kingdom's aircraft and arms sales.[5] Biden said in the speech that the United States would "continue to support and help Saudi Arabia defend its sovereignty and its territorial integrity."[6] How would that square with his promise to end support for the war?

The meaning of "offensive support," it turned out, would be highly contested. Regarding intelligence and logistical support, Pentagon spokesperson John Kirby clarified that all noncombat assistance to the coalition had been terminated, including "intelligence and some advice and best practices."[7] The Biden administration initially paused all ongoing weapons sales approved by the Trump administration for review, including a sale of F-35 fighter jets and drones to the UAE as part of the Abraham Accords.[8] The Biden administration did ultimately suspend two pending sales of precision-guided munitions to Saudi Arabia that were worth about $760 million.[9] However, in April 2021, the administration decided to move forward with some arms sales to Saudi Arabia and the UAE.[10]

Activists criticized the administration for failing to execute on Biden's promise to treat Saudi Arabia as an "international pariah." Hassan El-Tayyab, legislative manager for Middle East Policy at the Friends Committee on National Legislation (FCNL), said "the recent admission by the Department of Defense that U.S. companies are still authorized to maintain Saudi warplanes . . . means that our government is still enabling the Saudi operations."[11] Some also felt that the administration was not doing enough to remove restrictions on humanitarian goods and commodities entering Yemen's ports. Lenderking frequently pressed Saudi and Yemeni government interlocutors on this point. In a May briefing, Lenderking noted that "it is a fundamental pillar of the United States that all economic arteries, all ports, all airports in Yemen should be open."[12]

In late 2021, the Biden administration announced the first new arms sale to Saudi Arabia during Biden's tenure. The sale included $650 million worth of advanced medium-range air-to-air (AMRAAM) missiles.[13] Again, advocates argued that the sale was inconsistent with Biden's promise to end offensive support for the Saudi-led coalition. "Selling more arms to Saudi Arabia now rewards the country's worst behavior," wrote Sarah Leah Whitson, the executive director of Democracy for the Arab World Now (DAWN). "Americans should not be fooled by the semantics of 'defensive' weapons," she argued.[14] The Biden administration, for its part, claimed that the sale was "fully consistent" with the February announcement. It argued that the sale was in line with Biden's promise to ensure "that Saudi Arabia has the means to defend itself from Iranian-backed Houthi air attacks."[15] A Senate vote to block the sale failed.[16]

From the outset, Biden's Yemen policy illustrated a broader tension between his promise to place human rights and values at the center of his administration's foreign policy and the administration's strategic priorities. As the analyst Yasmine Farouk noted, "there is a tension between the administration's emphasis on those values and its de-emphasis of the Middle East as an area where the U.S. will be actively engaged."[17] This tension was also evident in the United

States' new approach to Yemen: after all, in order to facilitate diplomatic negotiations, U.S. officials would need to meet with Saudi
officials, precluding a "pariah" treatment.

Did Diplomacy Work?

As the fighting continued, and the Houthis consolidated territorial
gains in the north, the Biden administration's new approach to Yemen's war did not have a dramatic effect on the contours of the
conflict in 2021. In assessing the Biden administration's diplomatic
efforts, we must start with the question of what U.S. diplomacy could
reasonably be expected to achieve. The United States—or any outside actor—cannot single-handedly impose a peaceful settlement on
the actors fighting in Yemen; nor should it try to, since the specifics
of any peace agreement should be up to Yemenis themselves.

By 2021, the conflict had also evolved significantly since its start.
While the United States may have prevented (or at least curtailed)
its security partners' intervention in Yemen in March 2015, by 2021,
the withdrawal of the Saudi-led coalition would not be sufficient
to end the fighting among increasingly factionalized local actors.
Additionally, the coalition had become capable of carrying out some
operations, such as aerial refueling, without significant assistance. In
this context, a U.S. administration would not be able to unilaterally
end the conflict. However, the United States did have the ability,
as we have seen, to shape the incentives of different conflict actors
and to provide a platform for mediation efforts, as the United States
and the GCC did during the post–Arab Spring National Dialogue
Conference.

Critics on opposite sides argued that the Biden administration
was not doing enough to encourage a cease-fire, either because it
failed to place enough pressure on the Saudi-led coalition or because
it had not taken a harsh-enough stance against the Houthis. FCNL's
El-Tayyab argued that the fact that U.S. companies still provided
maintenance services to the Saudi Air Force "means that our government is still enabling offensive Saudi operations in Yemen."[18] In
contrast, by revoking the FTO designation "unconditionally," the
Biden administration "made a huge mistake," tweeted the Yemen

analyst Nadwa Al-Dawsari: "The expectation is that [the] Houthis will reciprocate [and] engage in peace talks in good faith. But that is not how [the] Houthis will interpret this."[19]

But the shift in U.S. policy did yield some important changes. The appointment of Special Envoy Lenderking revived the moribund UN negotiations. Soon after Biden's speech, Saudi Arabia announced a proposal to reopen the Sana'a airport and allow food and fuel imports through Hodeidah in exchange for a UN-monitored cease-fire.[20] The proposal was not new and in fact represented terms that Saudi officials had offered in private discussions. It was also quickly rejected by the Houthis. But the fact that Saudi officials offered what amounted to a public endorsement of the UN initiative still represented a step forward. Oman, a trusted interlocutor, also facilitated talks between Saudi Arabia and the Houthis that were reportedly "thrashing out terms for a peace deal."[21] The main points of contention, including a cease-fire and the opening of the Sana'a airport and lifting restrictions on Hodeidah, were the same as they had been for at least the past year. In contrast, "the good news is that there is clearly more focus on direct negotiations with the Houthi leadership in Sanaa," Peter Salisbury noted; "the bad news is that this hasn't yet closed the gap between the Houthis' and the Saudis' positions. Until that happens, we won't see much movement."[22] Nevertheless the appointment of Lenderking and a new UN special envoy for Yemen, Hans Grundberg, in August 2021 gave the UN-led process a second wind.

The Biden administration's approach also shifted the incentives faced by external regional actors, encouraging a thawing of tensions between Saudi Arabia and Iran. Saudi Arabia and Iran held indirect talks, convened by Iraq in the spring of 2021, in which Yemen was reportedly an issue under discussion.[23] Reaching a settlement in Yemen and ending cross-border attacks from the Houthis were among Saudi officials' top concerns in the talks. Saudi and Iranian officials held three rounds of talks in Baghdad and at least one on the sidelines of the UN General Assembly meeting in New York in September 2021. In October 2021, the move toward a détente progressed, in the context of flagging talks to revive the Iran nuclear deal, this time with direct talks between the new government in Iran and Saudi Arabia.[24] As Renad Mansour, an expert on Iraqi politics, noted, "The U.S. is pushing its Gulf allies to talk directly to Iran. That's part of the two-track approach that Biden is pursuing."[25] Likewise, MbS told a Saudi television channel of the talks, "we're working today with our partners in the region to find solutions to these issues, and we hope to overcome them and have a good and positive relationship with them."[26] This was an anodyne remark, to be sure, but it signaled more openness to engagement with Iran, in stark contrast with MbS's comment three years prior, when he said, "I believe the Iranian supreme leader makes Hitler look good."[27] Saudi Arabia and Iran could not simply strike a bilateral deal that would end the conflict, since Iran does not have direct command over the Houthis. However, such a deal could ease Saudi officials' concerns about Houthi missile and drone strikes on Saudi territory.

The move toward détente between Iran and Saudi Arabia was not only related to Yemen but part of a broader trajectory of successive U.S. administrations' attempts to pivot away from the Gulf. For Gulf states, this shift has motivated leadership to take greater ownership over their own security, with the goal of relying less on the assistance of the United States. "The perception is very clear that the U.S. is not as committed to the Gulf as it used to be in the views of many people in decision-making authority in the region," said the Gulf politics scholar Kristian Ulrichsen. "From the Saudi point of view, they now see Obama, Trump and Biden—three successive presidents—taking decisions that signify to some extent an abandonment."[28] But both countries also see de-escalation as in their own interests. For Saudi Arabia, "in order to end the war in Yemen, to address Vision 2030 and to attract serious investment into the kingdom, it can only achieve that through de-escalation with Iran," said the Middle East expert Sanam Vakil.[29] For Iranian leaders, de-escalation aligns with their own economic interests: the "bottom line is that Iran has a great interest in broadening regional trade relations," said Adnan Tabatabai, an Iran analyst.[30]

At the same time, the United States' active participation in the war since 2015 has indelibly shaped how many participants and observers view the U.S. role. For some, this history means that the United States cannot be a credible mediator. "When you're an active participant, you don't get to be a mediator," said Aisha Jumaan. When U.S. diplomats say they are acting as a mediator, she said, "I think they're lying to themselves and to us. The U.S. administration needs to admit to themselves and to us that they're part of the war."[31]

The Biden administration also confronted a complicated situation. A Houthi offensive in Marib intensified in 2021. Were the Houthis to seize this oil- and natural-gas-rich province, this would be a major tipping point in the war. By late 2021, the Houthis had won the battle for al-Bayda, next to Marib province, giving the offensive additional momentum. Winning Marib would mean that the Houthis are "the unchallenged military and political hegemon in Yemen's north," an International Crisis Group report noted. The offensive demonstrated that the Houthis are capable of "running a well-coordinated . . . military campaign on several fronts."[32]

The Houthi Marib offensive took a heavy toll on both fighting forces and civilians.[33] The fight for Marib threatened a large civilian population, including more than one million internally displaced persons who had already fled Houthi advances. Prior to 2020, Marib was described as a "beacon of relative stability" in the midst of conflict, a haven for people from other parts of the country who had been displaced by fighting.[34] Civilians in Marib were killed and injured by the fighting, including indiscriminate firing of missiles and artillery by the Houthis into densely populated areas, as Human Rights Watch documented.[35] But the intensified fighting also cut off humanitarian access and forced thousands of already-displaced people to flee once again.[36] Lenderking noted that the battle for Marib was "the stumbling block" in negotiations to end the fighting.[37] While the Houthis had the chance to win this key territory, they had little incentive to stop fighting. Furthermore, while the United States had considerable leverage over the Saudi-led coalition, it had very little leverage over the Houthis.[38] This accords with the academic literature on civil wars, which shows that while rebels have battlefield momentum, an agreement to end the fighting is less likely. James Fearon finds, for example, that "an advantage in . . . rebel capabilities will tend to reduce the odds of a negotiated settlement."[39]

Even with this shift in the U.S. approach, then, it will prove difficult to find a sustainable solution to the war in Yemen. Indeed, ending a civil war is notoriously difficult. As Barbara Walter's research has shown, civil wars have historically been less likely to end in negotiated settlements than in victory for one side because the parties face a commitment problem: it is difficult for the combatants themselves to agree to credible terms for disarmament. Negotiations to end civil wars often fail because parties are reluctant to lay down their own arms knowing that the other side could renege on a peace agreement. External mediators therefore play a critical role in helping to end civil wars by enforcing parties' commitment to an agreement.[40] But even with such a third-party actor willing to act as enforcer, building enough trust for each side that the other will adhere to a peace agreement is a major challenge.

In Yemen, these complications were added to the fact that several years of fighting had factionalized fighting forces on both sides, especially among nominally pro-Hadi forces. More factionalization, in turn, means more potential spoilers able to scuttle an agreement.[41] Even if the UN-led process is able to get the parties to agree to a cease-fire, though, the underlying causes of the conflict will remain. A political transition process will need to address transitional justice and accountability, questions around future governance and the structure of decentralization, and power sharing at the federal level, among other issues. As we have seen, many of these are long-standing issues that predate the current war and were not solved during the National Dialogue Conference. Resolving these underlying causes of conflict will therefore be yet another obstacle on the path to sustainable peace.

That does not mean, however, that the United States does not have an important role to play as diplomacy pushes forward against the odds. Indeed, the literature on the termination of civil war suggests that outside actors, even "biased" ones, can play an important role as mediators to end civil wars. The corollary to Walter's argument about the role of third-party mediators is that powerful external actors—like the United States—can help parties reach a negotiated settlement by helping to monitor and enforce the terms of an agreement. This may be true even in cases where a third-party mediator is seen as "biased"—in fact, biased mediators can help end civil wars more effectively because they can counsel the side that they support to accept costly concessions, ensure that "their" side's interests are represented in negotiations, and use the leverage that they have over one side to encourage them to negotiate in good faith.[42]

At the end of the day, few U.S. foreign policy shifts yield immediate gains. Yet by changing the incentives that other actors face, they can push toward a resolution to the conflict.

Did It Matter?

In hindsight, the fact that the Biden administration's approach to Yemen has yielded few quick victories has led some observers to assume that it did not matter. Yet the shift on Yemen policy was a watershed moment that should be seen both as a change in the direction of the conflict and as an extraordinary victory for democratic engagement in U.S. foreign policy within U.S. domestic politics.

Matt Duss, Senator Sanders's foreign policy advisor, said that Biden's announcement represented a major victory for the Yemen policy movement but also more broadly for efforts to bring progressive foreign policy into the mainstream of U.S. politics. It demonstrated that the Biden administration "understood that this was a major priority for the progressive movement and for the Democratic majority," he said. The announcement did not mark the end of the advocacy movement's work, of course: "Have they gone as far as we want them to go since that announcement? I don't think so," Duss noted. "But still, that was important—not only seriously diminishing support for the Saudi war but also empowering [the special envoy] to up the diplomacy."[43]

Geo Saba, Congressman Khanna's chief of staff, agreed, noting that the announcement marked a step on the path toward the movement's goal of ending the war in Yemen. "At the time, we viewed it as a victory. . . . It was a huge validation of what we had been saying for the past four years, especially at first, when we were met with opposition from those within our own party," Saba said. "So now to see the president and former vice president who oversaw the start of the war come out and validate our position was huge." Since February 2021, advocates have pressed the administration to step up diplomacy to end the war, "but that night we were celebrating," said Saba.[44]

CHAPTER TEN

Lessons Learned

THERE IS MUCH THAT we can learn from the story of U.S. engagement in Yemen about how to make U.S. policy both more just and more effective. The mistakes that U.S. policy makers made—as well as their successes— tell us a great deal about not only how to make U.S. policy in Yemen more effective but also how we can (and, indeed, must) revise U.S. Middle East policy broadly. The approach of the past decade or so—a narrow focus on counterterrorism operations, coupled with logistical and indirect support for regional actors' interventions in civil wars—is not working. In Yemen, supporting regional partners' intervention has driven instability, has associated the United States with civilian harm instead of the values we want to promote in the world, and has not made Americans demonstrably safer. In fact, as a driver of regional instability, support for the Saudi-led coalition has been *detrimental* to U.S. security goals.

The Obama administration knew when the war in Yemen began that it would be politically untenable to use maximal resources to pursue the objective of Houthi defeat, and in the context of Obama's aim of reducing the U.S. footprint in the Middle East and his antiwar 2008 campaign promises, direct U.S. intervention was untenable. Instead, the administration tried to split the difference by providing logistical military and diplomatic support to the intervening coalition.

The United States has pursued a similar approach to conflict and instability across the Middle East in recent years. U.S. strategic aims in the Middle East are often maximalist: not merely to mitigate the risk of terrorist attacks in the United States but to eradicate affiliates of al-Qaeda and ISIS wherever they may be found; not just to counter and contain Iranian influence in high-priority areas but to pressure the Iranian regime until it crumbles. At the same time, after the failures of U.S. military interventions in Afghanistan and Iraq, there is very little appetite for U.S. forces to be deployed on the ground in the Middle East—and little thought given in Washington, DC, to what a diplomacy-first approach might look like instead.

In other contexts in the Middle East (and indeed around the world), this halfway approach has worn different titles in recent years, such as "by, with, and through," a phrase used by then–CENTCOM commander General Joseph Votel to describe U.S. Special Forces' partnership with the forces of partner states in conducting counterterrorism operations.[1] In general, this approach involves empowering local state and nonstate actors, via direct and indirect U.S. support, to fight the wars that Americans are unwilling or unable to fight ourselves. This has meant arming proxy actors in some conflicts, as in Syria, or empowering security partners to do so themselves, as in Yemen and Libya. It has also meant supporting autocratic governments like President Ali Abdullah Saleh's because of their professed determination to fight terrorism. Indeed, proxy wars in the Middle East have not accomplished U.S. strategic goals, and in many cases, like in Yemen, they have actually done the opposite.

The story of U.S. engagement in Yemen's war yields three broad sets of lessons. Some readers may see these ideas as impractical, unrealistic, or even naïve. But in the face of the immense challenges that the Middle East faces, from tackling climate change to ongoing wars—and after decades of failed policies—they are worth serious consideration. As the Yemen advocacy movement demonstrated, it is possible for once seemingly improbable policy ideas to enter the realm of mainstream political discourse in a surprisingly short period of time.

Lesson 1: How Should We Think about U.S. Foreign Policy Interests Differently?

Prioritize Long-Term Stability

The United States consistently prioritizes short-term stability at the expense of addressing the root causes of conflicts and crises. This means that conflicts and crises are more likely to recur. Policy makers are stretched thin, with very limited time and resources, and are often forced to react to the latest crisis. But to get ahead of crises, we need to take a longer-term approach that insists on dealing with the underlying causes up front, rather than merely treating the symptoms of crises and conflicts. In Yemen, a failure to address the underlying causes of conflict—including regional grievances, government corruption, and transitional justice—has generated a succession of crises, including the failures of the U.S. counterterrorism campaign, the post–Arab Spring political transition, the failure of the National Dialogue Conference, and the onset of the ongoing war in 2014.

This approach to foreign policy may be messier in the short term. It will require more hands-on involvement from the international community to support local efforts to address these issues. Perhaps paradoxically, it will also require an acknowledgment from the United States and the rest of the international community that it cannot simply impose solutions on countries and communities. It can, however, provide support for local, community-led efforts to address the root causes of conflict. In the long term, however, this approach will be more likely to yield sustainable postconflict peace.

Mapping out long-term approaches to these problems that go beyond reaction will require the efforts and support not just of U.S. policy makers but also of the American public and, most importantly, the people who come from conflict-affected communities themselves. U.S. policy should seek to elevate and center the voices of people from the countries and regions it addresses.

Stability before Security

Preventing conflicts before they begin, and helping to end fighting when conflicts do break out, is the best way to ensure that substate violence does not transform into regional proxy wars. The proxy approach in the Middle East has not made Americans safer but instead has fostered instability and societal polarization.

Once conflicts begin, the United States can use its leverage, as we have seen, but the United States has relatively little leverage over actors like Russia and Iran. In fact, these actors—Iran in particular—often see direct and indirect intervention in substate conflicts as a source of leverage for themselves. Yet U.S. support for the Saudi-led coalition did little to limit Iranian influence. Instead, over the course of the war, Iranian support for the Houthis has increased, and the Houthis have gained the ability to launch ballistic missiles and drones targeting Saudi territory. Like proxy wars often do, the conflict has also only become more complex over time, as external support and the conflict itself have driven factionalization of fighting groups.

For these reasons and more, it is much easier to prevent a conflict that attracts third-party intervention than it is to try to end one. To do so, the U.S. could substantially increase its investments in conflict early warning and prevention tools. The Global Fragility Act (GFA), which was signed into law in December 2019, provides a platform for shifting the U.S. approach to security toward conflict prevention and mitigation instead of crisis reaction. The 2020 U.S. Strategy to Prevent Conflict and Promote Stability, produced by the State Department in response to this legislation, outlines steps that the United States will take to anticipate and prevent violent conflict and find locally driven political solutions to conflicts. These steps include everything from supporting local and international conflict early warning systems, "backed by preventative diplomacy," to promoting "meaningful reforms of governance" and "the rights of members of marginalized groups."[2] The GFA represents an important step forward in thinking about the U.S. approach to conflict and stability around the world.

Diplomatic and development tools will not achieve these goals without significant and sustained investment. The fact that the GFA authorizes $1.15 billion in funding in its first five years will be critical to its success.[3] The United States should continue to expand its investments in conflict prevention and mitigation efforts.

Support Genuinely Inclusive Peace Processes
and Political Transitions

The National Dialogue Conference and the more recent UN-led peace negotiations in Yemen have shown that political transition processes that are not genuinely inclusive are likely to fail. This accords with cross-national studies, which find that peace agreements signed by more women tend to be more durable and better implemented and that the participation of civil society groups in peace agreements makes them less likely to fail.[4] Séverine Autesserre's work shows that peace is more likely to be sustainable when international actors empower local communities and institutions to engage in peacebuilding, rather than attempting to impose a peace from the outside.[5]

Researchers at the Sana'a Center and the International Crisis Group have shown how the peace process in Yemen could be meaningfully inclusive of women. Women's civil society networks at the national and local level have successfully engaged in peacebuilding that is not part of the official UN initiative. For example, the Peace Track Initiative, an organization of Yemeni women, developed the *Feminist Peace Roadmap* in 2021.[6] Hadramawt Women for Peace successfully advocated for the opening of a vital road that had been closed by fighting.[7] International Crisis Group notes that in Yemen, "women and civil society organizations play a key role in local mediation and peacebuilding. Their support will be critical to supporting any ceasefire and subsequent stabilization efforts."[8] The Yemeni diplomat Jamila Ali Rajaa was one of only a few women who participated in the negotiations leading up to the Stockholm Agreement in late 2018. The talks in Stockholm "resulted in an agreement that was never truly implemented, not least because the parties . . . almost never met at one table," she noted.[9] An anecdote she tells from those negotiations demonstrates the importance of having different voices at the table: "The one time we got them together in one place was because I had maintained personal relationships with the leading negotiators from both sides for years," Rajaa said, "but if the UN had not insisted on women participating in the negotiations, they might not have exchanged a single word."[10]

Yet in an echo of the NDC, the official UN-led peace process has largely failed to meaningfully include women, civil society groups, and other voices from Yemeni communities. Sulaf al-Hanshi, a founder of Hadramawt Women for Peace, told the Sana'a Center that "women are not given opportunities and are eliminated in negotiations and committees working on peace."[11] This "outdated international approach to ending the war" is undergirded by UN Security Council Resolution 2216, which has been interpreted as a unilateral call for the Houthis to surrender and turn over their heavy weapons.[12] Passed in April 2016, this framework is unworkable today, but since the UN-led talks in Kuwait in 2016, it has been the framework for negotiations in Yemen. This framework effectively excludes women, civil society groups, and any Yemeni voices outside of the Houthis and the Hadi government, meaning that the visions and aspirations of the majority of Yemenis are not represented in these talks.[13]

Passing a new UN Security Council resolution to replace 2216 in order to create a more inclusive framework for negotiations is a worthwhile aspiration but is also likely to be a complicated process, as it will require getting all five of the veto-holding members of the Security Council, including China and Russia, on board. It would also require agreement around a replacement text, and while many commentators have called for 2216 to be replaced, there is little consensus about what exactly should replace it. Fortunately, as Peter Salisbury has noted, 2216 is open to alternative interpretations to the exclusive, two-party framework championed by Hadi's government and the Houthis, both of whom benefit from being the only two parties recognized by these formal talks. Indeed, the text of 2216 calls for a "consultative" and "inclusive" process, leaving an opening for the UN special envoy to include additional parties in negotiations.[14] The appointment of Hans Grundberg, previously the European Union ambassador to Yemen, as the UN special envoy in 2021 provided an opening for a change of course. Early signs are positive: Grundberg met with Aidarous al-Zubaidi, chairman of the Southern Transitional Council, leaders of the southern Hirak movement, women's rights activists, and civil society organizations as part of the listening tour he undertook shortly after his appointment. "There is an urgent need to change course and work toward an inclusive political settlement," Grundberg noted in October 2021.[15]

The United States should support international efforts toward a more inclusive peace process. The United States can support quotas for peace-talk delegations to make them more inclusive
and can provide support for a parallel peace process that incorpo-
rates civil society voices more directly.[16] At the same time, the UN
process should be careful not to inadvertently undermine ongoing
local-level peacebuilding efforts. Nadwa Al-Dawsari notes, for example, that while tribal mediation efforts have helped to mitigate
the effects of war on local communities, "engaging tribes in cease-
fire and de-escalation [efforts] without serious commitment by the
Houthis and Yemeni government can carry serious risks to tribal
mediators and to stability in tribal areas."[17] The UN and the international community should invest in deconfliction with local communities' peacebuilding efforts, incorporating them into national-level
processes where appropriate, while being mindful that engagement
without consultation at the local level can do more harm than good.

Make Accountability Part of Postconflict Transitions

The international community has focused overwhelmingly on
holding elections as the culmination of postconflict reconstruction
processes in recent years. Elections represent an important step in
restoring legitimate governing authority and in some contexts can
help to demilitarize politics.[18] But a focus on elections and rewriting
a state's constitution sidelines other critical parts of a transitional
political process. During the NDC process, key questions on both
of these points remained unresolved, making conflict down the line
more likely. Yemeni organizations and researchers point to the decision to give President Saleh unconditional immunity, for example, as
inextricably linked with the start of the war in 2014. Farea al-Muslimi
noted that the outcome of the NDC was not so much "a transition
to the future" but "was transporting the past to the future," because
it failed to deal with issues of restorative justice, human rights, and
compensation for harms. And as al-Muslimi pointed out, "the legacy
of un-accountability shaped" the conduct of the war.[19]

The war itself has inflicted immense harm on civilians, making
transitional justice and accountability all the more important today.
It has also strengthened the hand of armed groups like the Southern

Transition Council (STC), which is explicitly fighting for the right to secede from a future Yemeni state. Addressing the grievances of these regional actors and designing a future state that is acceptable to regional actors will be immensely challenging but is nevertheless vital to preventing future conflict. "Widespread and systematic human rights violations are an integral element of the conflict's causes, dynamics, and consequences," writes Hadil al-Mowafak of the Yemen Policy Center, "yet, despite being an important part of the problem, human rights have yet to constitute a part of the solution" in the UN-led peace efforts.[20]

Once the fighting ends, the United States and the international community should invest in efforts to promote postconflict justice and accountability and find a sustainable resolution to disagreements about what a future Yemeni state should look like. The international community should support local efforts rather than impose outside or top-down solutions and can play a vital role in supporting such efforts and linking them to a national-level transitional process. The United States can support justice and accountability mechanisms by facilitating the work of Yemeni human rights NGOs and through its role on the UN Human Rights Council.[21]

Radhya Al-Mutawakel, cofounder and chairperson of Mwatana for Human Rights, an independent Yemeni NGO, said that she discovered through her career in the human rights field that "information is power."[22] Mwatana's investigative research unit deploys field researchers across the country to document incidents of civilian harm by visiting field sites, interviewing survivors and eyewitnesses, and photographing weapons remnants. If civilians are dying in war but these events are not carefully documented, Al-Mutawakel said, these deaths will "be dealt with as if they are not happening." Documentation is "the first step toward advocacy, accountability, and transitional justice—if you don't have the information, if you don't document the details," then any movement toward justice or accountability will be incomplete. Mwatana is "building a human rights memory, not only for accountability for now but also for the future," she said.[23]

Mwatana and other Yemeni human rights organizations were deeply disappointed when the UN Human Rights Council discontinued the mandate of the Group of Eminent Experts on Yemen

(GEE), an impartial international body that investigated serious violations and abuses of human rights law by all parties to the conflict, in October 2021.[24] Amnesty International denounced the decision, arguing that the end of the GEE's mandate "will only entrench impunity, and act as a green light for all parties to the armed conflict to continue to commit war crimes and other serious violations."[25] Bahrain and Russia, with outside lobbying from Saudi Arabia, reportedly led the charge to end the GEE's mandate over objections from other members of the council. "I cannot help but feel that this Council has failed the people of Yemen," said the Dutch UN ambassador Peter Bekker.[26] The United States had withdrawn from the council during the Trump administration but rejoined soon after the decision to end the GEE's mandate for the session convening in January 2022. The decision in the United States' absence shows the importance of participating in such multilateral fora.

While addressing these critical issues in the present will be immensely challenging, to neglect them once again will only make the resumption of conflict more likely. The United States should support efforts to document human rights violations by conflict parties as part of a broader transitional justice and accountability process. And while supporting eventual elections, the international community should not push Yemeni parties to rush through the other critical pieces of a postconflict transitional process.

Revise the U.S. Approach to Counterterrorism

The United States' narrow focus on counterterrorism in Yemen prior to the Arab Spring created more problems than it resolved. While until 2014 this approach was held up as a success story, the narrow focus on targeting terrorist leaders and organizations at the expense of broader issues around corruption, stability, and governance was disrupted by the onset of the war in 2014. The U.S. partnership with President Ali Abdullah Saleh created perverse incentives for the regime and facilitated corruption. The literature on counterterrorism aid suggests that this problem is not unique to Yemen. Andrew Boutton has found that authoritarian regimes that rely on counterterrorism aid for their survival can become "racketeers" offering counterterrorism services in exchange for aid, even as they perpetuate the security threat.[27]

One step the United States can take on its own would be to severely limit, if not end, drone strikes in Yemen. As we have seen, the number of U.S. drone strikes in Yemen has increased substantially since 2009. Audrey Kurth Cronin argues that drone strikes can be tactically "successful" even as they undermine the strategic aims of U.S. counterterrorism efforts. While individual strikes may have successfully targeted members of terrorist organizations in Yemen, the drone campaign itself has increased animosity toward the United States and the central government, which is seen as collaborating with U.S. counterterrorism operations.[28]

At the same time, investigative reporting by journalists and human rights advocates has shown us that the underlying premise of the U.S. drone wars is simply wrong. The "Yemen model" promised a counterterrorism campaign that surgically targeted terrorists but spared civilians. In practice, the U.S. military appears to have systematically undercounted the civilian casualties associated with its drone campaigns across the Middle East and Afghanistan.[29] A U.S. approach to Yemen that is centered around the safety and well-being of Yemen's people, rather than narrowly defined counterterrorism goals, will help prevent terrorist groups from taking root without the use of drones.

Rethink Humanitarian Aid

The United States has provided Yemen with more than $4 billion in humanitarian aid since the war began in 2014.[30] Humanitarian assistance is much needed, and indeed there are still significant humanitarian needs that go unmet: in 2020, for example, only about 60 percent of the total amount requested by UN agencies for humanitarian aid in Yemen was actually funded.[31] Yet this amount far overshadows how much aid to Yemen goes toward sustainable economic development: in fiscal year 2021, over 98 percent of economic aid to Yemen from the United States was in the emergency response or food aid sectors.[32] Humanitarian aid is a stopgap measure (and a critical one at that) to prevent more widespread death and suffering in the largest humanitarian crisis in the world, but it is not helping Yemen to develop the building blocks of a sustainable economy. "It's an economic crisis, not a humanitarian one," says Summer Nasser, CEO of Yemen Aid: the approach of focusing primarily on humanitarian aid "isn't helping in the long term."[33]

While Yemen has experienced widespread hunger during the war, food shortages have not been the primary cause. While the coalition's blockade of ports has limited the import of food items and other goods in ways that are problematic for markets across the country, markets in Yemeni communities "have remained relatively stable in terms of food availability/supply."[34] Instead, fuel and food prices are so high that they are out of reach for many Yemenis, due to low currency reserves that make it difficult to finance imports, salaries that have gone unpaid for years, and inflation, among other factors. The problem is not necessarily whether there is enough food or fuel in Yemen but whether Yemenis can afford it.

Humanitarian aid in the form of in-kind goods can also have distorting effects on local markets. Yemeni development experts have called for humanitarian assistance to be provided as cash transfers rather than in food items, since "cash transfers have positive multiplier effects for local economies, assisting small vendors and the market as a whole to keep running, while also strengthening local credit systems."[35] As of 2020, however, more than 75 percent of emergency food assistance was in the form of in-kind food donations, while only 4 percent was in cash vouchers.[36] There are also numerous reports of in-kind food donations that were intended to be redistributed for free resurfacing for sale in markets.[37] Large-scale projects can be unwieldy to implement. Instead, research shows that "identifying and supporting the existing markets that have risen to provide essential goods and services to struggling Yemenis . . . could be an effective approach."[38] Indeed, some researchers charge that international humanitarian aid can sometimes cause more harm than good. "Much of the humanitarian aid that arrives in Yemen exacerbates the war by fostering a lucrative wartime economy, disincentivizing peaceful resolutions and prolonging national dependence on foreign aid," writes Asher Orkaby.[39]

The United States, the UN, and the international community should heed these warnings and revise their approach to humanitarian aid so that aid is not inadvertently fueling conflict, distorting local markets, or missing its intended recipients. A more sustainable approach to development aid should not have to wait until after the fighting ends. Yemenis "feel strongly that critical economic issues need to be addressed as a matter of urgency, not later as part of a political settlement," writes Rafat Al-Akhali.[40]

Invest in Sustainable Diplomacy and Development

In addition to revising our approach to humanitarian aid and investing in near-term conflict prevention, prioritizing stability and human well-being in the U.S. approach to Yemen will require an investment in sustainable diplomacy and development over the long term. This, in turn, will require a major shift in how we think about our bilateral relationships with states in the Middle East.

In recent decades, the United States has placed arms sales, security-sector assistance, and military basing at the center of its approach to security partners in the Middle East. Security partners have received considerable leeway with regard to both their regional security behavior and how they treat their own citizens, in exchange for staunch support for U.S. security objectives. U.S. support for the Saudi-led coalition in Yemen is emblematic of this approach.

The imbalance in U.S. aid to the MENA region reflects this securitized approach. The total amount of aid allocated to democracy and governance programs in the MENA region in President Biden's first budget request was more than double what President Trump requested in the last fiscal year of his presidency.[41] Nevertheless, 76 percent of the total request for aid to the MENA region, or $5.8 billion, under Biden's request was designated for security assistance, while less than 6 percent went toward all MENA democracy and human-rights-related programs.[42] Yemen also demonstrates the perils for U.S. administrations that attempt to pivot away from the Middle East. Subcontracting U.S. interests to security partners is not the most effective way to ensure that the United States does not get sucked into wars in the Middle East. The more effective way to keep the United States out of these wars is to ensure that proxy wars do not happen in the first place.

Preventing future proxy wars in the Middle East will require a substantial revision in U.S. relationships with security partners.

Instead of centering security arrangements, U.S. relationships with states in the Middle East could be rebuilt around the central challenges that these societies face. For countries without a significant natural resource base, like Lebanon, Egypt, and Jordan, as well as those involved in or emerging from conflict, like Yemen, Syria, and Libya, this will mean increased aid for sustainable development programming, as well as for human rights, anticorruption, democracy and governance, and conflict prevention, among other priorities. The wealthy GCC countries do not need development aid but are nevertheless facing critical challenges, including adapting to the effects of climate change and transitioning their economies away from dependence on fossil-fuel mining. The United States can partner with these countries by using diplomacy to encourage them to take the right steps (e.g., encouraging transparency and human rights in the tech sector) and providing technical capacity and assistance to further these transitions.

Climate change is the most critical challenge facing MENA countries within the next few decades, but it is also a ripe area for partnership. The Middle East is facing severe, near-term shocks due to environmental change. Anthropogenic change is "striking particularly hard" in the Middle East not just because many parts of the region are already especially hot and dry but also "because poor governance, weak institutions, and preexisting conflict offer dry kindling for environmentally driven instability," Peter Schwartzstein writes.[43] Of all countries in the MENA region, Yemen faces perhaps the largest challenges due to climate change. Already one of the most water-poor countries in the world, the availability of renewable water on a per capita basis is projected to shrink considerably in the next decade. The World Bank has predicted that Yemen will probably warm faster than the global average and will experience "more variability of rainfall patterns" as well as "an increased frequency of intense rainfall events and therefore an increased risk of floods."[44]

At the same time, reorienting U.S. relationships with countries in the MENA region around partnership to build resilience to climate change "can be part of a wider transition away from a military-dominated approach."[45] Bilateral partnerships built around preventing and adapting to environmental change would have positive ripple effects, not only on these countries' capacity to deal with climate change but also in helping to "lower tensions, better serve citizens, and tackle future sources of instability, rather than merely reacting to those that are already upon us," Schwartzstein notes.[46]

Lesson 2: What Can U.S. Policy Accomplish?
Using U.S. Leverage Effectively

The United States can use its leverage to help bring the war in Yemen to an end. In the instances when the United States historically exerted leverage over its security partners, this pressure played an important role in de-escalation. The Obama administration's public criticism of the civilian deaths caused by the coalition's bombing in the fall of 2016 appears to have temporarily reduced the overall tempo of coalition airstrikes and the proportion of strikes with civilian targets. When President Trump took office in January 2017, in contrast, the number of strikes rose considerably. The Trump administration's willingness to publicly admonish the coalition, alongside pressure from Congress, also played a role in the coalition's late 2017 decision to allow cranes purchased by USAID into the port of Hodeidah. Likewise, U.S. leverage is also linked to Saudi Arabia's agreement to the December 2018 Stockholm Agreement and the UAE's decision to redeploy and withdraw most of its forces from Yemen in the summer of 2019.

Nevertheless, U.S. administrations have sometimes hesitated to use U.S. leverage. After the murder of the journalist Jamal Khashoggi in 2018, for example, some analysts and policy makers fretted about using U.S. leverage because it could damage the U.S.-Saudi relationship. Some argued that the bilateral relationship is "mutually beneficial" in that the United States "gets some leverage over oil prices and supplies, gets a lot of petrodollar investments and huge contracts, and has a stable ally in a very unstable Middle East."[47] Such arguments risk becoming tautological: after all, what is the point of having leverage with U.S. security partners if we do not use it?

The story of U.S. engagement in Yemen's war demonstrates that the United States can fruitfully use the leverage it possesses to affect the behavior of its security partners—without destroying the bilateral relationship altogether. U.S. policy makers should therefore take advantage of opportunities where the United States does have leverage over partners to affect international outcomes, including external countries' interventions in their region's civil wars.

The U.S. Cannot Impose Solutions (but U.S. Policy Still Matters)

American analysts, from a diversity of perspectives, tend to make an implicit assumption that the United States is the primary or the most influential actor in conflicts in the Middle East. This approach can inadvertently strip agency from other conflict actors in our analyses. While the United States is an important actor, there are equally and more important actors in these conflicts, namely, local and regional actors. As a result, the United States does not have the final say in most outcomes—our recent history in Yemen, from U.S. counterterrorism policy to the failed NDC process and the intervening coalition's military failures, clearly demonstrates that this is true.

The implicit assumption that what the United States says or does matters most leads to analytical errors in understanding the impacts of U.S. policy choices. When we assume that any international outcome is the direct result of U.S. choices, we fail to acknowledge the incremental good—and harm—that U.S. policy can do.

Conversely, some analysis of the war in Yemen, and Middle East conflicts more broadly, significantly underplays the role of the United States. Some commentators assume that these conflicts are the result of ancient "ethnic hatreds" or that war in the Middle East is somehow both constant and inevitable. Some of these assumptions appear to ascribe conflict to the immutable features of the region and its people, rather than to the choices of leaders, including U.S. policy choices. This vein of analysis is also problematic because it can underestimate the effects of specific U.S. policy choices, as well as the leverage that the United States has in affecting outcomes— for example, in successfully pressuring the Saudi-led coalition to change its behavior.

Our analyses of U.S. policy must begin with an understanding of what U.S. policy can reasonably be expected to achieve in a given context and proceed from there, rather than assume that bad outcomes are either the direct result only of U.S. policy choices or that U.S. policy is completely ineffectual in the face of larger forces. The United States cannot unilaterally impose solutions in the Middle East, but it is also capable of doing a great deal to either exacerbate or ameliorate conflict.

Lesson 3: How Can We Change U.S. Policy?

Democracy Works

U.S. security policy tends to be static and immensely difficult to change, nowhere more so than in the Middle East. Our securitized approach to the MENA region today, with a focus on energy access, counterterrorism, arms sales, and basing rights, would be immediately recognizable to a security analyst in the 1970s or 1980s. In short, oil for security has been the quid pro quo since President Franklin Roosevelt's famous meeting with Saudi Arabia's King Abdulaziz Ibn Saud on board the USS *Quincy* on February 14, 1945, through Nixon's "twin pillars" policy of the 1970s and the Carter Doctrine of the 1980s. The question of how to change U.S. policy toward the Middle East for the better is therefore a crucial one: all of the well-intended policy recommendations in the world will not matter unless we can find a way to implement them.

This is where the Yemen advocacy movement comes in. It demonstrates that democratic engagement, activism, and organizing can change U.S. security policy for the better—and that U.S. security policy can be responsive to American public opinion. Americans do care about what their government does around the world, and that matters. Political scientists have traditionally assumed that public opinion does not matter in the foreign policy realm because it does not appear to affect voting decisions. The story of the Yemen advocacy movement complicates that narrative: U.S. citizens can weigh in on foreign policy decisions not just by voting once every two years but on a regular basis by lobbying their members of Congress. As we have seen, Congress, in turn, can have a significant role in pressuring the executive and U.S. security partners directly. In the meantime, these advocacy movements can also change our conversations around security policy, making policies that once seemed preposterous or naïve appear within reach within just a few years.

Researchers need to develop a better understanding of how the American public engages on foreign policy issues and the conditions under which such engagement is effective in actually shifting U.S. policy. This knowledge could help make U.S security policy more democratic but also make it more just and responsive to the aspirations of all Americans.

International Diplomacy Starts at Home

U.S. domestic policies that have an outsized effect on Yemeni Americans and Muslim Americans more generally deeply affect Yemenis' perceptions of the United States and its role in the world. "U.S. policy towards Yemen is not exclusive to what happens in Yemen—it includes how Yemenis view the U.S. too and how the U.S. domestically views Yemeni Americans or immigrants or refugees," said the Yemeni director and filmmaker Yousef Assabahi.[48] The Trump administration's immigration ban also affected Yemenis: the policy "left a huge wound on the image of what it means to be a (Yemeni) American that will be difficult for coming administrations to repair," al-Muslimi noted.[49]

To repair the damage of the Trump administration's policies toward immigrants and refugees, substantially lifting the cap on annual refugee admissions and taking steps to alleviate the harm that Islamophobia has caused for Muslim communities in the United States, for example, would both be important steps. The United States can also provide more support to countries in the Middle East that admit large numbers of refugees.

Rewriting the Narrative

This last point may seem out of place at the end of a book that focuses on war in Yemen, but it is of vital importance. As we have seen, U.S. policy toward Yemen in the past few decades has been taken up almost entirely by security concerns and more recently by the war itself. Yet, too often, Americans perceive the Middle East as a region dominated only by failed states, war, and misery. While governance failures, violent conflict, and human rights violations are an important part of the MENA region's story over the past century or more, there is also much more to the Middle East. U.S. media rarely tell the stories of everyday life in the Middle East. In crafting a U.S. approach toward the region, researchers and policy makers also tend to revert to these assumptions, instead of asking about the aspirations and visions of people from the region itself.

One step toward changing this will be rewriting the dominant Western narratives about the Middle East and about Yemen in particular. Yousef Assabahi acknowledges that criticizing this narrative when people in Yemen are suffering feels like a privileged conversation, but he notes, "My issue is not that these stories are being told—it's that they're the *only* stories being told." There are other stories we could tell about Yemen too: "Yes, there is hunger—but also a lot of villages in Yemen are using solar panels to get electricity. That's a story that no one talks about," Assabahi said. "People don't talk about young people in the capital who are putting on music events, playing music on the sidewalk. . . . That's resistance."[50]

Western media coverage of Yemen does not "allow us to be multidimensional," said Mariam Al-Dhubhani, a Yemeni Russian journalist and filmmaker. "Obviously the war is always in the background. It's always going to be there. But that doesn't mean that you are the war or you are the famine," she said. "You are a human who's trying to survive. You adapt. You still find laughter. You still find a way to pursue [your life]. . . . If you can allow the complexity to show, then people can relate and stories become less of a stereotype." "There is more than one way to live, so there is more than one way to tell a story," Al-Dhubhani said.[51]

Conclusion

U.S. officials have long seen Yemen as of peripheral interest to U.S. national security, but Yemen somehow continually inserted itself into the list of U.S. regional priorities in the second half of the twentieth century and early twenty-first century. During the civil war in North Yemen in the 1960s, U.S. officials tried to contain the conflict by pressuring Saudi Arabia to end its support for the royalists. In the 1970s, conflicts between the two countries of North and South Yemen, U.S. policy makers were primarily concerned about the potential spread of Soviet-sponsored communism in the Middle East. By the 1980s and 1990s, Yemen was again a lower priority for U.S. policy makers, and the 1986 and 1994 civil wars that bookended unification did not spark much concern.

However, Yemen became important to U.S. security interests as understood by policy makers in the age of the Global War on Terror, following the bombing of the USS *Cole* in 2000 and even more so after the "underwear bomber" failed to detonate an explosive on a flight to Detroit, Michigan, on Christmas Day 2009. But while the "Yemen model" of counterterrorism was initially held up as a success, it failed to foresee, let alone help prevent, the outbreak of the war in 2014.

Yemen made it through the early post–Arab Spring years as the only country in the Arab world with a negotiated settlement, transition plan, and plans for a national political dialogue.[52] But while the National Dialogue Conference, sponsored by the United States and the GCC, also appeared to be successful at first, it failed in its attempt to address Yemenis' grievances around regional autonomy, transitional justice, the distribution of resources, corruption, and the other issues that had ignited the Arab Spring protest movement in early 2011. These problems, which eventually led to the civil war beginning in 2014, were not unforeseeable to the astute eye: April Longley Alley wrote in 2013 that many Yemenis saw the NDC as a process to reshuffle "power among old-regime elites" rather than to create a true "power-sharing agreement to ensure a more democratic, accountable system. Even if one is reached, implementation will be difficult, especially in the south, where mobilization and demands for separation are high."[53]

Still, the civil war would most likely have ended, or at least transitioned into a phase of lower-level conflict, in early 2015 without external intervention. When the Saudi-led coalition intervened in March 2015, President Hadi was fleeing the country as Houthi forces advanced on Aden. Instead, the coalition intervention pushed back against Houthi advances, and Iran's escalating support for the Houthis facilitated their ability to push back against the coalition.

Years of fighting have driven factionalization among both sides: while the conflict is often depicted in Western media as the Hadi government facing off against the Houthis, in reality, these are "just two actors among a multiplicity of groups, and face their own internal divisions," as demonstrated by fighting between Houthi forces and Saleh loyalists in December 2017 in Sana'a and between southern separatists and Hadi's forces in January 2018 and in August 2019 in Aden.[54] Houthi forces still control much of northern Yemen, the majority of Yemen's population, and most government institutions and military resources. Southern Yemen has in many ways become de facto separated from the north, with military groups affiliated with the STC.

The Biden administration's diplomatic efforts may yet succeed in convincing Saudi Arabia to end its military intervention in Yemen, but without more sustained effort, Saudi Arabia's hypothetical withdrawal will not mean that Yemen's war is over. Rather, the war will most likely move into a new phase in which increasingly factionalized military groups are still fighting one another in the absence of a cease-fire and plan for a comprehensive political settlement. The international community has reached its last chance to strike a "grand bargain" that could knit Yemen back together as a unified state, a prospect that looks increasingly unlikely.[55] Without sustained international diplomacy, "Yemen could easily slip into a nightmare scenario," writes Gregory Johnsen, "in which Saudi Arabia strikes a deal with the Houthis, the local war is left unaddressed, international attention wanes with the Saudi withdrawal, and fighting continues on the ground."[56]

Still, the appointment of a new UN special envoy for Yemen in 2021 and the Biden administration's diplomatic engagement provide a small window of hope. "At best, a long process of negotiation and change has begun," Alley wrote in 2013.[57] This is still true today. Despite these many challenges, the United States could assist Yemenis in ending the war and welcoming in a new political future. But it cannot do so by sticking with the old approach.

Epilogue

I COMPLETED THE FIRST DRAFT of this book in January 2021. On April 1, 2022, something unexpected happened: UN Special Envoy Hans Grundberg announced that the conflict parties had agreed to a temporary truce.[1] In addition to a pause in the fighting, the terms included that the internationally recognized government would allow commercial flights to operate out of Sana'a Airport to certain destinations and fuel ships into Hodeidah port. The parties also agreed to discuss opening blocked roads around Taiz.

Initially slated to last two months, the truce was renewed in June and again in August before it formally lapsed in October 2022. Remarkably, the truce, the first nationwide cease-fire in Yemen since 2016, led to a sharp decline in violence across the country.[2] The six months of the truce saw the lowest levels of violence on a monthly basis since before the Saudi-led coalition's intervention began in March 2015. Coalition airstrikes ceased entirely, and ships and flights entered Hodeidah port and Sana'a Airport, respectively, on a somewhat regular basis.[3] The truce did not end the violence entirely, as armed clashes occurred at some points along existing front lines, particularly in Marib and Taiz governorates, although much of this was shelling that appeared aimed at maintaining a frontline presence and deterring the other side rather than escalation. Land mines also contributed to casualties, as did clashes in the south between the Southern Transition Council and al-Qaeda in the Arabian Peninsula. Still, the Armed Conflict Location & Event Data Project (ACLED) reported that during the truce, there were about 200 casualties per month, compared to an average monthly fatality rate of 1,750 from January 2015 through March 2022.[4]

Even more remarkably, perhaps, many of the truce's terms stayed in effect even when the truce itself formally lapsed in October. On February 22, 2023, the 113th round-trip flight of the truce took off from and returned to Sana'a Airport, although the rate of fuel ships cleared to enter Hodeidah had declined.[5] In a January 2023 briefing to the UN Security Council, Grundberg reported that the "military situation . . . remained stable," with no major fighting or shifts in the front lines.[6] While mediation efforts had yet to result in a breakthrough on a truce expansion, they nevertheless continued. The conflict parties appeared to pursue an economic war instead, with a rise in Houthi attacks on oil terminals controlled by the Islamic Revolutionary Guard Corps (IRGC) and retaliation from the IRGC, which placed sanctions on Houthi leaders as well as companies doing business in Houthi-controlled territory.[7]

Why was there a breakthrough in April 2022, after more than seven years of fighting and minimal progress on peace? At this moment, both sides of the conflict had reached a limit in their efforts to place themselves in a better battlefield position. The Houthi offensive on Marib, beginning in early 2020, would have yielded the Houthis a significant victory, giving them access to gas and oil infrastructure and therefore a significant source of income. But as the offensive stalled out, the benefits of continuing to fight apparently diminished. The Saudi-led coalition, for its part, has acknowledged that the conflict will not be resolved on the battlefield and appears to be looking for a face-saving way out of the war. The increased tempo of Houthi UAV and missile attacks on Saudi and Emirati territory had significantly escalated the costs of the war for the coalition.[8] In a surprise move on April 7, at talks in Riyadh, President Hadi, long seen as an obstacle to negotiations, was ousted in favor of an eight-member Presidential Leadership Council (PLC) that balanced Saudi and Emirati loyalists and included representatives of the major factions in the anti-Houthi coalition. While the PLC has struggled to get off the ground, its formation in Riyadh demonstrated the coalition's willingness to push negotiations forward at least.[9]

The Biden administration's investment in diplomacy, and its support for a reinvigorated UN-led negotiation process, was also a necessary, if not sufficient, condition for the truce agreement, in my view.

The people of Yemen are not in the clear. Rising global food prices and retaliatory economic moves by the conflict parties have complicated the economic picture even further, while the UN's humanitarian fundraising efforts in 2023 have fallen far short of their goals.[10] Two-thirds of Yemen's population still needs life-saving humanitarian support. In 2022, the UN was forced to cut back on humanitarian programming in Yemen due to funding gaps.[11]

As you know after reading this book, significant obstacles remain on Yemen's path to peace. But the truce demonstrates that forward movement in peace negotiations is possible—and that U.S. diplomacy can play a supportive role in moving negotiations forward.

February 2023

Acknowledgments

This book was completed before I began working at RAND and does not reflect RAND views.

There are so many people who helped me in some way with the creation of this book, and it would be impossible for me to thank them all here. But a big thank-you up front to everyone who has supported me and encouraged my academic explorations.

I first began to understand the United States' role in the war in Yemen through the incredible advocacy work of Kate Gould and the Friends Committee on National Legislation. I am grateful for all of the wisdom that Kate has shared with me and for her and FCNL's early leadership in this work.

I am especially grateful to those who have produced knowledge and writing about Yemen and U.S. foreign policy that I have drawn on in my own work (whether or not they are aware of it!). Again, there are too many wonderful scholars, researchers, and practitioners whose work has informed mine, but a special thanks to ACAPS, ACLED, Noha Aboueldahab, Nadwa Al-Dawsari, Maysaa Shuja al-Deen, Ahmad Algohbary, Abdul-Ghani al-Iryani, Farea Al-Muslimi, Radhya Al-Mutawakel, Adam Baron, Kristine Beckerle, Eric Eikenberry, Kate Gould, Ibrahim Jalal, Gregory Johnsen, Thomas Juneau, Kate Kizer, Ahmed Nagi, Afrah Nasser, Asher Orkaby, Scott Paul, Layla Picard, Peter Salisbury, and Stacey Philbrick Yadav. Any errors are, of course, my own.

My dissertation research set me on the path to writing this book, and my dissertation committee—Lise M. Howard, Daniel Byman, and Andrew Bennett—are a wise and wonderful group who provided the best advice and support I could imagine. There is no way I would have made it through my PhD without my friends and colleagues in the PhD program at Georgetown and my officemates at the Belfer Center Lilly Frost and Yuree Noh.

I conducted research that appears in sections of Chapter 4 while I worked at New America for the report *The Monarchs' Pawns? Gulf State Proxy Warfare 2011–Today* (June 15, 2020). I am grateful for the time I spent at New America, and for the leadership and support of Anne-Marie Slaughter, Heather Hurlburt, Peter Bergen, and Mark Schmitt, as well as for the friendship of so many of my colleagues there.

My thanks to all of the folks I interviewed for this book and for my dissertation research, whose views and ideas shaped my own, some of whom are named here and some who are not.

Thanks to the wonderful people who patiently read early drafts of this book and gave me great advice: Alexandra Evans, Heather Hurlburt, Andrew Leber, Jane Morency, and my parents.

Thank you to the two anonymous reviewers whose thoughtful comments helped to substantially improve the manuscript. I am incredibly grateful for the guidance of the Yale University Press team, including Jaya Chatterjee, who has guided me down the book path from the beginning, Jeffrey Schier, and Amanda Gerstenfeld. Thanks also to Ghaidaa Alrashidy for creating the wonderful illustrations, Enid Zafran for the index, Judy Loeven for proofreading, and Andrew Katz for copyediting.

Thank you to my grandparents and extended family who taught me the history of two genocides through a personal lens and provided a supportive, creative, joy-filled, intellectual environment to grow up in. A special thanks to my loving parents, who have nurtured my love for reading, loved me unconditionally, and served as role models (not to mention driven me to many, many swim meets!). And finally, thank you to Winnie, Samantha, and especially Andrew Leber, bearer of coffee, knowledge, comfort, and support and my partner in life. I couldn't imagine a more perfect person for me. I love you all!

Notes

Introduction

Epigraph: Mwatana for Human Rights, "US Weapons Responsible for Civilian Deaths in Yemen," September 20, 2018, https://mwatana.org/en/us-weapons/.

1. Quoted in Elbagir et al., "Bomb That Killed 40 Children in Yemen."
2. Ibid.
3. Bruce and Karl, "White House Continues to Back Yemen as Model for Successful Counterterrorism."
4. Dresch, *History of Modern Yemen*, xv.

Chapter One. A Brief History of External Intervention in Yemen's Wars

Epigraph: Memo from Thomas L. Hughes, State Department Bureau of Intelligence and Research, June 7, 1963, National Security Files, Country Files—Yemen, Box 208a, Folder: Yemen General, 6/63, John F. Kennedy Presidential Library (JFK Library).

1. Dresch, *History of Modern Yemen*, i.
2. Ibid.
3. Mackintosh-Smith, *Yemen*, 116.
4. Schmidt, *Yemen*, 272–273; Kerr, *Arab Cold War*.
5. Clark, *Yemen*, 95.
6. Orkaby, *Beyond the Arab Cold War*, 130.
7. Ferris, *Nasser's Gamble*, 30.
8. Orkaby, *Beyond the Arab Cold War*, 49.
9. State Dept. Incoming Telegram (Hart), March 2, 1963, National Security Files, Country Files—Yemen, Box 208, Folder: Yemen General, Saudi Arabian Cables, 1/63–3/63, JFK Library.

10. See, e.g., State Dept. Incoming Telegram (Macomber), November 12, 1962, National Security Files, Country Files—Yemen, Box 207, Folder: Yemen General, 11/1/62–11/15/62, JFK Library.

11. State Dept. Incoming Telegram (Macomber), November 10, 1962, ibid.

12. State Dept. Incoming Telegram (Macomber), November 22, 1962, ibid.

13. National Security Action Memorandum No. 227, from McGeorge Bundy to the Secretary of State, "Subject: Decisions Taken at President's Meeting on Yemen Crisis," February 25, 1963, National Security Files, Robert W. Komer Files, Box 447, Folder: Yemen 1961–4/63, JFK Library.

14. Memorandum of Conversation, Participants: Prince Faysal, Deputy Foreign Minister Sayyid 'Umar Saqqaf, Amb Parker T. Hart, President's special envoy Amb. Ellsworth Bunker, Isa K. Sabbagh, PAO, U.S. Embassy, Jidda, at Crown Prince Faysal's home, March 17, 1963, National Security Files, Country Files—Yemen, Box 208, Folder: Yemen General, 3/63, JFK Library.

15. Memorandum for the President, from Robert Komer, July 12, 1962, National Security Files, Country Files—Yemen, Box 208a, Folder: Yemen General, 7/63, JFK Library.

16. Dresch, *History of Modern Yemen*, 101.

17. Halliday, *Revolution and Foreign Policy*, 181.

18. Brehony, *Yemen Divided*, xix.

19. Halliday, *Revolution and Foreign Policy*, 202.

20. Westad, *Global Cold War*, 382.

21. Halliday, *Revolution and Foreign Policy*, 79.

22. Westad, *Global Cold War*, 329.

23. Halliday, *Revolution and Foreign Policy*, 87.

24. Quoted ibid., 93.

25. Ibid., 93.

26. Brehony, *Yemen Divided*, 155.

27. Halliday, *Revolution and Foreign Policy*, 42.

28. Brehony, *Yemen Divided*, 157.

29. Ibid.

30. Westad, *Global Cold War*, 382.

31. Ibid., 385.

32. Quoted in Halliday, *Revolution and Foreign Policy*, 95.

33. Brehony, *Yemen Divided*, 157.

34. Ibid.

35. Rabi, *Yemen*, 122.

36. Durac, "Joint Meeting Parties," 348.

37. Alley, "Yemen's Multiple Crises," 74.

38. Hudson, "Bipolarity, Rational Calculation, and War in Yemen," 10.

39. Clark, *Yemen*, 135.

40. Ibid.; Dresch, *History of Modern Yemen*, 186.

41. Vreeland and Dreher, *Political Economy of the United Nations Security Council*, 68.

42. International Crisis Group, *Yemen: Coping with Terrorism.*
43. Brehony, *Yemen Divided*, 194.
44. Ibid., 195.
45. Ibid., 196.
46. Ibid.
47. Hudson, "Bipolarity, Rational Calculation, and War in Yemen."
48. Day, *Political Challenge of Yemen's Southern Movement*, 10.
49. Dresch, *History of Modern Yemen*, 197.
50. Ibid.
51. Day, *Regionalism and Rebellion in Yemen*, 157.
52. International Crisis Group, *Breaking Point?*, 8.
53. Day, *Political Challenge of Yemen's Southern Movement.*
54. International Crisis Group, *Yemen: Coping with Terrorism.*
55. Shuja Al-Deen, "Iran and Houthis."
56. Salmoni, Loidolt, and Wells, *Regime and Periphery in Northern Yemen*, 67.
57. Ibid.
58. Baron, *Mapping the Yemen Conflict.*
59. Brandt, *Tribes and Politics in Yemen*, 21.
60. Lackner, *Yemen in Crisis*, 3.
61. For a detailed timeline of the Saada wars, see Salmoni, Loidolt, and Wells, *Regime and Periphery in Northern Yemen.*
62. Hill, *Yemen Endures*, 194–195.
63. Salmoni, Loidolt, and Wells, *Regime and Periphery in Northern Yemen*, 10.
64. Hill, *Yemen Endures*, 178, 176.
65. Egel et al., *Building an Enduring Peace in Yemen*, 10.
66. Alley, "Shifting Light in the Qamariyya."
67. International Crisis Group, *Yemen: Coping with Terrorism.*
68. Hales, *Fault Lines.*
69. World Bank, "World Development Indicators 2016."
70. Durac, "Joint Meeting Parties and the Politics of Opposition in Yemen," 2.
71. Day, *Regionalism and Rebellion in Yemen*, 240.
72. Ibid.
73. Alley, "Yemen's Multiple Crises," 72.

Chapter Two. The U.S. Counterterrorism War in Yemen

Epigraph: Quoted in Schwartz, "ABC's Karl Hammers WH's Earnest."
1. Shane, *Objective Troy*, 6.
2. Quoted in McCrisken, "Ten Years On," 785.
3. Shane, *Objective Troy*, 20.
4. Hennessy, "In Devising a Plan in Iraq, U.S. Looks to Its Yemen Model."
5. White House, "Remarks by the President on the Situation in Iraq."
6. White House, "Statement by the President on ISIL."
7. Zimmerman, "Yemen Model Won't Work in Iraq, Syria."

8. Summer Nasser, author interview, October 2021, Zoom.
9. Ibid.
10. Taub, "Obama's Love of the 'Yemen Model.'"
11. Tharoor, "Yemen and Somalia Are Examples of U.S. Mission Creep."
12. Quoted in Shane, *Objective Troy*, 211.
13. National Commission on Terrorist Attacks upon the United States, *Ninth Public Hearing*.
14. Johnsen, *Last Refuge*, 90.
15. Ibid., 92.
16. Ibid., 122–123.
17. Shane, *Objective Troy*, 203.
18. Quoted ibid., 203.
19. Ibid.
20. Quoted ibid.
21. Quoted ibid., 206.
22. Ibid., 207–208.
23. Ibid., 208.
24. Ibid., 209.
25. U.S. Senate Committee on Foreign Relations, *Al Qaeda in Yemen and Somalia*.
26. U.S. Department of Justice, "Umar Farouk Abdulmutallab Sentenced to Life in Prison."
27. U.S. Senate Committee on Foreign Relations, *Al Qaeda in Yemen and Somalia*.
28. Shane, *Objective Troy*, 21.
29. Johnsen, *Last Refuge*, 262–263.
30. Klaidman, *Kill or Capture*, 256.
31. Ryan and Dwyer, "Terror Threat 'Most Heightened' since 9/11."
32. White House, "Press Briefing by Press Secretary Josh Earnest, 3/23/2015."
33. White House, "Press Briefing by Press Secretary Josh Earnest, 9/26/2014."
34. Bergen, Sterman, and Salyk-Virk, "America's Counterterrorism Wars."
35. Ibid.
36. Sanger, *Confront and Conceal*, 243.
37. Shane, *Objective Troy*, 211.
38. Ibid.
39. Quoted in Sanger, *Confront and Conceal*, 251.
40. Shane, *Objective Troy*, 218–224.
41. ACLU, "Al-Aulaqi v. Panetta."
42. Shiel and Woods, "Legacy of Unrecognized Harm."
43. BBC, "Obituary: Anwar al-Awlaki."
44. Shane, "Enduring Influence of Anwar al-Awlaki," 15.
45. Shane, *Objective Troy*, 216–217.
46. Shane, "Enduring Influence of Anwar al-Awlaki."
47. Farley, "Targeting Anwar Al-Aulaqi," 58–59.

48. Quoted ibid., 59.
49. Bergen, Sterman, and Salyk-Virk, "America's Counterterrorism Wars."
50. Finn and Miller, "Anwar al-Awlaki's Family Speaks Out against His, Son's Death."
51. Al-Muslimi, testimony in *Drone Wars*, 16; Zakaria, "Yemeni at U.S. Hearing"; Hsieh, "Watch: Yemeni Activist."
52. Pew Research Center, "Global Opposition to U.S. Surveillance and Drones."
53. Kilcullen and Exum, "Death from Above."
54. Shane, Mazzetti, and Worth, "Secret Assault on Terrorism Widens."
55. Mazzetti, "U.S. Is Said to Expand Secret Actions in Mideast."
56. Ross et al., "Obama Ordered U.S. Military Strike."
57. Mazzetti, "U.S. Is Said to Expand Secret Actions in Mideast"; Security Assistance Monitor, "Foreign Military Training."
58. Priest, "U.S. Military Teams, Intelligence Deeply Involved."
59. *Reuters*, "Yemen Offered U.S. 'Open Door' to al Qaeda."
60. Hill, *Yemen Endures*, 149.
61. White House, "Weekly Address."
62. Human Rights Watch, "US: Investigate Counterterrorism Assistance to Yemen."
63. Worth, "Man Who Danced on the Heads of Snakes."
64. Knights, "Military Role in Yemen's Protests," 266.
65. Human Rights Watch, "US: Investigate Counterterrorism Assistance to Yemen."
66. Ibid.
67. Day, *Regionalism and Rebellion in Yemen*, 203.
68. Watling and Shabibi, "How the War on Terror Failed Yemen."
69. Johnsen, *Last Refuge*, 144.
70. U.S. Senate Committee on Foreign Relations, *Al Qaeda in Yemen and Somalia*.
71. Watling and Shabibi, "How the War on Terror Failed Yemen."
72. Karman, "Yemen's Unfinished Revolution."
73. Quoted in Cook, *Woman's Place*, 248–249.
74. Clinton, *Hard Choices*, 335.
75. Priest, "U.S. Military Teams, Intelligence Deeply Involved."
76. Watling and Shabibi, "How the War on Terror Failed Yemen."
77. Gerald Feierstein, author interview, September 2017, in person.

Chapter Three. Arab Spring, Arab Fall

Epigraph: Friedman, "Yemeni Way."
1. Ibid.
2. White House, "Remarks by the President on the Situation in Iraq."
3. Karman, "Our Revolution's Doing What Saleh Can't."

4. Alley, "Yemen on the Brink"; Abdullah and Ghobari, "Thousands March in Yemen."
5. Kasinof, "Are Yemen's Protests Going to Bring Another Revolution?"
6. Baron, "Despite the War, Yemenis Still Crave Dignity, Justice, and the Rule of Law."
7. Karman, "Our Revolution's Doing What Saleh Can't."
8. Baron, "Despite the War, Yemenis Still Crave Dignity, Justice, and the Rule of Law."
9. Finn, "Yemen Arrests Anti-government Activist."
10. Daragahi and Browning, "Tens of Thousands Turn Out."
11. Sherwood and Finn, "Thousands Join 'Day of Rage.'"
12. Almasmari, "Yemen Imposes State of Emergency."
13. Quoted in *Reuters*, "U.S. 'Alarmed' at Yemen Violence."
14. Alley, "Yemen on the Brink."
15. Barker, "US Ratchets Up Pressure on Yemen's President."
16. *Al Jazeera*, "Reports: Saleh Refuses to Sign Exit Deal."
17. Londono and Miller, "Yemen's Saleh Refuses to Sign Deal to Quit."
18. BBC, "Yemen: President Saleh Injured in Attack on Palace."
19. Almasmari, "More Protests Demand Ouster of Yemen's Leader."
20. Rashad, "Yemen's Saleh Signs Deal to Give Up Power."
21. Obama, *Promised Land*, 643.
22. Crowley, "'We Caved.'"
23. Quoted ibid.
24. Brennan, *Undaunted*, 341.
25. Ibid.
26. Hill, *Yemen Endures*, 257.
27. Brennan, *Undaunted*, 342.
28. Malley and Pomper, "Accomplice to Carnage."
29. Hill, *Yemen Endures*, 238.
30. White House, "Statement by the Press Secretary on Violence in Yemen."
31. Ibid.
32. Gaston, *Process Lessons Learned*, 2.
33. Day, "'Non-Conclusion' of Yemen's National Dialogue."
34. Ibid.
35. International Crisis Group, *Case for More Inclusive—and More Effective—Peacemaking in Yemen*.
36. Schmitz, *Yemen's National Dialogue*, 6.
37. Hill, *Yemen Endures*, 261.
38. International Crisis Group, *Case for More Inclusive—and More Effective—Peacemaking in Yemen*.
39. Among them, the GPC had 112 seats, Islah had 50, and YSP held 37; International Crisis Group, *Yemen's Southern Question*.
40. Aboueldahab, *Transitional Justice*, 106.

41. E.g., Hagopian, "Democracy by Undemocratic Means"; Durant and Weintraub, "How to Make Democracy Self-Enforcing."
42. Yadav, "'Yemen Model' as a Failure of Political Imagination," 145.
43. Ibid.
44. Al-Mowafak, "Yemen's Political Activists Find New Spaces."
45. Jamshidi, "How Transitional Justice Can Affect Yemen's Future."
46. International Crisis Group, *Yemen's Southern Question*.
47. Ibid.
48. Schmitz, *Yemen's National Dialogue*, 2.
49. International Crisis Group, *Yemen's Southern Question*.
50. Gaston, *Process Lessons Learned*, 6.
51. Schmitz, *Yemen's National Dialogue*.
52. Jamshidi, "How Transitional Justice Can Affect Yemen's Future."
53. Gerald Feierstein, author interview.
54. Schmitz, *Yemen's National Dialogue*.
55. Farea al-Muslimi, author interview, January 2021, Zoom.
56. Snyder, "Where the US Fell Down in Yemen."
57. Farea al-Muslimi, author interview.
58. Snyder, "Where the US Fell Down in Yemen."
59. Aboueldahab, *Transitional Justice*, 106.
60. Hill, *Yemen Endures*, 269.
61. Egel et al., *Building an Enduring Peace in Yemen*, 6.

Chapter Four. Regional Proxy Wars before 2015

1. Hiro, *Cold War in the Islamic World*, 244–245.
2. Yom and Gause, "Resilient Royals," 80; Ulrichsen, *United Arab Emirates*, 192; Ulrichsen writes that "there was virtually no prospect of any mass protest in the UAE."
3. Ulrichsen, *United Arab Emirates*, 191; Broomhall, "Arab Spring Has Cost Gulf Arab States $150bn."
4. Bronner and Slackman, "Saudi Troops Enter Bahrain to Help Put Down Unrest."
5. Matthiesen, *Sectarian Gulf*.
6. Ulrichsen, *United Arab Emirates*, 198.
7. Hassan, "Gulf States," 20.
8. Blanga, "Saudi Arabia's Motives in the Syrian Civil War."
9. Ulrichsen, *Qatar and the Arab Spring*, 130–138.
10. Abboud, *Syria*, 125.
11. Hassan, "Gulf States," 21.
12. Weiss and Hassan, *ISIS*.
13. Abboud, *Syria*, 146.
14. Obama, *Promised Land*, 651.

15. Morris and Naylor, "Arab States Fear Nuclear Deal."
16. Entessar, "Regional Great Game?"
17. Obama, *Promised Land*, 652.
18. Hubbard, *MBS*, 88.
19. Brandt, "Hidden Realities."
20. Al-Enazy, "International Boundary Treaty," 161.
21. Brandt, *Tribes and Politics in Yemen*, 75–76.
22. Ibid., 76.
23. Esfandiary and Tabatabai, "Yemen," 155.
24. *Time*, "Crown Prince Mohammed bin Salman Talks to *Time*."
25. Ibid.
26. O'Donnell, "Saudi Arabia's Heir to the Throne Talks to *60 Minutes*."
27. Ibid.
28. Ibid.
29. Flanders et al., "Saudi Crown Prince Discusses Trump, Aramco, Arrests."
30. Al-Rashed, "Al-Tadkheel fi al-Yemen minah al-kartha" (translation by the author).
31. Lackner, *Yemen in Crisis*, 82.
32. Quoted in Filkins, "Saudi Prince's Quest."
33. Quoted in Aboudi, "UAE Says Sees Systematic Iranian Meddling."
34. Akbarzadeh and Conduit, "Rouhani's First Two Years in Office," 10.
35. Bonnefoy, "Sunni Islamist Dynamics in Context of War," 23.
36. Worth, "Mohammed bin Zayed's Dark Vision."
37. Hertog, *Princes, Brokers, and Bureaucrats*, 12.
38. Hertog, "Rentier Militaries in the Gulf States," 400.
39. Ulrichsen, "Endgames for Saudi Arabia and the United Arab Emirates," 31.
40. Gause, "United States Is the Last Check on MBS's Power."
41. Almezaini, *UAE and Foreign Policy*, 29.
42. Ulrichsen, "Endgames for Saudi Arabia and the United Arab Emirates," 32.
43. Ibid.
44. Stephens, *Arab Cold War Redux*, 17.
45. Ostovar, *Vanguard of the Imam*, 205.
46. Tabatabai, *No Conquest, No Defeat*, 255, 274.
47. Memarian, "Iran's Green Movement Never Went Away"; Akbarzadeh and Conduit, "Rouhani's First Two Years in Office," 2.
48. Tabatabai, *No Conquest, No Defeat*, 256; Haghighatjoo, "Green Movement and Political Change in Iran," 250.
49. Tabatabai, *No Conquest, No Defeat*, 277.
50. Quoted in Fürtig, "Iran and the Arab Spring," 5; also see Maloney, "Iran."
51. Fürtig, "Iran and the Arab Spring," 5.
52. Ostovar, *Vanguard of the Imam*, 192.
53. Ibid., 193.
54. Ibid., 277.
55. Cordesman et al., *US-Iranian Competition*.

56. Tabatabai, *No Conquest, No Defeat*, 267.
57. Ibid., 290.
58. Ibid., 277.
59. Byman, "Confronting Iran," 110.
60. Ostovar, *Vanguard of the Imam*, 206.
61. Maloney, "Iran," 259.
62. Goodarzi, "Iran," 27.
63. Ibid.
64. Ibid., 26.
65. Byman, "Confronting Iran," 110–111.
66. Ostovar, *Vanguard of the Imam*, 290–291.
67. Ibid., 260.
68. Tabatabai, *No Conquest, No Defeat*, 278.
69. Karon, "Hamas Signals Break with Iran."
70. Jones, "Hope and Disappointment," 77.
71. Ibid., 73.
72. International Institute for Strategic Studies, *Iran's Networks of Influence in the Middle East*.
73. Ibid.
74. Ostovar, *Vanguard of the Imam*, 281.
75. Ibid., 289.
76. Esfandiary and Tabatabai, *Triple-Axis*, 161.
77. Esfandiary and Tabatabai, "Yemen," 156.
78. Tabatabai, Martini, and Wasser, *Iran Threat Network*, 14.
79. Ostovar, *Vanguard of the Imam*, 256.
80. Esfandiary and Tabatabai, "Yemen," 164.
81. Quoted ibid.
82. Quoted in Esfandiary and Tabatabai, "Yemen," 165.
83. Esfandiary and Tabatabai, *Triple-Axis*, 165.

Chapter Five. Descent into "Chaos"

Epigraph: Salisbury, *Yemen*, 2.
1. Ibid.
2. Ibid., 45.
3. Ibid., 2.
4. UNICEF, "What UNICEF Is Doing in Yemen."
5. UNHCR, "Yemen Fact Sheet."
6. Magdy, "UN Warns of Mass Famine."
7. Coalition members include Saudi Arabia and the UAE, the de facto leaders of the coalition, as well as Bahrain, Kuwait, Morocco, Senegal, and Sudan. Qatar was also a coalition member until 2017.
8. Hager and Mazzetti, "Emirates Secretly Sends Colombian Mercenaries."
9. Knights, "Lessons from the UAE War in Yemen."

10. Al-Dawsari, "Fantasies of State Power Cannot Solve Yemen's War."

11. Knights and Almeida, "Saudi-UAE War Effort in Yemen (Part 1)"; Knights and Almeida, "Saudi-UAE War Effort in Yemen (Part 2)."

12. Kirkpatrick, "On the Front Line of the Saudi War in Yemen."

13. Ibid.

14. United Nations Office of the Special Representative of the Secretary-General for Children and Armed Conflict, "Child Recruitment and Use."

15. Quoted in *Reuters*, "Saudi-Led Coalition Announces End to Yemen Operation."

16. Knights and Almeida, "Saudi-UAE War Effort in Yemen (Part 1)."

17. Ulrichsen, *United Arab Emirates*, 210.

18. Ibid., 209.

19. Lackner, *Yemen in Crisis*, 55.

20. Katzman, *United Arab Emirates*, 16.

21. Baron, *Yemen's Forgotten War*.

22. Des Roches, "Prize Deferred."

23. Mwatana for Human Rights, *Starvation Makers*, 184. For the full account of this incident, see 184–189.

24. Ibid., 184.

25. Yemen Data Project, "Data."

26. Mwatana for Human Rights, *Starvation Makers*, 17.

27. Ibid.

28. Chapter 6 provides more detail about how the Obama administration responded to these strikes, including its attempts to reduce the number of civilian casualties due to coalition airstrikes.

29. Advani, *Constructing Commercial Empire*.

30. Ardemagni and Al-Hamdani, *Yemen*; Roston, "Middle East Monarchy Hired American Ex-Soldiers."

31. Fuller, "Targeting Islamists."

32. Roy, "UAE's Sphere of Influence in Southern Yemen."

33. Al-Dawsari, "Fantasies of State Power Cannot Solve Yemen's War."

34. For more on these complex relationships, two comprehensive guides may be especially useful to the reader: Al-Dawsari, "Fantasies of State Power Cannot Solve Yemen's War"; and DeLozier, "Yemen Matrix."

35. Al-Dawsari, "Fantasies of State Power Cannot Solve Yemen's War."

36. Ibid.

37. Egel et al., *Building an Enduring Peace in Yemen*, 22.

38. Ibid., 21–22.

39. DeLozier, "Yemen Matrix," 25.

40. Salisbury, "Yemen's Southern Transitional Council."

41. Fuller, "Yemen."

42. Ibid.

43. *Al Jazeera*, "Battle for Aden."

44. Freer, *Rentier Islamism*.

45. Salisbury, "Beginning of the End of Yemen's Civil War?"
46. Jalal, "Riyadh Agreement." The full text of the Riyadh Agreement can be found here: https://www.peaceagreements.org/masterdocument/2235.
47. Salisbury, "Beginning of the End of Yemen's Civil War?"
48. Ibid.
49. Jalal, "Riyadh Agreement."
50. Ibid.
51. Salisbury, "Yemen's Southern Transitional Council."
52. Al-Madhaji, "Riyadh Agreement."
53. Salisbury, *Yemen*, 32.
54. Schmitt and Worth, "With Arms for Yemen Rebels."
55. International Crisis Group, *Yemen: Is Peace Possible?*, 11.
56. United Nations Security Council Panel of Experts on Yemen, *Final Report* (2021), 26.
57. Ibid., 2.
58. Knights, "Yemen's 'Southern Hezbollah.'"
59. Ibid.
60. Ibid.
61. United Nations Verification & Inspection Mechanism for Yemen, "About UNVIM."
62. United Nations Security Council Panel of Experts on Yemen, *Final Report* (2021), 3; Faucon and Nissenbaum, "Iran Navy Port Emerges as Key."
63. Quoted Faucon and Nissenbaum, "Iran Navy Port Emerges as Key."
64. Nichols, "Exclusive."
65. World Food Programme, "Yemen Facts and Figures."
66. UNHCR, "Statement to the Security Council."
67. ACAPS, "Yemen: Global Wheat Supply Dynamics and Their Impact."
68. ACAPS, "Yemen: Al Hodeidah Fuel Import and Fuel Price Modelling."
69. Oxfam America, "Blockade and Violence in Yemen."
70. Editorial Board, "Slaughter of Children in Yemen."
71. WHO, "Yemeni Health System Crumbles."
72. Ibid.
73. Federspiel and Ali, "Cholera Outbreak in Yemen."
74. ACLED, "Battle of Hodeidah Has Started."
75. United Nations Office of the Resident Coordinator and Humanitarian Coordinator for Yemen, "Military Assault on Hodeidah," 1.
76. Salisbury, "Yemen."
77. *Saudi Press Agency*, "General" (author's translation from Arabic).
78. Human Rights Watch, "Yemen: Coalition Blockade Imperils Civilians."
79. For more detail about U.S. engagement around the cranes, see chapter 8; and for more on advocacy coalitions and the blockade, see chapter 9.
80. International Crisis Group, *Yemen: Averting a Destructive Battle.*
81. Ibid., 6.
82. Ibid.

83. Roy, "Battle of Hodeidah Has Started."
84. International Crisis Group, *Yemen: Averting a Destructive Battle*, 1.
85. United Nations Office of the Resident Coordinator and Humanitarian Coordinator for Yemen, "Military Assault on Hodeidah," 1.
86. ACLED, "Battle of Hodeidah Has Started."
87. Horton, "What the Battle for Hodeidah Means."
88. Roy, "Who Are the UAE-Backed Forces Fighting on the Western Front in Yemen?"
89. Nebehay, "Yemen Peace Talks Collapse."
90. Quoted in Carboni and D'Hauthuille, *Yemen's Urban Battleground*, 50.
91. Al Mujahed and Raghavan, "Hundreds of Thousands of Yemenis Trapped."
92. Quoted ibid.
93. Dijkstal, "Yemen and the Stockholm Agreement."
94. Office of the Special Envoy of the Secretary-General for Yemen, "Year after the Stockholm Agreement."
95. International Crisis Group, *Saving the Stockholm Agreement*, i.
96. DeLozier, "In Damning Report, UN Panel Details War Economy."
97. United Nations Security Council Panel of Experts on Yemen, *Final Report* (2021), 3.
98. World Food Programme, "WFP Demands Action."
99. Quoted ibid.
100. BBC, "Yemen's Houthis Step Back on Threats to Tax Aid."
101. *Al Jazeera*, "UN: Houthi Rebels Impeding Aid Flow."
102. Al-Shamahi, "Egregious Record."
103. Human Rights Watch, *Deadly Consequences*.
104. Ryan, "As Coronavirus Looms."
105. Carboni, "Myth of Stability."
106. United Nations Security Council Panel of Experts on Yemen, *Final Report* (2021), 17.
107. Egel et al., *Building an Enduring Peace in Yemen*, 7.
108. Carboni, "Myth of Stability."
109. Ibid.
110. Al-Dawsari, "Fantasies of State Power Cannot Solve Yemen's War."

Chapter Six. "Dumb Wars"

Epigraph: Quoted in Goldberg, "Obama Doctrine."
1. *NPR*, "Transcript: Obama's Speech against the Iraq War."
2. White House, "Remarks by the President at Cairo University, 6-04-09."
3. Black and Tran, "Barack Obama Pledges New Beginning"; Holzman, "Obama Seeks 'New Beginning.'"
4. *All Things Considered*, "Obama Speech Adviser Compares 2009 Speech."
5. Power, *Education of an Idealist*, 298.
6. Quoted in Goldberg, "Obama Doctrine."

7. Obama, "Remarks by the President."

8. Obama, *Promised Land*, 655.

9. Power, *Education of an Idealist*, 367.

10. Quoted in Goldberg, "Obama Doctrine."

11. National Security Action, "Former Senior Obama Administration Officials Call for Halt."

12. *Al Jazeera*, "Saudi and Arab Allies Bomb Houthi Positions."

13. Niarchos, "How the U.S. Is Making the War in Yemen Worse."

14. Brennan, *Undaunted*, 339.

15. White House, "Statement by NSC Spokesperson Bernadette Meehan."

16. U.S. Senate Committee on Armed Services, *Hearing to Receive Testimony on U.S. Central Command*, 612.

17. Byman, "U.S. 'Yellow Light' in Yemen."

18. Malley and Pomper, "Accomplice to Carnage."

19. Ibid.

20. Ibid.

21. Quoted in Goldberg, "Obama Doctrine." For an example of the response from the Gulf, see the op-ed in *Arab News* written by Saudi Prince Turki Al-Faisal: Al-Faisal, "Mr. Obama, We Are Not 'Free Riders.'"

22. Goldberg, "Obama Doctrine."

23. Obama, *Promised Land*, 651.

24. Rhodes, "Remarks by Deputy National Security Advisor."

25. Arms Control Association, "Timeline of Nuclear Diplomacy with Iran."

26. Cordesman, "More than Keeping Up the Façade."

27. Molavi, *Iran and the Gulf States*.

28. Stark, "Gun at a Knife Fight."

29. Quoted in Niarchos, "How the U.S. Is Making the War in Yemen Worse."

30. Quoted ibid.

31. Crowley, "Obama's Mideast 'Free Fall.'"

32. White House, "On-the-Record Conference Call."

33. Klion, "When Will Washington End the Forever War?"

34. Malley and Pomper, "Accomplice to Carnage."

35. Ibid.

36. Stewart, "Exclusive."

37. Hosenball, Stewart, and Strobel, "Exclusive."

38. White House, "Statement by NSC Spokesperson Ned Price on Reports of Civilian Deaths."

39. Walsh and Schmitt, "Arms Sales to Saudis."

40. White House, "Press Gaggle by Principal Deputy Press Secretary Eric Schultz."

41. White House, "Letter from the President."

42. Becca Wasser, author interview, July 2020, Zoom.

43. Fred Dews, "Watch: Sen. Chris Murphy on Revisiting U.S.-Saudi Relationship."

44. Niarchos, "How the U.S. Is Making the War in Yemen Worse."
45. Graham and McCain, "Statement by Senators John McCain and Lindsey Graham."
46. Taylor, "Yemen Crisis Threatens Obama Iran Nuclear Talks."
47. Oakford and Salisbury, "Yemen."
48. Rhodes, "Remarks by Deputy National Security Advisor."
49. White House, "Remarks by President Obama in Q&A with the Press."
50. Emmons, "27 U.S. Senators Rebel against Arming Saudi Arabia."
51. Sharp, Blanchard, and Collins, *Congress and the War in Yemen*, 3.
52. White House, "Press Gaggle by Press Secretary Eric Schultz."
53. See chapter 5.
54. Knights and Almeida, "Saudi-UAE War Effort in Yemen (Part 2)."
55. Kouddous, "With US Help, Saudi Arabia Is Obliterating Yemen."
56. *MSNBC*, "Secretary Kerry on Yemen Conflict."
57. Emmons, "John Kerry Gives Saudis a Big Pass."
58. Malley and Pomper, "Accomplice to Carnage."
59. Strobel and Landay, "Exclusive."
60. Niarchos, "How the U.S. Is Making the War in Yemen Worse."
61. Becca Wasser, author interview.
62. Strobel and Landay, "Exclusive."
63. Ibid.
64. Quoted in Niarchos, "How the U.S. Is Making the War in Yemen Worse."
65. Strobel and Landay, "Exclusive."
66. Quoted in Hosenball, Stewart, and Strobel, "Exclusive."
67. Niarchos, "How the U.S. Is Making the War in Yemen Worse."
68. Larry Lewis, author interview, July 2020, Zoom.
69. Ibid.
70. UNOHCHR, *Situation of Human Rights in Yemen*, 7.
71. Larry Lewis, author interview.
72. Ibid.
73. Anonymous defense analyst, author interview, 2020.
74. Larry Lewis, author interview.
75. Colville, "Press Briefing Notes on Yemen."
76. Human Rights Watch, *What Military Target Was in My Brother's House*.
77. Draper, "Tragic Civilian Toll of Airstrikes in Yemen."
78. Mundy, *Strategies of the Coalition in the Yemen War*, 18.
79. International Committee of the Red Cross, "Yemen."
80. Human Rights Watch, "Yemen: Coalition Strikes on Residence."
81. *Guardian*, "Missile Attack on Yemen Wedding Kills 131"; United Nations Secretary-General, "Statement Attributable to the Spokesman."
82. Quoted in *Guardian*, "Missile Attack on Yemen Wedding Kills 131."
83. Embassy of the Kingdom of Saudi Arabia in the United Kingdom, "Statement from the Royal Embassy."
84. Quoted in Walsh and Schmitt, "Arms Sales to Saudis."

85. Larry Lewis, author interview.
86. Ibid.
87. Anonymous defense analyst, author interview, 2020.
88. Khan, "Hidden Pentagon Records."
89. Ibid.
90. Khan and Gopal, "Uncounted."
91. Sengupta, "Pressure Mounting."
92. *Guardian*, "Saudi-Led Coalition Admits to Bombing."
93. United Nations Security Council Panel of Experts on Yemen, *Final Report* (2017), 49, 214.
94. Nichols, "Saudi Coalition Violated Law."
95. White House, "Statement by National Security Council Spokesperson Ned Price."
96. White House, "Press Briefing by Press Secretary Josh Earnest and Ben Rhodes."
97. White House, "Statement by NSC Spokesperson Ned Price on Additional U.S. Humanitarian Aid."
98. Niarchos, "How the U.S. Is Making the War in Yemen Worse."
99. Ibid.
100. Ibid.
101. Larry Lewis, author interview.
102. Quoted in Niarchos, "How the U.S. Is Making the War in Yemen Worse."
103. White House, "Statement by NSC Spokesperson Ned Price on Yemen."
104. Ryan, "With Small Changes, U.S. Maintains Military Aid."
105. Cooper, "U.S. Blocks Arms Sale to Saudi Arabia."
106. Stewart and Strobel, "U.S. to Halt Some Arms Sales to Saudi."
107. Ryan, "With Small Changes, U.S. Maintains Military Aid."
108. Sullivan, "U.S. Policy in the Arabian Peninsula."
109. Yemen Peace Project, *America's Role in Yemen 2017 and Beyond*, 9.
110. Stewart and Strobel, "U.S. to Halt Some Arms Sales to Saudi."
111. De Luce, Mcleary, and Lynch, "How the U.S. Got Dragged into Yemen."
112. Salisbury, *Yemen*, 35.
113. Ibid.
114. United Nations, "Secretary-General Appoints Ismail Ould Cheikh Ahmed."
115. Nordland, "Talks to End War in Yemen Are Suspended."
116. Salisbury, "Why US, Britain Are Key."
117. Sharp, *Yemen: Recent Attacks against U.S. Naval Vessels.*

Chapter Seven. Maximum Pressure

1. Specia and Yuhas, "Two Speeches, a Decade Apart."
2. Ibid.
3. Wolff, *Fire and Fury*, 225.

4. International Crisis Group, *Failure of U.S. "Maximum Pressure" against Iran.*
5. U.S. Department of State, "Briefing with Special Representative for Iran and Senior Advisor to the Secretary Brian Hook."
6. Schmitt, "Saudi Arabia Tries to Ease Concerns."
7. Moshashai, Leber, and Savage, "Saudi Arabia Plans for Its Economic Future."
8. Hubbard, *MBS*, 219.
9. Landler, "Saudi Prince's White House Visit."
10. Ignatius, "Saudi Crown Prince Just Made a Very Risky Power Play."
11. Wolff, *Fire and Fury*, 227.
12. Kushner, *Breaking History.*
13. Kirkpatrick et al., "Wooing of Jared Kushner."
14. Ibid.
15. Ibid.
16. Wolff, *Fire and Fury*, 229.
17. Karni, "Jared Kushner's Mission Impossible."
18. Kirkpatrick et al., "Wooing of Jared Kushner."
19. De Luce, Mcleary, and Lynch, "How the U.S. Got Dragged into Yemen."
20. Schmitt, "Saudi Arabia Tries to Ease Concerns."
21. Quoted in De Luce, Mcleary, and Lynch, "How the U.S. Got Dragged into Yemen."
22. Quoted ibid.
23. Quoted ibid. The *Atlantic* reported in December 2018 that although the Defense Department had claimed that the UAE and Saudi Arabia reimbursed the United States for the cost of aerial refueling, they had not actually been "charged adequately"; Oakford and Goodman, "U.S. Is Paying More than It Bargained For."
24. De Luce, Mcleary, and Lynch, "How the U.S. Got Dragged into Yemen."
25. Quoted in Salisbury, *Yemen*, 37.
26. Quoted in DeYoung and Ryan, "Trump Administration Weighs Deeper Involvement."
27. Yemen Data Project, "Data."
28. Quoted in De Luce, Mcleary, and Lynch, "How the U.S. Got Dragged into Yemen."
29. Savage and Schmitt, "Trump Administration Is Said to Be Working to Loosen Counterterrorism Rules."
30. Ibid.
31. Ibid.
32. Schmitt and Sanger, "Raid in Yemen."
33. White House, "President Trump Announces Iran Strategy."
34. *NPR*, "Transcript: Trump's Remarks on Iran Nuclear Deal."
35. Robert Greenway, author interview, July 2021.
36. Schenker and Satloff, "Middle East Policy from Trump to Biden."

37. Robert Greenway, author interview.
38. Ibid.
39. Ibid.
40. See, e.g., U.S. Department of State, "Iran-Backed Houthi Attacks against Saudi Arabia"; U.S. Department of State, "Iranian-Backed Houthis Sentencing 30 Political Prisoners"; U.S. Department of State, "Houthi Attack on Abha Airport."
41. U.S. Department of State, "Remarks to the Traveling Press."
42. Robert Greenway, author interview.
43. Matt Duss, author interview, October 2021, Zoom.
44. Author interviews with congressional staffers and other U.S. officials.
45. U.S. Department of State, "Senior State Department Official on Developments in Yemen."
46. Schenker and Satloff, "Middle East Policy from Trump to Biden."
47. Emmons, "U.S. Ambassador to Yemen's Hard-Line Approach."
48. Gebrekidan and Saul, "Special Report."
49. World Food Programme, "Four USAID-Funded Mobile Cranes Arrive."
50. Quoted in Sharp, *Yemen: Civil War and Regional Intervention*, 3.
51. *Reuters*, "Saudi Arabia Deposits $2 Billion"; Kalin, "Saudi-Led Coalition to Give $1.5 Billion."
52. Kirkpatrick et al., "Wooing of Jared Kushner."
53. For more on Congress's and advocates' role in this issue, see chapter 9.
54. U.S. Department of State, "U.S.-Funded Cranes Offloading Goods in Yemen."
55. Emmons, "U.S. Is Exacerbating the World's Worst Humanitarian Crisis."
56. Ibid.
57. Emmons, "U.S. Ambassador to Yemen's Hard-Line Approach."
58. Nissenbaum, "U.S. Deepens Role in Yemen Fight."
59. Ibid.
60. Ibid.
61. Author interview with a former U.S. official. For a longer analysis of Congress's role in Yemen policy, see chapter 8.
62. Robert Greenway, author interview.
63. Author interview with a former U.S. official.
64. Matt Duss, author interview.
65. Office of Congressman Ro Khanna, "US Aerial Support for Saudi-Led Campaign"; Michaels, "U.S. Military Refueling Saudi Planes."
66. Michaels, "U.S. Military Refueling Saudi Planes."
67. Kate Kizer, author interview, July 2021, Zoom.
68. Oakford and Goodman, "U.S. Is Paying More than It Bargained For."
69. Oakford, "U.S. Doubled Fuel Support."
70. *CSPAN*, "User Clip."
71. Oakford, "U.S. Military Can't Keep Track."
72. Gould, "US to Bill UAE, Saudi Arabia."

73. *Security Council Report*, "Penholders and Chairs."
74. Cumming-Bruce, "In a Compromise, U.N. Rights Experts Will Examine Abuses."
75. Office of the Director of National Intelligence, *Assessing the Saudi Government's Role in the Killing of Jamal Khashoggi.*
76. Hubbard, *MBS*, 271.
77. Ibid.
78. Stewart, "U.S. Halting Refueling."
79. Harb, "Pompeo's Departing Sabotage in Yemen."
80. Schwartz and Lang, "Six Reasons."
81. Schenker and Satloff, "Middle East Policy from Trump to Biden."
82. Miller, "Biden Revokes Terrorist Designation."

Chapter Eight. Congress and the Yemen Advocacy Coalition

1. Kate Gould, author interview, June 2021, Zoom.
2. Author interview with anonymous House staffer, 2021.
3. Silverstein, "Behind the Cover."
4. Boone and McElwee, "On Yemen, the Right Choice Is the Popular One."
5. Author interviews, 2021.
6. Emmons, Chavez, and Lacy, "Joe Biden."
7. White House, "Remarks by President Biden."
8. Author interviews, 2021.
9. Stark, "Mohammed bin Salman's Collapsing Coalition."
10. Fearon, "Signaling Foreign Policy Interests."
11. Sharp, Blanchard, and Collins, *Congress and the War in Yemen*, 11.
12. Democratic Party, "2020 Democratic Platform."
13. Picard, "About Layla."
14. Eric Eikenberry, author interview, July 2021.
15. Picard, "About Layla."
16. Oxfam America, "Blockade and Violence in Yemen."
17. Scott Paul, author interview, July 2021.
18. O'Brien, "Yemen Doesn't Need the Obama Administration's 'Deep Concern.'"
19. Ibid.
20. Aisha Jumaan, author interview, October 2021.
21. Ibid.
22. Mercer, Jumaan, and Kimball, "Why Are We Waging War on the People of Yemen?"
23. Author interviews.
24. Scott Paul, author interview.
25. Fahim, "Saudis Face Mounting Pressure."
26. Lieu, letter to Honorable Ashton Carter and John F. Kerry.
27. Zornick, "Why Is the United States Risking Involvement?"

28. Newton, "Assessment of the Legality of Arms Sales," 22–23.

29. Sharp, Blanchard, and Collins, *Congress and the War in Yemen*, 3.

30. Quoted in Warikoo, "Yemeni-Americans Stuck in Yemen."

31. Stark, *Managing U.S. Security Partnerships*.

32. Ibid., 26.

33. The rules of privilege around joint resolutions of disapproval of arms sales are a bit more complicated on the House side.

34. Saturno, *Privileged Business on the House Floor*.

35. Author interviews.

36. Sharp, Blanchard, and Collins, *Congress and the War in Yemen*, 3.

37. Ibid., 4.

38. Ibid., 52.

39. Ibid., 5.

40. Kate Gould, author interview.

41. Barrett, "Senate Rejects Bid to Block US-Saudi Arabia Arms Deal."

42. Quoted in Beauchamp, "Why the Hell Is the US Helping Saudi Arabia Bomb Yemen?"

43. Editorial Board, "America Is Complicit in the Carnage in Yemen."

44. Beauchamp, "Why the Hell Is the US Helping Saudi Arabia Bomb Yemen?"

45. Vlahos, "Critics Try."

46. Kate Gould, author interview.

47. Ibid.

48. S.J.Res.39, A joint resolution relating to the disapproval of the proposed foreign military sale to the Government of the Kingdom of Saudi Arabia of M1A1/A2 Abrams Tank structures and other major defense equipment, 114th Congress (2015–16); and S.J.Res.42, A joint resolution relating to the disapproval of the proposed export to the Government of the Kingdom of Saudi Arabia of certain defense articles, 115th Congress (2017–18), respectively.

49. Author interviews.

50. Author interviews.

51. Elbagir, Abdelaziz, and Smith-Spark, "Made in America."

52. Kate Gould, author interview.

53. Matt Duss, author interview, October 2021, Zoom.

54. Author interviews.

55. Author interviews.

56. Kizer, "Hitting Iran Where It Doesn't Hurt."

57. Author interviews.

58. Hurlburt and Polimedio, *Can Transpartisan Coalitions Overcome Polarization?*, 2.

59. Paul and Khanna, "Case for Restraint."

60. Geo Saba, author interview, August 2021.

61. Kelety, "Can Sarah Smith Be Seattle's Alexandria Ocasio-Cortez?"

62. Grim, "Primaries Matter."
63. Ibid.
64. Ibid.; Smith, "HASC Ranking Member Adam Smith."
65. Matt Duss, author interview.
66. Author interview with anonymous congressional staffer, 2021.
67. Kate Kizer, author interview.
68. Cornell Law School, "War Powers."
69. Weed, *War Powers Resolution*.
70. See ibid., 6–9.
71. First War Powers Act, 50a U.S.C. §§ 601–622 (1946).
72. Weed, *War Powers Resolution*, 5.
73. Corey Jacobson, author interview, September 2021.
74. Author interviews.
75. Office of Congressman Mark Pocan, "Bipartisan Effort."
76. Directing the President Pursuant to Section 5(c) of the War Powers Resolution to Remove United States Armed Forces from Unauthorized Hostilities in the Republic of Yemen, H.Con.Res.81, 115th Cong. (2017–2018), https://www.congress.gov/bill/115th-congress/house-concurrent-resolution/81.
77. Expressing the Sense of the House of Representatives with Respect to United States Policy towards Yemen, and for Other Purposes, H.Res.599, 115th Cong. (2017–2018), https://www.congress.gov/bill/115th-congress/house-resolution/599.
78. Geo Saba, author interview.
79. Kate Gould, author interview.
80. Castle, Letter to Honorable Mitchell "Mitch" McConnell.
81. Hathaway and Haviland, "Legality of U.S. Support."
82. Quoted in Bridgeman, *War Powers Resolution Reporting*, 30.
83. Khanna, Pocan, and Jones, "Stop the Unconstitutional War in Yemen."
84. A Joint Resolution to Direct the Removal of United States Armed Forces from Hostilities in the Republic of Yemen That Have Not Been Authorized by Congress, S.J.Res.54, 115th Cong. (2017–2018), https://www.congress.gov/bill/115th-congress/senate-joint-resolution/54/text/is.
85. Geo Saba, author interview.
86. Matt Duss, author interview.
87. Goodman, "Annotation of Sec. Pompeo's Certification of Yemen War."
88. Author interviews.
89. Certification under Section 1290 of the John S. McCain National Defense Authorization Act for Fiscal Year 2019 (DIV A, P.L. 115-232) Related to Military Assistance for Saudi Arabia and the United Arab Emirates.
90. Author interviews.
91. Goodman, "Annotation of Sec. Pompeo's Certification of Yemen War."
92. Quoted in Nissenbaum, "Top U.S. Diplomat Backed Continuing Support."
93. Author interviews.

94. Author interviews.
95. Ruffalo, Twitter post.
96. Author interviews.
97. Booker, "Who Is the Senate Parliamentarian?"
98. H.J.Res.37, Directing the removal of United States Armed Forces from hostilities in the Republic of Yemen that have not been authorized by Congress, 116th Congress (2019–20).
99. Nelson, "Trump's First Veto Averted."
100. Ackerman, "Bernie Sanders Moves to Rescue Yemen Withdrawal."
101. U.S. Senate, "Vetoes by President Donald J. Trump."
102. Cooper, "Senate Narrowly Backs Trump Weapons Sale."
103. Menendez, Letter to Honorable Michael Pompeo and Honorable James Mattis.
104. Sharp, Blanchard, and Collins, *Congress and the War in Yemen*, 16.
105. Ibid., 16–17.
106. Edmondson, "Senate Fails to Override Trump's Veto."
107. Edmondson, "Ousted Watchdog Says State Dept. Official Pressured Him."
108. Ibid; Verma and Wong, "Another Inspector General Resigns."
109. U.S. House of Representatives, Foreign Affairs Committee, "Engel Releases Witness Affidavit."
110. Spindel, "Beyond Military Power."
111. Author interview.
112. Young, "Young Continues to Press Saudi Government."
113. Anonymous, author interview.
114. Jim Cason, author interview, July 2021.
115. Sharp, Blanchard, and Collins, *Congress and the War in Yemen*, 9.
116. Kate Gould, author interview.
117. Author interviews.
118. U.S. Department of State, "Deputy Secretary Sullivan's Meeting on Yemen."
119. Author interview.
120. U.S. Department of State, Twitter post.
121. Anonymous Trump administration official, author interview.
122. U.S. Department of State, "Ending the Conflict in Yemen."
123. United States Institute of Peace, "James Mattis: Yemen Needs a Truce."
124. Salisbury, "Making Yemen's Hodeida Deal Stick."
125. Ibid.
126. See, e.g., DeLozier, "UAE Drawdown May Isolate Saudi Arabia in Yemen"; Knights, *"Miss Me Yet?"*
127. Anonymous Trump administration official, author interview.
128. Walsh and Kirkpatrick, "U.A.E. Pulls Most Forces."
129. Yemen Data Project, "Data."
130. Author interview.

Chapter Nine. The Biden Administration

Epigraph: White House, "Remarks by President Biden."

1. Ibid.
2. Ibid.
3. Hansler, "Biden Administration to Remove Houthis."
4. Foran, "Lawmakers Call Biden's Yemen Policy a 'Historic Shift.'"
5. Ward, "US May Still Be Helping Saudi Arabia."
6. White House, "Remarks by President Biden."
7. Kirby, "Defense Department Briefing."
8. Defense Security Cooperation Agency, "Saudi Arabia—GBU-39"; Mcleary, "State Dept. Pauses New Arms Exports."
9. Gould and Mehta, "Boeing, Raytheon Missile Sales."
10. *Reuters* and Zengerle, "Biden Administration Proceeding."
11. Ward, "US May Still Be Helping Saudi Arabia."
12. Lenderking, "Special Briefing via Telephone."
13. Defense Security Cooperation Agency, "Saudi Arabia—AIM-120C."
14. Whitson, "Congress Must Halt Biden's Arms Sales."
15. Executive Office of the President, "Statement of Administration Policy."
16. Desiderio, "Senate Backs Biden Admin Weapons Sale to Saudi Arabia."
17. Mezher, "Why Biden White House Lifted Arms Sales Freeze."
18. Quoted in Office of Senator Elizabeth Warren, "Warren, Colleagues to Biden Admin."
19. Al-Dawsari, Twitter post.
20. Naar and Elkatouri, "Full Text of Saudi Arabia's New Peace Initiative."
21. El Yaakoubi, "End of Yemen Quagmire?"
22. Quoted in Al-Shamahi, "Bitter Pill to Swallow."
23. Al Ansary, Motevalli, and Fattah, "Iraq Brings Saudi and Iran Closer."
24. *Reuters*, "Saudi Confirms First Round of Talks."
25. Quoted in Al Ansary, Motevalli, and Fattah, "Iraq Brings Saudi and Iran Closer."
26. Ibid.
27. Goldberg, "Saudi Crown Prince."
28. Quoted in Gambrell, "US Pulls Missile Defenses."
29. Quoted in Holleis, "Why Saudi-Iran Relations Are Thawing."
30. Ibid.
31. Aisha Jumaan, author interview, October 2021.
32. International Crisis Group, *After al-Bayda*.
33. O'Grady and Al-Mujahed, "Battle for the Badlands."
34. Baron, *Marib Paradox*.
35. Human Rights Watch, "Yemen: Houthis Attacking Displaced People's Camps."
36. International Organization for Migration, "Thousands of People Forced to Flee."

37. O'Grady and Al-Mujahed, "Battle for the Badlands."
38. Johnsen, "How the U.S. Can Create Leverage."
39. Fearon, "Why Do Some Civil Wars Last So Much Longer than Others?," 297.
40. Walter, "Critical Barrier to Civil War Settlement," 335–336.
41. Stedman, "Spoiler Problems in Peace Processes."
42. Savun, "Information, Bias, and Mediation Success"; Kydd, "Which Side Are You On?"
43. Matt Duss, author interview, October 2021, Zoom.
44. Geo Saba, author interview, August 2021.

Chapter Ten. Lessons Learned

1. Robinson, "SOF's Evolving Role."
2. U.S. Department of State, *United States Strategy*.
3. United States Institute of Peace, "Global Fragility Act."
4. Krause, Krause, and Bränfors, "Women's Participation"; Nilsson, "Anchoring the Peace."
5. Autesserre, *Frontlines of Peace*.
6. Peace Track Initiative, *Feminist Peace Roadmap*.
7. International Crisis Group, *Case for More Inclusive—and More Effective—Peacemaking in Yemen*.
8. Ibid.
9. Rajaa and Schmid, "Two Top Diplomats."
10. Ibid.
11. Mutaher, *Yemen's New Networks*, 13.
12. International Crisis Group, *Rethinking Peace in Yemen*.
13. Salisbury, "New UN Envoy."
14. Ibid.
15. Office of the Special Envoy of the Secretary-General for Yemen, "US Special Envoy Hans Grundberg."
16. International Crisis Group, *Case for More Inclusive—and More Effective—Peacemaking in Yemen*.
17. Al-Dawsari, *Peacebuilding in the Time of War*, 5.
18. Reilly, "Elections in Post-conflict Scenarios"; Lyons, "Post-conflict Elections."
19. Farea al-Muslimi, author interview, January 2021, Zoom.
20. Al-Mowafak, "For Sustainable Peace."
21. Mwatana for Human Rights, "Civil Society Groups Seek Urgent UN Action."
22. Radhya Al-Mutawakel, author interview.
23. Ibid.
24. UNOHCHR, "Statement by Group of Experts."
25. Amnesty International, "Yemen."

26. *Deutsche Welle*, "UN Human Rights Council Votes."
27. Boutton, "Of Terrorism and Revenue."
28. Cronin, "Why Drones Fail."
29. Khan, "Hidden Pentagon Records."
30. Blinken, "United States Announces Additional Humanitarian Assistance."
31. UNOCHA, "Yemen 2020."
32. ForeignAssistance.gov, "U.S. Foreign Assistance by Country."
33. Summer Nasser, author interview, October 2021, Zoom.
34. Baladauf, *Reframing Famine.*
35. Sana'a Center, *Increasing the Effectiveness of the Humanitarian Response*, 3.
36. Baladauf, *Reframing Famine.*
37. Ibid.
38. Wood, Huddleston, and Ghoorhoo, "Best Way to Help Yemenis Survive."
39. Orkaby, "Benefiting from the Misery of Others."
40. Al-Akhali, "Yemen's Most Pressing Problem Isn't War."
41. The budget that is actually enacted is passed by Congress and signed into law by the president, so there is often a difference between the levels of funding requested by a president and the size of any actual budget item. Nevertheless, the president's budget request is "one of the foundational documents" of a president's agenda, "and an early indication of [an] administration's global priorities and approach"; Binder, *Back to Business as Usual*, 4.
42. Ibid., 2.
43. Schwartzstein, "Bringing the Natural World into America's Middle East Policy."
44. Lackner and Al-Eryani, *Yemen's Environmental Crisis.*
45. Schwartzstein, "Bringing the Natural World into America's Middle East Policy."
46. Ibid.
47. Ward, "Why the US Won't Break Up with Saudi Arabia."
48. Yousef Assabahi, author interview, October 2021.
49. Farea al-Muslimi, author interview.
50. Yousef Assabahi, author interview.
51. Mariam Al-Dhubhani, author interview, October 2021.
52. Alley, "Tracking the 'Arab Spring,'" 74.
53. Ibid.
54. Salisbury, *Yemen*, 8.
55. Johnsen, "Grand Bargain for Yemen."
56. Ibid.
57. Alley, "Tracking the 'Arab Spring,'" 74.

Epilogue

1. Office of the Special Envoy of the Secretary-General for Yemen, "Press Statement."

2. *Guardian*, "John Kerry Says Yemen's Houthis and Saudi Coalition Agree."
3. Office of the Special Envoy of the Secretary-General for Yemen, "Timeline."
4. ACLED, "Violence in Yemen."
5. Office of the Special Envoy of the Secretary-General for Yemen, "Timeline."
6. Office of the Special Envoy of the Secretary-General for Yemen, "Briefing to the United Nations Security Council."
7. Sana'a Center, "Govt Pushes Ahead with Terrorism Designation."
8. Stark, "Can the Riyadh Reshuffle Bring Peace to Yemen?"
9. Sana'a Center, "Govt Pushes Ahead with Terrorism Designation."
10. Magdy, "UN Raises $1.2 Billion for Yemen Humanitarian Crisis."
11. Blinken, "Additional Humanitarian Assistance."

Bibliography

Abboud, Samer Nassif. *Syria*. Cambridge, UK: Polity, 2015.

Abdullah, Khaled, and Mohammed Ghobari. "Thousands March in Yemen to Demand Change of Government." *Reuters*, January 27, 2011.

Aboudi, Sami. "UAE Says Sees Systematic Iranian Meddling in Yemen, Region." *Reuters*, April 8, 2015.

Aboueldahab, Noha. *Transitional Justice and the Prosecution of Political Leaders in the Arab Region: A Comparative Study of Egypt, Libya, Tunisia and Yemen*. London: Hart, 2017.

ACAPS. "Yemen: Al Hodeidah Fuel Import and Fuel Price Modelling." April 4, 2022.

ACAPS. "Yemen: Global Wheat Supply Dynamics and Their Impact." August 25, 2022.

Ackerman, Spencer. "Bernie Sanders Moves to Rescue Yemen Withdrawal after House Screwed It Up." *The Daily Beast*, February 26, 2019.

ACLED (Armed Conflict Location & Event Data Project). "The Battle of Hodeidah Has Started." June 21, 2018.

ACLED (Armed Conflict Location & Event Data Project). "Violence in Yemen during the UN-Mediate Truce: April–October 2022." October 14, 2022.

ACLU. "Al-Aulaqi v. Panetta—Constitutional Challenge to Killing of Three U.S. Citizens." June 4, 2014. https://www.aclu.org/cases/al-aulaqi-v-pane tta-constitutional-challenge-killing-three-us-citizens.

Advani, Rohan. *Constructing Commercial Empire: The United Arab Emirates in the Red Sea and the Horn*. Washington, DC: Century Foundation, 2019.

Akbarzadeh, Shahram, and Dara Conduit. "Future Prospects." In *Iran in the World: President Rouhani's Foreign Policy*, edited by Shahram Akbarzadeh and Dara Conduit, 177–181. London: Palgrave Macmillan, 2016.

Akbarzadeh, Shahram, and Dara Conduit. "Rouhani's First Two Years in Office: Opportunities and Risks in Contemporary Iran." In *Iran in the World:*

President Rouhani's Foreign Policy, edited by Shahram Akbarzadeh and Dara Conduit, 1–15. London: Palgrave Macmillan, 2016.

Al-Akhali, Rafat. "Yemen's Most Pressing Problem Isn't War. It's the Economy." *Foreign Policy*, October 8, 2021.

Al Ansary, Khalid, Golnar Motevalli, and Zainab Fattah. "Iraq Brings Saudi and Iran Closer as Biden Resets Policy." *Bloomberg*, May 7, 2021.

Al Arabiya. "GCC Troops Dispatched to Bahrain to Maintain Order." March 14, 2011.

Al-Dawsari, Nadwa. "Fantasies of State Power Cannot Solve Yemen's War." Century Foundation, July 13, 2021.

Al-Dawsari, Nadwa. *Peacebuilding in the Time of War: Tribal Cease-Fire and De-escalation*. Washington, DC: Middle East Institute, 2021.

Al-Dawsari, Nadwa. Twitter post. February 6, 2021, 6:32 a.m. https://twitter .com/ndawsari/status/1358015813635211264?lang=en.

Al-Enazy, Askar Halwan. "'The International Boundary Treaty' (Treaty of Jeddah) Concluded between the Kingdom of Saudi Arabia and the Yemeni Republic on June 12, 2000." *American Journal of International Law* 96, no. 1 (2002): 161–173.

Al-Faisal, Turki. "Mr. Obama, We Are Not 'Free Riders.'" *Arab News*, March 14, 2016.

Al Jazeera. "Battle for Aden: Who Is Fighting Who and How Things Got Here." August 29, 2019.

Al Jazeera. "Reports: Saleh Refuses to Sign Exit Deal." April 30, 2011.

Al Jazeera. "Saudi and Arab Allies Bomb Houthi Positions in Yemen." March 26, 2015.

Al Jazeera. "Saudi Oil Attack: All the Latest Updates." September 30, 2019.

Al Jazeera. "UN: Houthi Rebels Impeding Aid Flow in Yemen." February 19, 2020.

Alley, April Longley. "Shifting Light in the Qamariyya: The Reinvention of Patronage Networks in Contemporary Yemen." PhD diss., Georgetown University, 2008.

Alley, April Longley. "Tracking the 'Arab Spring': Yemen Changes Everything . . . and Nothing." *Journal of Democracy* 24, no. 4 (2013): 74–85.

Alley, April Longley. "Yemen on the Brink." *Foreign Affairs*, April 4, 2011.

Alley, April Longley. "Yemen's Multiple Crises." *Journal of Democracy* 21, no. 4 (2010): 72–86.

All Things Considered. "Obama Speech Adviser Compares 2009 Speech in Cairo with Pompeo's Address." NPR, January 11, 2019.

Al-Madhaji, Maged. "The Riyadh Agreement: Saudi Arabia Takes the Helm in Southern Yemen." Sana'a Center for Strategic Studies, November 5, 2019.

Almasmari, Hakim. "More Protests Demand Ouster of Yemen's Leader." *CNN*, September 9, 2011.

Almasmari, Hakim. "Yemen Imposes State of Emergency after Deadly Attack on Protesters." *Washington Post*, March 18, 2011.

Almezaini, Khalid S. *The UAE and Foreign Policy: Foreign Aid, Identities and Interests*. London: Routledge, 2012.

Al-Mowafak, Hadil. "For Sustainable Peace, Human Rights Must Be Front and Center of Yemen's Peace Process." Yemen Policy Center, November 15, 2021. https://www.yemenpolicy.org/for-sustainable-peace-human-rights-must-be-front-and-center-of-yemens-peace-process/.

Al-Mowafak, Hadil. "Yemen's Political Activists Find New Spaces for Mobilization." Italian Institute for International Political Studies, March 26, 2021. https://www.ispionline.it/en/publication/yemens-political-activists-find-new-spaces-mobilization-29776.

Al Mujahed, Ali, and Sudarsan Raghavan. "Hundreds of Thousands of Yemenis Trapped as Fighting Escalates in Strategic Port City." *Washington Post*, November 8, 2018.

Al-Muslimi, Farea. Testimony in *Drone Wars: The Constitutional and Counterterrorism Implications of Targeted Killing: Hearing before the Subcommittee on the Constitution, Civil Rights and Human Rights of the Committee on the Judiciary, United States Senate*. 113th Cong., 1st sess. (April 23, 2013).

Al-Rashed, Abdulrahman. "Al-Tadkheel fi al-Yemen minah al-kartha / The Intervention in Yemen Prevented a Disaster." *Asharq al-Awsat*, March 27, 2015. Translation by the author.

Al-Shamahi, Abubakr. "'Bitter Pill to Swallow': Saudis Grapple with Yemen Peace Deal." *Al Jazeera*, June 29, 2021.

Al-Shamahi, Abubakr. "'Egregious Record': Yemen's Houthis Denounced for Blocking Aid." *Al Jazeera*, September 14, 2020.

Amnesty International. "Yemen: UN Human Rights Council Member States' Abject Failure to Renew Yemen Investigation Is a Wake-Up Call." October 13, 2021.

Arab Barometer. "Data Analysis Tool." Accessed September 27, 2021. https://www.arabbarometer.org/survey-data/data-analysis-tool/.

Ardemagni, Eleanora, and Raiman Al-Hamdani. *Yemen: The GPC and Islah after 2011*. Milan: Institute for International Political Studies, 2021.

Arms Control Association. "Timeline of Nuclear Diplomacy with Iran." October 2021.

Autesserre, Séverine. *The Frontlines of Peace: An Insider's Guide to Changing the World*. New York: Oxford University Press, 2021.

Baladauf, Maia. *Reframing Famine: New Approaches and Food System Accountability in Yemen*. Sana'a, Yemen: Sana'a Center for Strategic Studies.

Barker, Anne. "US Rachets Up Pressure on Yemen's President." *ABC News*, April 4, 2011.

Baron, Adam. "Despite the War, Yemenis Still Crave Dignity, Justice, and the Rule of Law." *Newlines Magazine*, March 2, 2021.

Baron, Adam. *Mapping the Yemen Conflict*. Berlin: European Council on Foreign Relations, 2015.

Baron, Adam. *The Marib Paradox: How One Province Succeeds in the Midst of Yemen's War*. Berlin: European Council on Foreign Relations, 2018.

Baron, Adam. *Yemen's Forgotten War: How Europe Can Lay the Foundations for Peace*. Berlin: European Council on Foreign Relations, December 20, 2016.

Barrett, Ted. "Senate Rejects Bid to Block US-Saudi Arabia Arms Deal." *CNN*, September 21, 2016.

BBC. "Obituary: Anwar al-Awlaki." September 30, 2011.

BBC. "Yemen: President Saleh Injured in Attack on Palace." June 3, 2011.

BBC. "Yemen's Houthis Step Back on Threats to Tax Aid." February 14, 2020.

Beauchamp, Zach. "Why the Hell Is the US Helping Saudi Arabia Bomb Yemen? A Brief Guide." *Vox*, October 14, 2016.

Bergen, Peter, David Sterman, and Melissa Salyk-Virk. "America's Counterterrorism Wars." New America, June 17, 2021. https://www.newamerica.org/international-security/reports/americas-counterterrorism-wars/the-war-in-yemen/#us-drone-strikes-in-yemen.

Binder, Seth. *Back to Business as Usual: President Biden's First Foreign Affairs Budget for the Middle East and North Africa*. Washington, DC: Project on Middle East Democracy, 2021.

Black, Ian, and Mark Tran. "Barack Obama Pledges New Beginning between US and Muslims." *The Guardian*, June 4, 2009.

Blanga, Yehuda U. "Saudi Arabia's Motives in the Syrian Civil War." *Middle East Policy Council Journal* 24, no. 4 (Winter 2017).

Blinken, Antony. "Additional Humanitarian Assistance for the People of Yemen." U.S. Department of State, February 27, 2023.

Blinken, Antony. "United States Announces Additional Humanitarian Assistance for the People of Yemen." U.S. State Department, September 22, 2021.

Bonnefoy, Laurent. "Sunni Islamist Dynamics in Context of War: What Happened to al-Islah and the Salafis?" In *Politics, Governance, and Reconstruction in Yemen*, edited by Stacey Philbrick Yadav and Marc Lynch, 23–26. Washington, DC: POMEPS, 2018.

Booker, Brakkton. "Who Is the Senate Parliamentarian Who Ruled against a Minimum Wage Increase?" *NPR*, February 26, 2021.

Boone, Jeb, and Sean McElwee. "On Yemen, the Right Choice Is the Popular One." *Fellow Travelers Blog*, December 5, 2018.

Boucek, Christopher. *War in Saada: From Local Insurrection to National Challenge*. Washington, DC: Carnegie Endowment for International Peace, 2010.

Boutton, Andrew. "Of Terrorism and Revenue: Why Foreign Aid Exacerbates Terrorism in Personalist Regimes." *Conflict Management and Peace Science* 36, no. 4 (2016).

Brandt, Marieke. "The Hidden Realities behind Saudi Arabia's Operation Decisive Storm in Yemen." *Focal Blog*, May 15, 2015, http://www.focaalblog.com/2015/05/15/marieke-brandt-the-hidden-realities-behind-saudi-arabias-operation-decisive-storm-in-yemen/.

Brandt, Marieke. *Tribes and Politics in Yemen: A History of the Houthi Conflict.* London: Hurst, 2017.

Brehony, Noel. *Yemen Divided: The Story of a Failed State in South Arabia.* New York: I. B. Tauris, 2013.

Brennan, John O. *Undaunted: My Fight against America's Enemies, at Home and Abroad.* New York: Celadon Books, 2020.

Bridgeman, Tess. *War Powers Resolution Reporting: Presidential Practice and the Use of Armed Forces Abroad, 1973–2019.* New York: Reiss Center on Law and Security, NYU Law School, January 2020.

Bronner, Ethan, and Michael Slackman. "Saudi Troops Enter Bahrain to Help Put Down Unrest." *New York Times*, March 14, 2011.

Broomhall, Elizabeth. "Arab Spring Has Cost Gulf Arab States $150bn." *Arabian Business*, September 8, 2011.

Bruce, Mary, and Jonathan Karl. "White House Continues to Back Yemen as Model for Successful Counterterrorism." *ABC News*, March 25, 2015.

Byman, Daniel. "Confronting Iran." *Survival* 60, no. 1 (2018): 107–128.

Byman, Daniel. "The U.S. 'Yellow Light' in Yemen." Brookings Institute, August 3, 2018.

Carboni, Andrea. "The Myth of Stability: Infighting and Repression in Houthi-Controlled Territories." Armed Conflict Location & Event Data Project, February 9, 2021.

Carboni, Andrea, and Valentin D'Hauthuille. *Yemen's Urban Battlegrounds: Violence and Politics in Sana'a, Aden, Ta'izz and Hodeidah.* Madison, WI: Armed Conflict Location & Event Data Project, 2018.

Castle, William S., General Counsel of the Department of Defense. Letter to Honorable Mitchell "Mitch" McConnell. February 27, 2018. Accessed at House Foreign Affairs Committee website, https://foreignaffairs.house.gov/wp-content/uploads/2019/02/02-27-2018-Acting-GC-re-Yemen-Joint-Res.pdf.

CBS News. "Saudi King Orders Troops to Join Yemen Campaign." April 21, 2015.

Chandraeskaran, Rajiv. "In the UAE, the United States Has a Quiet, Potent Ally Nicknamed 'Little Sparta.'" *Washington Post*, November 9, 2014.

Clark, Victoria, *Yemen: Dancing on the Heads of Snakes.* New Haven, CT: Yale University Press, 2010.

Clinton, Hillary. *Hard Choices.* New York: Simon and Schuster, 2014.

Clinton, Hillary. "Ongoing Situation in Yemen." U.S. Department of State, May 22, 2011.

Colville, Rupert (spokesperson for the United Nations High Commissioner for Human Rights). "Press Briefing Notes on Yemen, Central African Republican and Escalating Tensions in East Jerusalem and West Bank."

United Nations Office of the High Commissioner for Human Rights, September 29, 2015.

Cook, Joana. *A Woman's Place: US Counterterrorism since 9/11*. New York: Oxford University Press, 2020.

Cooper, Helene. "Senate Narrowly Backs Trump Weapons Sale to Saudi Arabia." *New York Times*, June 13, 2017.

Cooper, Helene. "U.S. Blocks Arms Sale to Saudi Arabia amid Concerns over Yemen War." *New York Times*, December 13, 2016.

Cooper, Helene, and Robert F. Worth. "In Arab Spring, Obama Finds a Sharp Test." *New York Times*, September 24, 2012.

Cordesman, Anthony H. "More than Keeping Up the Façade: The U.S.-GCC Summit at Camp David." Center for Strategic and International Studies, May 15, 2015.

Cordesman, Anthony H., Alexander Wilner, Michael Gibbs, and Scott Modell. *US-Iranian Competition: The Gulf Military Balance—I: The Conventional and Asymmetric Dimensions*. Washington, DC: Center for Strategic and International Studies, 2013.

Cornell Law School. "War Powers." Accessed October 26, 2020. https://www.law.cornell.edu/wex/war_powers.

Cronin, Audrey Kurth. "Why Drones Fail: When Tactics Drive Strategy." *Foreign Affairs*, July–August 2013.

Crowley, Michael. "Obama's Mideast 'Free Fall.'" *Politico*, March 26, 2015.

Crowley, Michael. "'We Caved.'" *Politico*, January 7, 2016.

CSPAN. "User Clip: Elizabeth Warren Questions Gen. Joseph Votel on Yemen Targeting." Video, March 13, 2018. https://www.c-span.org/video/?c4718581/user-clip-elizabeth-warren-questions-gen-joseph-votel-yemen-targeting.

Cumming-Bruce, Nick. "In a Compromise, U.N. Rights Experts Will Examine Abuses in Yemen's War." *New York Times*, September 29, 2017.

Daragahi, Borzou, and Noah Browning. "Tens of Thousands Turn Out for Rival Rallies in Yemen." *Los Angeles Times*, February 3, 2011.

Day, Stephen W. "The 'Non-Conclusion' of Yemen's National Dialogue." *Foreign Policy*, January 27, 2014.

Day, Stephen W. *The Political Challenge of Yemen's Southern Movement*. Washington, DC: Carnegie Endowment for International Peace, 2010.

Day, Stephen W. *Regionalism and Rebellion in Yemen: A Troubled National Union*. New York: Cambridge University Press, 2012.

Defense Security Cooperation Agency. "Saudi Arabia—AIM-120C Advanced Medium Range Air-to-Air Missiles (AMRAAM)." November 4, 2021.

Defense Security Cooperation Agency. "Saudi Arabia—GBU-39 Small Diameter Bomb I (SDB I) Munitions." December 29, 2020.

DeLozier, Elana. "In Damning Report, UN Panel Details War Economy in Yemen." Washington Institute for Near East Policy, January 25, 2019.

DeLozier, Elana. "UAE Drawdown May Isolate Saudi Arabia in Yemen." Washington Institute for Middle East Peace, July 2, 2019.

DeLozier, Elana. "Yemen Matrix: Allies and Adversaries." Washington Institute for Near East Policy, September 17, 2020. https://www.washington institute.org/policy-analysis/yemen-matrix-allies-adversaries.

De Luce, Dan, Paul Mcleary, and Colum Lynch. "How the U.S. Got Dragged into Yemen." *Foreign Policy*, December 11, 2017.

Democratic Party. "The 2020 Democratic Platform." Accessed October 19, 2021. https://democrats.org/where-we-stand/party-platform/.

Dergham, Raghida. "'Decisive Storm' Responds to Iran's Encroachment on Saudi Borders." *Al Arabiya*, March 30, 2015.

Desiderio, Andrew. "Senate Backs Biden Admin Weapons Sale to Saudi Arabia." *Politico*, December 7, 2021.

Des Roches, D. B. "The Prize Deferred: Stumbling toward Hodeidah." Arab Gulf States Institute in Washington, March 31, 2017.

Deutsche Welle. "UN Human Rights Council Votes to End Yemen War Crimes Inquiry." October 7, 2021.

Dews, Fred. "Watch: Sen. Chris Murphy on Revisiting U.S.-Saudi Relationship." Brookings Institution, April 22, 2016.

DeYoung, Karen, and Missy Ryan. "Trump Administration Weighs Deeper Involvement in Yemen War." *Washington Post*, March 26, 2017.

Dijkstal, Haydee. "Yemen and the Stockholm Agreement: Background, Context, and the Significance of the Agreement." *American Society of International Law* 25, no. 5 (2019).

Draper, Lucy. "The Tragic Civilian Toll of Airstrikes in Yemen." *Newsweek*, October 12, 2015.

Dresch, Paul. *A History of Modern Yemen*. New York: Cambridge University Press, 2001.

Durac, Vincent. "The Joint Meeting Parties and the Politics of Opposition in Yemen." *British Journal of Middle Eastern Studies* 38, no. 3 (2011): 343–365.

Durant, T. Clark, and Michael Weintraub. "How to Make Democracy Self-Enforcing after Civil War: Enabling Credible yet Adaptable Elite Pacts." *Conflict Management and Peace Science* 31, no. 5 (2014): 521–540.

Editorial Board. "America Is Complicit in the Carnage in Yemen." *New York Times*, August 17, 2016. https://www.nytimes.com/2016/08/17/opinion/stop-saudi-arms-sales-until-carnage-in-yemen-ends.html.

Editorial Board. "The Slaughter of Children in Yemen." *New York Times*, August 25, 2017.

Edmonson, Catie. "Ousted Watchdog Says State Dept. Official Pressured Him to End Investigation into Pompeo." *New York Times*, June 3, 2020.

Edmonson, Catie. "Senate Fails to Override Trump's Veto on Saudi Arms Sales." *New York Times*, July 29, 2019.

Egel, Daniel, Trevor Johnston, Ashley L. Rhoades, and Eric Robinson. *Building an Enduring Peace in Yemen: Lessons from Five Years of RAND Research*. Santa Monica, CA: RAND, 2021.

Elbagir, Nima, Salma Abdelaziz, Ryan Browne, Barbara Arvanitidis, and Laura Smith-Spark. "Bomb That Killed 40 Children in Yemen Was Supplied by the US." *CNN*, August 17, 2018.

Elbagir, Nima, Salma Abdelaziz, and Laura Smith-Spark. "Made in America." *CNN*, September 2018.

El Yaakoubi, Aziz. "End of Yemen Quagmire? Saudi-Led Coalition, Houthis Near Peace Deal." *Reuters*, June 21, 2021.

Embassy of the Kingdom of Saudi Arabia in the United Kingdom. "Statement from the Royal Embassy of the Kingdom of Saudi Arabia, London." October 7, 2015.

Emmons, Alex. "John Kerry Gives Saudis a Big Pass on Indiscriminate Bombing of Civilians in Yemen." *The Intercept*, June 3, 2016.

Emmons, Alex. "27 U.S. Senators Rebel against Arming Saudi Arabia." *The Intercept*, September 21, 2016.

Emmons, Alex. "The U.S. Ambassador to Yemen's Hard-Line Approach Is Jamming Up Peace Efforts." *The Intercept*, December 13, 2017.

Emmons, Alex. "The U.S. Is Exacerbating the World's Worst Humanitarian Crisis by Outsourcing Its Yemen Policy." *The Intercept*, June 16, 2018.

Emmons, Alex, Aida Chavez, and Akela Lacy. "Joe Biden, in Departure from Obama Policy, Says He Would Make Saudi Arabia a 'Pariah.'" *The Intercept*, November 21, 2019.

Entessar, Nader. "A Regional Great Game? Iran-Saudi Relations in Flux." In *The Changing Security Dynamics of the Persian Gulf*, edited by Kristian Coates Ulrichsen. London: Hurst, 2017.

Esfandiary, Dina, and Ariane Tabatabai. *Triple-Axis: Iran's Relations with Russia and China*. London: I. B. Tauris, 2021.

Esfandiary, Dina, and Ariane Tabatabai. "Yemen: An Opportunity for Iran-Saudi Dialogue?" *Washington Quarterly* 39, no. 2 (April 2, 2016): 155–174.

Executive Office of the President. "Statement of Administration Policy: S.J. Res 31—Providing for Congressional Disapproval of the Proposed Foreign Military Sales Case to the Kingdom of Saudi Arabia of Certain Defense Articles." December 7, 2021.

Fahim, Kareem. "Saudis Face Mounting Pressure over Civilian Deaths in Yemen Conflict." *New York Times*, September 29, 2015.

Farley, Benjamin F. "Targeting Anwar Al-Aulaqi: A Case Study in U.S. Drone Strikes and Targeted Killings." *American University National Security Law Brief* 2, no. 3 (2012): 57–87.

Faucon, Benoit, and Dion Nissenbaum. "Iran Navy Port Emerges as Key to Alleged Weapons Smuggling to Yemen, U.N. Report Says." *Wall Street Journal*, January 9, 2022.

Fearon, James D. "Signaling Foreign Policy Interests: Tying Hands versus Sinking Costs." *Journal of Conflict Resolution* 41, no. 1 (1997): 68–90.

Fearon, James D. "Why Do Some Civil Wars Last So Much Longer than Others?" *Journal of Peace Research* 41, no. 3 (2004): 275–301.

Federspiel, Frederik, and Mohammad Ali. "The Cholera Outbreak in Yemen: Lessons Learned and Way Forward." *BMC Public Health*, no. 18 (2018).

Ferris, Jesse. *Nasser's Gamble: How Intervention in Yemen Caused the Six-Day War and the Decline of Egyptian Power*. Princeton, NJ: Princeton University Press, 2012.

Filkins, Dexter. "A Saudi Prince's Quest to Remake the Middle East." *New Yorker*, April 9, 2018.

Finn, Peter, and Greg Miller. "Anwar al-Awlaki's Family Speaks Out against His, Son's Death." *Washington Post*, October 17, 2011.

Finn, Tom. "Yemen Arrests Anti-government Activist." *The Guardian*, January 23, 2011.

Flanders, Stephanie, Vivian Nereim, Donna Abu-Nasr, Nayla Razzouk, Alaa Shahine, and Riad Hamade. "Saudi Crown Prince Discusses Trump, Aramco, Arrests: Transcript." *Bloomberg*, October 5, 2018.

Foran, Clare. "Lawmakers Call Biden's Yemen Policy a 'Historic Shift' in US Foreign Relations." *CNN*, March 11, 2021.

ForeignAssistance.gov. "U.S. Foreign Assistance by Country." Accessed October 29, 2021. https://www.foreignassistance.gov/cd/yemen/2021/obligations/0.

Freer, Courtney Jean. *Rentier Islamism: The Influence of the Muslim Brotherhood in Gulf Monarchies*. New York: Oxford University Press, 2018.

Friedman, Thomas L. "The Yemeni Way." *New York Times*, May 11, 2013.

Fuller, Braden. "Targeting Islamists: Assassinations in South Yemen." Armed Conflict Location & Event Data Project, November 8, 2018.

Fuller, Braden. "Yemen—The Battle of Aden." Armed Conflict Location & Event Data Project, February 16, 2018.

Fürtig, Henner. "Iran and the Arab Spring: Between Expectations and Disillusion." Working Paper No. 241. German Institute for Global and Area Studies (GIGA), 2013.

Gambrell, Jon. "US Pulls Missile Defenses in Saudi Arabia amid Yemen Attacks." *Associated Press*, September 11, 2021.

Gaston, Erica. *Process Lessons Learned in Yemen's National Dialogue*. Washington, DC: United States Institute of Peace, 2014.

Gause, F. Gregory, III. "Saudi Arabia's Regional Security Strategy." In *The International Politics of the Persian Gulf*, edited by Mehran Kamrava. Syracuse, NY: Syracuse University Press, 2011.

Gause, F. Gregory, III. "The United States Is the Last Check on MBS's Power." *Foreign Affairs*, March 30, 2021.

Gebrekidan, Selam, and Jonathan Saul. "Special Report: In Blocking Arms to Yemen, Saudi Arabia Squeezes a Starving Population." *Reuters*, October 11, 2017.

Ghattas, Kim. *Black Wave: The Saudi-Iran Wars on Religion and Culture That Destroyed the Middle East*. New York: Henry Holt, 2020.

Goldberg, Jeffrey. "The Obama Doctrine." *The Atlantic*, April 2016.

Goldberg, Jeffrey. "Saudi Crown Prince: Iran's Supreme Leader 'Makes Hitler Look Good.'" *The Atlantic*, April 2, 2018.

Goodarzi, Jubin. "Iran: Syria as the First Line of Defence." In *The Regional Struggle for Syria*, edited by Julien Barnes-Dacey and Daniel Levy, 25–32. London: European Council on Foreign Relations, 2013.

Goodman, Ryan. "Annotation of Sec. Pompeo's Certification of Yemen War: Civilian Casualties and Saudi-Led Coalition." *Just Security*, October 15, 2018.

Gould, Joe. "US to Bill UAE, Saudi Arabia $331M for Yemen Refueling." *Defense News*, December 13, 2018.

Gould, Joe, and Aaron Mehta. "Boeing, Raytheon Missile Sales to Saudi Arabia Paused by Biden Administration." *Defense News*, February 5, 2021.

Gould, Kate. "47 Senators Say No to Weapons of Mass Starvation." FCNL, June 13, 2017.

Graham, Lindsey, and John McCain III. "Statement by Senators John McCain and Lindsey Graham on Saudi Arabia Leading Air Strikes in Yemen." March 25, 2015. Accessed at John McCain's Senate website (no longer accessible).

Grim, Ryan. "Primaries Matter: How a Long-Shot Challenge Shifted the Debate on the War in Yemen." *The Intercept*, January 30, 2019.

Guardian, The. "John Kerry Says Yemen's Houthis and Saudi Coalition Agree to Ceasefire." November 15, 2016.

Guardian, The. "Missile Attack on Yemen Wedding Kills 131." September 29, 2015.

Guardian, The. "Saudi-Led Coalition Admits to Bombing Yemen Funeral." October 15, 2016.

Hager, Emily B., and Mark Mazzetti. "Emirates Secretly Sends Colombian Mercenaries to Yemen Fight." *New York Times*, November 25, 2015.

Haghighatjoo, Fatemeh. "The Green Movement and Political Change in Iran." In *Power and Change in Iran: Politics of Contention and Conciliation*, edited by Daniel Brumberg and Farideh Farhi, 224–250. Bloomington: Indiana University Press, 2016.

Hagopian, Frances. "'Democracy by Undemocratic Means'? Elites, Political Pacts, and Regime Transition in Brazil." *Comparative Political Studies* 23, no. 2 (1990): 147–170.

Hales, Gavin. *Fault Lines: Tracking Armed Violence in Yemen*. Geneva: Small Arms Survey, 2010.

Halliday, Fred. *Revolution and Foreign Policy: The Case of South Yemen 1967–1987*. New York: Cambridge University Press, 2002.

Hanna, Michael. Twitter post. April 21, 2021, 11:25 a.m. https://twitter.com/mwhanna1/status/1384891020731731969?s=20.

Hansler, Jennifer. "Biden Administration to Remove Houthis from Terrorist List, Reversing Trump's Decision." *CNN*, February 5, 2021.

Harb, Imad K. "Pompeo's Departing Sabotage in Yemen." Arab Center, Washington, DC, January 19, 2021.

Hassan, Hassan. "The Gulf States: United against Iran, Divided over Islamists." In *The Regional Struggle for Syria*, edited by Julien Barnes-Dacey and Daniel Levy, 17–24. Berlin: European Council on Foreign Relations, 2013.

Hathaway, Oona, and Aaron Haviland. "The Legality of U.S. Support for the Saudi-Led Campaign in Yemen." *Just Security*, March 1, 2018.

Hedges, Matthew. *Reinventing the Sheikhdom: Clan, Power and Patronage in Mohammed bin Zayed's UAE*. Oxford: Oxford University Press, 2021.

Hennessy, Kathleen. "In Devising a Plan in Iraq, U.S. Looks to Its Yemen Model." *Los Angeles Times*, June 22, 2014.

Hertog, Steffen. *Princes, Brokers, and Bureaucrats: Oil and the State in Saudi Arabia*. Ithaca, NY: Cornell University Press, 2010.

Hertog, Steffen. "Rentier Militaries in the Gulf States: The Price of Coup-Proofing." *International Journal of Middle East Studies* 43, no. 3 (2011): 400–402.

Hill, Ginny. *Yemen Endures*. London: Hurst, 2017.

Hiro, Dilip. *Cold War in the Islamic World: Saudi Arabia, Iran and the Struggle for Supremacy*. New York: Oxford University Press, 2018.

Holleis, Jennifer. "Why Saudi-Iran Relations Are Thawing—for Now." *Deutsche Welle*, October 16, 2021.

Holzman, Todd. "Obama Seeks 'New Beginning' with Muslim World." *NPR*, June 4, 2009.

Horton, Michael. "What the Battle for Hodeidah Means for Yemen and the Region." Jamestown Foundation, August 10, 2018.

Hosenball, Mark, Phil Stewart, and Warren Strobel. "Exclusive: U.S. Expands Intelligence Sharing with Saudis in Yemen Operation." *Reuters*, April 10, 2015.

Hsieh, Steven. "Watch: Yemeni Activist Tells Senators That Drone Strike on His Village 'Empowers Militants.'" *Alternet*, April 24, 2013.

Hubbard, Ben. *MBS: The Rise to Power of Mohammed Bin Salman*. New York: Penguin Random House, 2021.

Hudson, Michael C. "Bipolarity, Rational Calculation, and War in Yemen." *Arab Studies Journal* 3, no. 1 (Spring 1995): 9–19.

Hughes, Thomas L. Memo from State Department Bureau of Intelligence and Research, June 7, 1963. National Security Files, Country Files—Yemen,

Box 208a, Folder: Yemen General, 6/63, John F. Kennedy Presidential Library.

Human Rights Watch. *Deadly Consequences: Obstruction of Aid in Yemen during Covid-19*. Washington, DC: Human Rights Watch, 2020.

Human Rights Watch. "US: Investigate Counterterrorism Assistance to Yemen." December 11, 2010.

Human Rights Watch. *What Military Target Was in My Brother's House: Unlawful Coalition Airstrikes in Yemen*. Washington, DC: Human Rights Watch, 2015.

Human Rights Watch. "Yemen: Coalition Blockade Imperils Civilians." December 7, 2017.

Human Rights Watch. "Yemen: Coalition Strikes on Residence Apparent War Crime." July 27, 2015.

Human Rights Watch. "Yemen: Houthis Attacking Displaced People's Camps." March 23, 2021.

Human Rights Watch. "Yemen: Houthis Block Vital Goods into Taizz." January 31, 2016.

Hurlburt, Heather, and Chayenne Polimedio. *Can Transpartisan Coalitions Overcome Polarization? Lessons from Four Case Studies*. Washington, DC: New America, 2016.

Ignatius, David. "The Saudi Crown Prince Just Made a Very Risky Power Play." *Washington Post*, November 5, 2017.

International Committee of the Red Cross. "Yemen: Attacks on Health Care Facilities Must Stop." November 10, 2015.

International Crisis Group. *After al-Bayda, the Beginning of the Endgame for Northern Yemen?* Brussels: International Crisis Group, 2021.

International Crisis Group. *Breaking Point? Yemen's Southern Question*. Brussels: International Crisis Group, 2011.

International Crisis Group. *The Case for More Inclusive—and More Effective—Peacemaking in Yemen*. Brussels: International Crisis Group, 2021.

International Crisis Group. *The Failure of U.S. "Maximum Pressure" against Iran*. Brussels: International Crisis Group, 2021.

International Crisis Group. *Iran's Priorities in a Turbulent Middle East*. Brussels: International Crisis Group, 2018.

International Crisis Group. *Rethinking Peace in Yemen*. Brussels: International Crisis Group, 2020.

International Crisis Group. *Saving the Stockholm Agreement and Averting a Regional Conflagration in Yemen*. Brussels: International Crisis Group, 2019.

International Crisis Group. *Yemen: Averting a Destructive Battle for Hodeida*. Brussels: International Crisis Group, 2018.

International Crisis Group. *Yemen: Coping with Terrorism and Violence in a Fragile State*. Brussels: International Crisis Group, 2003.

International Crisis Group. *Yemen: Is Peace Possible?* Middle East Report No. 167. Brussels: International Crisis Group, February 9, 2016. https://icg-prod.s3.amazonaws.com/167-yemen-is-peace-possible.pdf.

International Crisis Group. *Yemen's Southern Question: Avoiding a Breakdown*. Brussels: International Crisis Group, 2013.

International Institute for Strategic Studies (IISS). *Iran's Networks of Influence in the Middle East*. New York: Routledge, 2020. https://www.iiss.org/publi cations/strategic-dossiers/iran-dossier.

International Organization for Migration. "Thousands of People Forced to Flee Escalating Hostilities in Yemen's Ma'rib." October 7, 2021.

Jalal, Ibrahim. "The Riyadh Agreement: Yemen's New Cabinet and What Remains to Be Done." Middle East Institute, February 1, 2021.

Jamshidi, Maryam. "How Transitional Justice Can Affect Yemen's Future." *Washington Post*, December 20, 2018.

Johnsen, Gregory D. "A Grand Bargain for Yemen." Arab Gulf States Institute in Washington, June 30, 2021.

Johnsen, Gregory D. "How the U.S. Can Create Leverage with the Houthis in Yemen." Arab Gulf States Institute in Washington, March 15, 2021.

Johnsen, Gregory D. *The Last Refuge: Yemen, Al-Qaeda, and America's War in Arabia*. New York: Norton, 2012.

Jones, Peter. "Hope and Disappointment: Iran and the Arab Spring." *Survival* 55, no. 4 (2013): 73–84.

Kalin, Stephen. "Saudi-Led Coalition to Give $1.5 Billion in Yemen Aid, Expand Port Capacity." *Reuters*, January 21, 2018.

Karman, Tawakkol. "Our Revolution's Doing What Saleh Can't—Uniting Yemen." *The Guardian*, April 8, 2011.

Karman, Tawakkol. "Yemen's Unfinished Business." *New York Times*, June 18, 2011.

Karni, Annie. "Jared Kushner's Mission Impossible." *Politico Magazine*, February 11, 2017.

Karon, Tony. "Hamas Signals Break with Iran, but Is That Good for Israel?" *Time*, February 29, 2012.

Kasinof, Laura. "Are Yemen's Protests Going to Bring Another Revolution?" *Christian Science Monitor*, January 27, 2011.

Katzman, Kenneth. *The United Arab Emirates (UAE): Issues for U.S. Policy*. Washington, DC: Congressional Research Service, 2018.

Kelety, Josh. "Can Sarah Smith Be Seattle's Alexandria Ocasio-Cortez?" *Seattle Weekly*, July 11, 2018.

Kerr, Malcolm. *The Arab Cold War, 1958–1964: A Study of Ideology in Politics*. London: Oxford University Press, 1965.

Khan, Azmat. "Hidden Pentagon Records Reveal Patterns of Failure in Deadly Airstrikes." *New York Times*, December 18, 2021.

Khan, Azmat, and Anand Gopal. "The Uncounted." *New York Times*, November 16, 2017.

Khanna, Ro, Mark Pocan, and Walter Jones. "Stop the Unconstitutional War in Yemen." *New York Times*, October 10, 2017.

Kilcullen, David, and Andrew McDonald Exum. "Death from Above, Outrage Down Below." *New York Times*, May 16, 2009.

Kirby, John. "Defense Department Briefing." U.S. Department of Defense, February 5, 2021.

Kirkpatrick, David D. "On the Front Line of the Saudi War in Yemen: Child Soldiers from Darfur." *New York Times*, December 28, 2018.

Kirkpatrick, David D., Ben Hubbard, Mark Landler, and Mark Mazzetti. "The Wooing of Jared Kushner: How the Saudis Got a Friend in the White House." *New York Times*, December 8, 2018.

Kizer, Kate. "Hitting Iran Where It Doesn't Hurt: Why U.S. Intervention in Yemen Will Backfire." *Just Security*, March 8, 2017.

Klaidman, Daniel. *Kill or Capture: The War on Terror and the Soul of the Obama Presidency*. New York: Mariner Books, 2013.

Klion, David. "When Will Washington End the Forever War?" *The Nation*, May 13, 2019.

Knights, Michael. "Lessons from the UAE War in Yemen." *Lawfare*, August 18, 2019.

Knights, Michael. "The Military Role in Yemen's Protests: Civil-Military Relations in the Tribal Republic." *Journal of Strategic Studies* 36, no. 2 (2013): 261–288.

Knights, Michael. *"Miss Me Yet?": What the UAE Drawdown Means for the United States and UN in Yemen*. Washington, DC: Washington Institute for Near East Peace, 2019.

Knights, Michael. "Yemen's 'Southern Hezbollah': Implications of Houthi Missile and Drone Improvements." Washington Institute for Near East Policy, April 1, 2021.

Knights, Michael, and Alex Almeida. "The Saudi-UAE War Effort in Yemen (Part 1): Operation Golden Arrow in Aden." Washington Institute for Near East Policy, August 10, 2015.

Knights, Michael, and Alex Almeida. "The Saudi-UAE War Effort in Yemen (Part 2): The Air Campaign." Washington Institute for Near East Policy, August 11, 2015.

Kouddous, Sharif Abdel. "With US Help, Saudi Arabia Is Obliterating Yemen." *PRI*, November 30, 2015.

Krause, Jana, Werner Krause, and Piia Bränfors. "Women's Participation in Peace Negotiations and the Durability of Peace." *International Interactions* 44, no. 6 (2018): 985–1016.

Kushner, Jared. *Breaking History: A White House Memoir*. New York: Broadside Books, 2022.

Kydd, Andrew. "Which Side Are You On? Bias, Credibility, and Mediation." *American Journal of Political Science* 47, no. 4 (2003): 597–611.

Lackner, Helen. *Yemen in Crisis: Autocracy, Neo-liberalism and the Disintegration of the State*. London: Saqi Books, 2017.

Lackner, Helen, and Abdulrahman Al-Eryani. *Yemen's Environmental Crisis Is the Biggest Risk for Its Future*. Washington, DC: Century Foundation, December 14, 2020.

Landler, Mark. "Saudi Prince's White House Visit Reinforces Trump's Commitment to Heir Apparent." *New York Times*, March 20, 2018.

Lenderking, Timothy. "Special Briefing via Telephone with Timothy Lenderking U.S. Special Envoy for Yemen." U.S. Department of State, May 20, 2021.

Lieu, Ted W. Letter to Honorable Ashton Carter and John F. Kerry. November 2, 2016. Accessed at Ted Lieu's House website, https://lieu.house.gov/sites/lieu.house.gov/files/documents/2016-11-02%20Lieu%20Letter%20to%20Sec.%20Defense%20and%20State.pdf.

Lockheed Martin. "U.S. Air Force Awards Lockheed Martin $87 Million for Paveway II Plus Laser Guided Bombs." September 19, 2016, https://news.lockheedmartin.com/2016-09-19-U-S-Air-Force-Awards-Lockheed-Martin-87-Million-Contract-for-Paveway-II-Plus-Laser-Guided-Bombs.

Londono, Ernesto, and Greg Miller. "Yemen's Saleh Refuses to Sign Deal to Quit." *Washington Post*, May 23, 2011.

Lyons, Terrence. "Post-conflict Elections and the Process of Demilitarizing Politics: The Role of Electoral Administration." *Democratization* 11, no. 3 (2004): 36–62.

Mackintosh-Smith, Tim. *Yemen: Adventures in Dictionary Land*. London: John Murray, 1997.

Madhani, Aamer. "Cleric al-Awlaki Dubbed 'bin Laden of the Internet.'" *USA Today*, August 24, 2010.

Magdy, Samy. "UN Raises $1.2 Billion for Yemen Humanitarian Crisis, Far Below Its 2023 Target." *PBS NewsHour*, February 27, 2023.

Magdy, Samy. "UN Warns of Mass Famine in Yemen Ahead of Donor Conference." *Associated Press*, February 28, 2021.

Malley, Robert, and Stephen Pomper. "Accomplice to Carnage: How America Enables War in Yemen." *Foreign Affairs*, March–April 2021.

Maloney, Suzanne. "Iran: The Bogeyman." In *The Arab Awakening: America and the Transformation of the Middle East*, edited by Kenneth M. Pollack and Daniel L. Byman, 258–267. Washington, DC: Brookings Institution Press, 2011.

Matthiesen, Toby. *Sectarian Gulf: Bahrain, Saudi Arabia, and the Arab Spring That Wasn't*. Redwood City, CA: Stanford University Press, 2013.

Mazzetti, Mark. "U.S. Is Said to Expand Secret Actions in Mideast." *New York Times*, May 24, 2010.

McCrisken, Trevor. "Ten Years On: Obama's War on Terrorism in Rhetoric and Practice." *International Affairs* 87, no. 4 (2011): 781–801.

Mcleary, Paul. "State Dept. Pauses New Arms Exports: UAE, Saudi Deals Hanging." *Breaking Defense*, January 27, 2021.

Memarian, Omid. "Iran's Green Movement Never Went Away." *Foreign Affairs*, June 14, 2019.

Menendez, Robert. Letter to Honorable Michael Pompeo and Honorable James Mattis. June 28, 2018. Accessed at Robert Menendez's Senate

website, https://www.menendez.senate.gov/newsroom/press/menendez-de
mands-more-answers-from-trump-admin-before-letting-arms-sales-to
-united-arab-emirates-and-saudi-arabia-move-forward.

Mercer, Mary Anne, Aisha Jumaan, and Ann Marie Kimball. "Why Are We Waging War on the People of Yemen?" *Huffington Post*, December 6, 2017.

Mezher, Chyrine. "Why Biden White House Lifted Arms Sales Freeze to UAE, KSA." *Breaking Defense*, April 23, 2021.

Michaels, Jim. "U.S. Military Refueling Saudi Planes for Yemen Airstrikes." *USA Today*, April 8, 2015.

Miller, Zeke. "Biden Revokes Terrorist Designation for Yemen's Houthis." *Associated Press*, February 5, 2021.

Mohiedeen, Naba. "PM: Sudan Cuts Troops in Yemen by Two-Thirds." *Voice of America*, December 11, 2019.

Molavi, Afshin. *Iran and the Gulf States*. Washington, DC: United States Institute of Peace, 2018.

Morris, Loveday, and Hugh Naylor. "Arab States Fear Nuclear Deal Will Give Iran a Bigger Regional Role." *Washington Post*, July 14, 2015.

Moshashai, Daniel, Andrew M. Leber, and James D. Savage. "Saudi Arabia Plans for Its Economic Future: Vision 2030, the National Transformation Plan and Saudi Fiscal Reform." *British Journal of Middle Eastern Studies* 47, no. 3 (2020): 381–401.

MSNBC. "Secretary Kerry on Yemen Conflict." June 1, 2016.

Mundy, Martha. *The Strategies of the Coalition in the Yemen War: Aerial Bombardment and Food War*. Somerville, MA: World Peace Foundation, October 9, 2018.

Mutaher, Fatima. *Yemen's New Networks in Women's Peacebuilding*. Sana'a, Yemen: Yemen Peace Forum and the Sana'a Center for Strategic Studies, 2021.

Mwatana for Human Rights. "Civil Society Groups Seek Urgent UN Action on Yemen." December 2, 2021.

Mwatana for Human Rights. *Starvation Makers: The Use of Starvation by Warring Parties in Yemen*. Sana'a, Yemen: Mwatana for Human Rights, 2021.

Mwatana for Human Rights. "US Weapons Responsible for Civilian Deaths in Yemen." September 20, 2018. https://mwatana.org/en/us-weapons/.

Naar, Ismaeel, and Omar Elkatouri. "Full Text of Saudi Arabia's New Peace Initiative to End Yemen War." *Al Arabiya*, March 22, 2021.

National Commission on Terrorist Attacks upon the United States. *Ninth Public Hearing*. April 8, 2004.

National Security Action. "Former Senior Obama Administration Officials Call for Halt to All U.S. Support for the War in Yemen." November 10, 2018.

NBC News. "Yemen Crisis: Saudi Arabia Masses 150,000 Troops to Support Airstrikes." March 26, 2015.

Nebehay, Stephanie. "Yemen Peace Talks Collapse in Geneva after Houthi No-Show." *Reuters*, September 8, 2018.

Nelson, Steven. "Trump's First Veto Averted as Senate Parliamentarian Derails Yemen War Vote." *Washington Examiner*, February 25, 2019.

Newton, Michael. "An Assessment of the Legality of Arms Sales to the Kingdom of Saudi Arabia in the Context of the Conflict in Yemen." American Bar Association, May 19, 2017.

Niarchos, Nicholas. "How the U.S. Is Making the War in Yemen Worse." *New Yorker*, January 15, 2018.

Nichols, Michelle. "Exclusive: U.N. Investigators Find Yemen's Houthis Did Not Carry Out Saudi Oil Attack." *Reuters*, January 8, 2020.

Nichols, Michelle. "Saudi Coalition Violated Law with Yemen Funeral Strike: U.S. Monitors." *Reuters*, October 20, 2016.

Nilsson, Desirée. "Anchoring the Peace: Civil Society Actors in Peace Accords and Durable Peace." *International Interactions* 38, no. 2 (2012): 243–266.

Nissenbaum, Dion. "Top U.S. Diplomat Backed Continuing Support for Saudi War in Yemen over Objections of Staff." *Wall Street Journal*, September 20, 2018.

Nissenbaum, Dion. "U.S. Deepens Role in Yemen Fight, Offers Gulf Allies Airstrike-Target Assistance." *Wall Street Journal*, June 12, 2018.

Nordland, Rod. "Talks to End War in Yemen Are Suspended." *New York Times*, August 6, 2016.

NPR. "Transcript: Obama's Speech against the Iraq War." January 20, 2009.

NPR. "Transcript: Trump's Remarks on Iran Nuclear Deal." October 13, 2017.

Oakford, Samuel. "U.S. Doubled Fuel Support for Saudi Bombing Campaign in Yemen after Deadly Strike on Funeral." *The Intercept*, July 13, 2017.

Oakford, Samuel. "The U.S. Military Can't Keep Track of Which Missions It's Fueling in Yemen War." *The Intercept*, September 18, 2017.

Oakford, Samuel, and Ryan Goodman. "The U.S. Is Paying More than It Bargained For in the Yemen War." *The Atlantic*, December 8, 2018.

Oakford, Samuel, and Peter Salisbury. "Yemen: The Graveyard of the Obama Doctrine." *The Atlantic*, September 23, 2016.

Obama, Barack. *A Promised Land*. New York: Crown, 2020.

Obama, Barack. "Remarks by the President in Address to the Nation on Libya." National Defense University, March 28, 2011.

O'Brien, Paul. "Yemen Doesn't Need the Obama Administration's 'Deep Concern.'" *Foreign Policy*, October 8, 2015.

O'Donnell, Norah. "Saudi Arabia's Heir to the Throne Talks to *60 Minutes*." *60 Minutes*, CBS, March 19, 2018.

Office of Congressman Mark Pocan. "Bipartisan Effort: 55 U.S. Representatives Call on Trump to Come to Congress before Taking Military Action in Yemen." April 11, 2017.

Office of Congressman Ro Khanna. "US Aerial Support for Saudi-Led Campaign in Yemen Soars under Trump." November 16, 2017.

Office of Senator Elizabeth Warren. "Warren, Colleagues to Biden Admin: Use All Tools to End Saudi Coalition's Blockade of Yemen." May 20, 2021.

Office of the Director of National Intelligence. *Assessing the Saudi Government's Role in the Killing of Jamal Khashoggi*. February 11, 2021. Declassified February 25, 2021.

Office of the Special Envoy of the Secretary-General for Yemen. "Briefing to the United Nations Security Council by the Special Envoy for Yemen Hans Grundberg." January 16, 2023. https://osesgy.unmissions.org/briefing-united-nations-security-council-special-envoy-yemen-hans-grundberg-9.

Office of the Special Envoy of the Secretary-General for Yemen. "Press Statement by the UN Special Envoy for Yemen Hans Grundberg on a Two-Month Truce." April 1, 2022. https://osesgy.unmissions.org/press-statement-un-special-envoy-yemen-hans-grundberg-two-month-truce.

Office of the Special Envoy of the Secretary-General for Yemen. "Timeline on the Progress of the Truce Implementation." Accessed February 28, 2023. https://osesgy.unmissions.org/timeline-progress-truce-implementation.

Office of the Special Envoy of the Secretary-General for Yemen. "US Special Envoy Hans Grundberg Concludes His First Visit to Yemen." October 6, 2021.

Office of the Special Envoy of the Secretary-General for Yemen. "A Year after the Stockholm Agreement: Where Are We Now?" Accessed September 16, 2021. https://osesgy.unmissions.org/year-after-stockholm-agreement-where-are-we-now.

O'Grady, Siobhán, and Ali Al-Mujahed. "Battle for the Badlands." *Washington Post*, October 1, 2021.

Orkaby, Asher. "Benefiting from the Misery of Others." Middle East Research and Information Project, May 5, 2021.

Orkaby, Asher. *Beyond the Arab Cold War*. New York: Oxford University Press, 2017.

Ostovar, Afshon. *Vanguard of the Imam: Religion, Politics, and Iran's Revolutionary Guards*. New York: Oxford University Press, 2016.

Oweis, Khaled Yacoub. "Qatar Emir Suggests Sending Arab Troops to Syria." *Reuters*, January 13, 2012.

Oxfam America. "Blockade and Violence in Yemen Pushing an Additional 25,000 People into Hunger Daily." July 27, 2015.

Oxfam America. "Yemen Fighting near Hodeidah Port Threatens to Cut Lifeline to Millions." June 6, 2018.

Paul, Rand, and Ro Khanna. "The Case for Restraint in American Foreign Policy." *Los Angeles Times*, June 1, 2017.

Peace Track Initiative. *The Feminist Peace Roadmap in Yemen: A Guiding Framework for Transforming the Peace Process*. Ottawa, ON: Peace Track Initiative, June 2021.

Pew Research Center. "Global Opposition to U.S. Surveillance and Drones, but Limited Harm to America's Image." July 14, 2014.

Phillips, Christopher. *The Battle for Syria: International Rivalry in the New Middle East.* New Haven, CT: Yale University Press, 2016.

Picard, Layla E. "About Layla." Layla Picard's website. Accessed September 30, 2021. https://laylapicard.com/about/.

Power, Samantha. *The Education of an Idealist.* New York: HarperCollins, 2019.

Power, Samantha. *A Problem from Hell.* New York: Basic Books, 2002.

Priest, Dana. "U.S. Military Teams, Intelligence Deeply Involved in Aiding Yemen on Strikes." *Washington Post*, January 27, 2010.

Putnam, Robert D. "Diplomacy and Domestic Politics: The Logic of Two-Level Games." *International Organization* 42, no. 3 (1988): 427–460.

Rabi, Uzi. *Yemen: Revolution, Civil War and Unification.* New York: I. B. Tauris, 2014.

Ragab, Eman. "Beyond Money and Diplomacy: Regional Policies of Saudi Arabia and UAE after the Arab Spring." *International Spectator* 52, no. 2 (2017): 37–53.

Rajaa, Jamila Ali, and Helga Schmid. "Two Top Diplomats on Why Peace Lasts Longer When It Is Not Made by Men Only." Sana'a Center for Strategic Studies, June 15, 2021.

Rashad, Marwa. "Yemen's Saleh Signs Deal to Give Up Power." *Reuters*, November 23, 2011.

Reilly, Benjamin. "Elections in Post-conflict Scenarios: Constraints and Dangers." *International Peacekeeping* 9, no. 2 (2002): 118–139.

Reuters. "Saudi Arabia Deposits $2 Billion in Yemen Central Bank to Back Currency." January 17, 2018.

Reuters. "Saudi Confirms First Round of Talks with New Iranian Government." October 3, 2021.

Reuters. "Saudi-Led Coalition Announces End to Yemen Operation." April 21, 2015.

Reuters. "U.S. 'Alarmed' at Yemen Violence, Calls for Restraint." March 18, 2011.

Reuters. "Yemen Offered U.S. 'Open Door' to al Qaeda: Wikileaks." December 3, 2010.

Reuters and Patricia Zengerle. "Biden Administration Proceeding with $23 Billion Weapon Sales to UAE." April 13, 2021.

Rhodes, Ben. "Remarks by Deputy National Security Advisor Ben Rhodes at the Iran Project." White House, June 16, 2016.

Rhodes, Ben. *The World as It Is.* New York: Random House, 2018.

Roberts, David B. "Qatar and the UAE: Exploring Divergent Responses to the Arab Spring." *Middle East Journal* 71, no. 4 (2017): 544–562.

Robinson, Linda. "SOF's Evolving Role: Warfare 'By, With, and Through' Local Forces." *Cipher Brief*, May 9, 2017.

Ross, Brian, Richard Esposito, Matthew Cole, Luis Martinez, and Kirit Radia. "Obama Ordered U.S. Military Strike on Yemen Terrorists." *New York Times*, December 18, 2009.

Roston, Aram. "A Middle East Monarchy Hired American Ex-Soldiers to Kill Its Political Enemies. This Could Be the Future of War." *BuzzFeed News*, October 16, 2018.

Roy, Emile. "The Battle of Hodeidah Has Started." Armed Conflict Location & Event Data Project, June 21, 2018.

Roy, Emile. "UAE's Sphere of Influence in Southern Yemen." Armed Conflict Location & Event Data Project, March 9, 2018.

Roy, Emile. "Who Are the UAE-Backed Forces Fighting on the Western Front in Yemen?" Armed Conflict Location & Event Data Project, July 20, 2018.

Ruffalo, Mark. Twitter post. February 28, 2018, 5:30 p.m. https://twitter.com/markruffalo/status/968976607850278912.

Ryan, Jason, and Devin Dwyer. "Terror Threat 'Most Heightened' since 9/11, Napolitano Says." *ABC News*, February 9, 2011.

Ryan, Missy. "As Coronavirus Looms, U.S. Proceeding with Major Reduction of Aid to Yemen." *Washington Post*, March 26, 2020.

Ryan, Missy. "With Small Changes, U.S. Maintains Military Aid to Saudi Arabia Despite Rebukes over Yemen Carnage." *Washington Post*, December 13, 2016.

Salisbury, Peter. "The Beginning of the End of Yemen's Civil War?" International Crisis Group, November 5, 2019.

Salisbury, Peter. "Making Yemen's Hodeida Deal Stick." International Crisis Group, December 19, 2018.

Salisbury, Peter. "A New UN Envoy Is an Opportunity for a New Approach in Yemen." International Crisis Group, June 18, 2021.

Salisbury, Peter. "Why US, Britain Are Key to Ending Yemen Horror." *CNN*, August 26, 2016.

Salisbury, Peter. "Yemen: After Hodeidah." Arab Gulf States Institute in Washington, June 19, 2018.

Salisbury, Peter. *Yemen: National Chaos, Local Order*. London: Chatham House, 2017.

Salisbury, Peter. "Yemen's Southern Transitional Council: A Delicate Balancing Act." Institute for International Political Studies, March 29, 2021.

Salmoni, Barak A., Bryce Loidolt, and Madeleine Wells. *Regime and Periphery in Northern Yemen: The Huthi Phenomenon*. Santa Monica, CA: RAND, 2010.

Sana'a Center. "Govt Pushes Ahead with Terrorism Designation as Port Attacks Continue." December 16, 2022.

Sana'a Center. *Increasing the Effectiveness of the Humanitarian Response in Yemen*. Sana'a, Yemen: Sana'a Center, April 10, 2018.

Sanger, David E. *Confront and Conceal: Obama's Secret Wars and Surprising Use of American Power*. New York: Penguin Random House, 2013.

Saturno, James V. *Privileged Business on the House Floor*. Washington, DC: Congressional Research Service, 2017.

Saudi Press Agency. "General / The Coalition Announces the Temporary Closure of All Yemeni Air, Sea and Land Ports, a First and Last Addition." November 6, 2017. www.spa.gov.sa/1684681.

Savage, Charlie, and Eric Schmitt, "Trump Administration Is Said to Be Working to Loosen Counterterrorism Rules." *New York Times*, March 12, 2017.

Savun, Burcu. "Information, Bias, and Mediation Success." *International Studies Quarterly* 52, no. 1 (2008): 25–47.

Schenker, David, and Robert Satloff. "Middle East Policy from Trump to Biden: Views from Inside the State Department's Near East Bureau." Washington Institute for Near East Peace, March 10, 2021.

Schmidt, Dana Adams. *Yemen: The Unknown War*. New York: Holt, Rinehart, and Winston, 1968.

Schmitt, Eric. "Saudi Arabia Tries to Ease Concerns over Civilian Deaths in Yemen." *New York Times*, June 14, 2017.

Schmitt, Eric, and David Sanger. "Raid in Yemen: Risky from the Start and Costly in the End." *New York Times*, February 1, 2017.

Schmitt, Eric, and Robert F. Worth. "With Arms for Yemen Rebels, Iran Seeks Wider Mideast Role." *New York Times*, March 15, 2012.

Schmitz, Charles. *Yemen's National Dialogue*. Washington, DC: Middle East Institute, 2014.

Schwartz, Eric, and Hardin Lang. "Six Reasons Why a Terrorist Designation for Yemen's Houthis Is a Bad Idea." *Just Security*, December 3, 2020.

Schwartz, Ian. "ABC's Karl Hammers WH's Earnest: 'Astounding' That You Still See Yemen as Model for Success Despite Chaos." *Real Clear Politics*, March 25, 2015.

Schwartzstein, Peter. "Bringing the Natural World into America's Middle East Policy: Averting a Crisis Foretold." Century Foundation, December 14, 2020.

Security Assistance Monitor. "Foreign Military Training." Accessed December 25, 2020. https://securityassistance.org/foreign-military-training/.

Security Council Report. "Penholders and Chairs." February 20, 2018.

Sengupta, Somini. "Pressure Mounting on Saudis' Coalition in Yemen." *New York Times*, June 30, 2015.

Shane, Scott. "The Enduring Influence of Anwar al-Awlaki in the Age of the Islamic State." *CTC Sentinel* 9, no. 3 (2016): 15–19.

Shane, Scott. *Objective Troy: A Terrorist, a President, and the Rise of the Drone*. New York: Penguin Random House, 2015.

Shane, Scott, and Andrew W. Lehren. "Leaked Cables Offer Raw Look at U.S. Diplomacy." *New York Times*, November 28, 2010.

Shane, Scott, Mark Mazzetti, and Robert F. Worth. "Secret Assault on Terrorism Widens on Two Continents." *New York Times*, August 14, 2010.

Sharp, Jeremy M. *Yemen: Civil War and Regional Intervention.* Washington, DC: Congressional Research Service, 2018.

Sharp, Jeremy M. *Yemen: Recent Attacks against U.S. Naval Vessels in the Red Sea.* Washington, DC: Congressional Research Service, 2016.

Sharp, Jeremy M., Christopher M. Blanchard, and Sarah R. Collins. *Congress and the War in Yemen: Oversight and Legislation, 2015–2020.* Washington, DC: Congressional Research Service, 2020.

Sherwood, Harriet, and Tom Finn. "Thousands Join 'Day of Rage' across the Middle East." *The Guardian*, February 25, 2011.

Shiel, Annie, and Chris Woods. "A Legacy of Unrecognized Harm: DoD/s 2020 Civilian Casualties Report." *Just Security*, June 7, 2021.

Shuja Al-Deen, Maysaa. "Iran and Houthis: Between Political Alliances and Sectarian Tensions." Sana'a Center for Strategic Studies, June 17, 2017.

Silverstein, Jake. "Behind the Cover: Can Yemen Survive Saudi Arabia's War?" *New York Times Magazine*, November 1, 2018.

Sly, Liz. "The UAE's Ambitions Backfire as It Finds Itself on the Front Line of U.S.-Iran Tensions." *Washington Post*, August 11, 2019.

Smith, Adam. "HASC Ranking Member Adam Smith, Rep. Ro Khanna, CPC Co-Chair Mark Pocan Announce Plan to Introduce a War Powers Resolution to Withdraw U.S. Forces from the War in Yemen." Adam Smith's U.S. House website, September 6, 2018. https://adamsmith.house.gov/2018/9/hasc-ranking-member-adam-smith-rep-ro-khanna-cpc-co-chair-mark-pocan.

Snyder, Stephen. "Where the US Fell Down in Yemen, as War Clouds Gathered." *The World*, May 26, 2016.

Specia, Megan. "Yemen's War Is a Tragedy. Is It Also a Crime?" *New York Times*, November 22, 2017.

Specia, Megan, and Alan Yuhas. "Two Speeches, a Decade Apart: How Pompeo Departed from Obama." *New York Times*, January 10, 2019.

Spindel, Jennifer. "Beyond Military Power: The Symbolic Politics of Conventional Weapons Transfers." PhD diss., University of Minnesota, 2018.

Stark, Alexandra. "Can the Riyadh Reshuffle Bring Peace to Yemen?" *War on the Rocks*, April 29, 2022.

Stark, Alexandra. "Gun at a Knife Fight: Regional Intervention in Civil Wars in the Middle East and North Africa, 1957–2017." PhD diss., Georgetown University, 2019.

Stark, Alexandra. *Managing U.S. Security Partnerships: A Toolkit for Congress.* Washington, DC: New America, October 26, 2020.

Stark, Alexandra. "Mohammed bin Salman's Collapsing Coalition in Yemen Means Trouble for Trump." *Foreign Policy*, August 23, 2019.

Stedman, Stephen John. "Spoiler Problems in Peace Processes." *International Security* 22, no. 2 (1997): 5–53.

Stephens, Michael. *The Arab Cold War Redux: The Foreign Policy of the Gulf Cooperation Council States since 2011*. New York: Century Foundation, 2017.

Stewart, Phil. "Exclusive: U.S. Withdraws Staff from Saudi Arabia Dedicated to Yemen Planning." *Reuters*, August 19, 2016.

Stewart, Phil. "U.S. Halting Refueling of Saudi-Led Coalition Aircraft in Yemen's War." *Reuters*, November 9, 2018.

Stewart, Phil, and Warren Strobel. "U.S. to Halt Some Arms Sales to Saudi, Citing Civilian Deaths in Yemen Campaign." *Reuters*, December 13, 2016.

Strobel, Warren, and Jonathan Landay. "Exclusive: As Saudis Bombed Yemen, U.S. Worried about Legal Blowback." *Reuters*, October 10, 2016.

Sullivan, Jake. Written testimony, U.S. House of Representatives Committee on Foreign Affairs hearing: "U.S. Policy in the Arabian Peninsula." February 6, 2019.

Tabatabai, Ariane M. *No Conquest, No Defeat: Iran's National Security Strategy*. London: Hurst, 2020.

Tabatabai, Ariane M., Jeffrey Martini, and Becca Wasser. *The Iran Threat Network (ITN): Four Models of Iran's Nonstate Client Partnerships*. Santa Monica, CA: RAND, 2021.

Taub, Amanda. "Obama's Love of the 'Yemen Model' Sums Up His Disastrously Shortsighted Foreign Policy." *Vox*, March 30, 2015.

Taylor, Guy. "Yemen Crisis Threatens Obama Iran Nuclear Talks, Further Clouds Middle East Policy." *Washington Times*, March 26, 2015.

Tharoor, Ishaan. "Yemen and Somalia Are Examples of U.S. Mission Creep, Not Success." *Washington Post*, September 11, 2014.

Time. "Crown Prince Mohammed bin Salman Talks to *Time* about the Middle East, Saudi Arabia's Plans and President Trump." April 5, 2018.

Ulrichsen, Kristian Coates. "Endgames for Saudi Arabia and the United Arab Emirates in Yemen." In *Politics, Governance, and Reconstruction in Yemen*, edited by Stacey Philbrick Yadav and Marc Lynch, 31–33. Washington, DC: POMEPS, 2018.

Ulrichsen, Kristian Coates. *Qatar and the Arab Spring*. London: Hurst, 2014.

Ulrichsen, Kristian Coates. *The United Arab Emirates: Power, Politics and Policymaking*. New York: Routledge, 2017.

UNHCR (United Nations High Commissioner for Refugees). "Statement to the Security Council on Missions to Yemen, South Sudan, Somalia and Kenya and an Update on the Oslo Conference on Nigeria and the Lake Chad Region." March 10, 2017.

UNHCR (United Nations High Commissioner for Refugees). "Yemen Fact Sheet." July 2021.

UNICEF (United Nations Children's Fund). "What UNICEF Is Doing in Yemen." Accessed September 15, 2021. https://www.unicef.org/emergencies/yemen-crisis#what-unicef-is-doing.

United Nations. "Secretary-General Appoints Ismail Ould Cheikh Ahmed of Mauritania as His Special Envoy for Yemen." April 25, 2016.

United Nations Office of the Resident Coordinator and Humanitarian Coordinator for Yemen. "A Military Assault on Hodeidah Will Almost Certainly Have Catastrophic Humanitarian Impact." June 8, 2018.

United Nations Office of the Special Representative of the Secretary-General for Children and Armed Conflict. "Child Recruitment and Use." Accessed November 20, 2021. https://childrenandarmedconflict.un.org/six-grave-vi olations/child-soldiers/#::text=Recruiting%20and%20using%20children %20under,by%20the%20International%20Criminal%20Court.

United Nations Secretary-General. "Statement Attributable to the Spokesman for the Secretary-General on Yemen." September 28, 2015.

United Nations Security Council Panel of Experts on Yemen. *Final Report of the Panel of Experts on Yemen.* S/2018/193. January 27, 2017.

United Nations Security Council Panel of Experts on Yemen. *Final Report of the Panel of Experts on Yemen.* S/2021/79. January 25, 2021.

United Nations Verification & Inspection Mechanism for Yemen. "About UNVIM." Accessed September 15, 2021. https://www.vimye.org/about.

United States Institute of Peace. "Global Fragility Act: A New U.S. Approach." January 15, 2020.

United States Institute of Peace. "James Mattis: Yemen Needs a Truce within 30 Days." October 31, 2018.

UNOCHA (United Nations Office for the Coordination of Humanitarian Affairs). "Yemen 2020." Accessed October 29, 2021. https://fts.unocha.org/ appeals/925/summary.

UNOHCHR (United Nations Office of the High Commissioner for Human Rights). *Situation of Human Rights in Yemen, including Violations and Abuses since September 2014: Report of the United Nations High Commissioner for Human Rights containing the Findings of the Group of Independent Eminent International and Regional Experts and a Summary of Technical Assistance Provided by the Office of the High Commissioner to the National Commission of Inquiry.* Annual report. August 17, 2018.

UNOHCHR (United Nations Office of the High Commissioner for Human Rights). "Statement by Group of Experts on Yemen on HRC Rejection of Resolution to Renew Their Mandate." October 8, 2021.

U.S. Department of Justice. "Umar Farouk Abdulmutallab Sentenced to Life in Prison for Attempted Bombing of Flight 253 on Christmas Day 2009." February 16, 2012.

U.S. Department of State. "Briefing with Special Representative for Iran and Senior Advisor to the Secretary Brian Hook." February 20, 2020.

U.S. Department of State. "Condemning the Houthi Missile Strike against Saudi Arabia." Heather Nauert, spokesperson. December 19, 2017.

U.S. Department of State. "Deputy Secretary Sullivan's Meeting on Yemen." Office of the Spokesperson, December 18, 2017.

U.S. Department of State. "Ending the Conflict in Yemen." Secretary of State Michael R. Pompeo, October 30, 2018.

U.S. Department of State. "Houthi Attack on Abha Airport." Secretary of State Michael R. Pompeo, June 24, 2019.

U.S. Department of State. "Iran-Backed Houthi Attacks against Saudi Arabia." Office of the Spokesperson, October 29, 2020.

U.S. Department of State. "Iranian-Backed Houthis Sentencing 30 Political Prisoners to Death in Yemen." Morgan Ortagus, spokesperson, July 13, 2019.

U.S. Department of State. "Remarks to the Traveling Press." Secretary of State Michael R. Pompeo, September 18, 2019.

U.S. Department of State. "Senior State Department Official on Developments in Yemen." February 25, 2020.

U.S. Department of State. Twitter post. December 18, 2017, 3:08 p.m. https://twitter.com/StateDept/status/942849061849313283?s=20.

U.S. Department of State. United States Strategy to Prevent Conflict and Promote Stability. Washington, DC: U.S. State Department, 2020.

U.S. Department of State. "U.S.-Funded Cranes Offloading Goods in Yemen." Heather Nauert, spokesperson, February 9, 2018.

U.S. Government Accountability Office. Defense Logistics Agreements: DOD Should Improve Oversight and Seek Payment from Foreign Partners for Thousands of Orders It Identifies as Overdue. Washington, DC: GAO Report to Congressional Committees, 2020.

U.S. House of Representatives, Foreign Affairs Committee. "Engel Releases Witness Affidavit in Committee's Investigation into Firing of State Department Inspector General." November 24, 2020.

U.S. Senate. "Vetoes by President Donald J. Trump." Accessed June 17, 2023. https://www.senate.gov/legislative/vetoes/TrumpDJ.htm.

U.S. Senate Committee on Armed Services. Hearing to Receive Testimony on U.S. Central Command, U.S. Africa Command and U.S. Special Operations Command Programs and Budget in Review of the Defense Authorization Request for Fiscal Year 2016 and the Future Years Defense Program. March 26, 2015.

U.S. Senate Committee on Foreign Relations. Al-Qaeda in Yemen and Somalia: A Ticking Time Bomb: A Report to the Committee on Foreign Relations, United States Senate. 111th Cong., 2nd sess. (January 21, 2010).

Verma, Pranshu, and Edward Wong. "Another Inspector General Resigns amid Questions about Pompeo." New York Times, August 5, 2020.

Vlahos, Kelley Beaucar. "Critics Try, but Fail to Kill $1 Billion Weapons Deal for Saudi Arabia." Fox News, December 20, 2015.

Vreeland, James, and Axel Dreher. The Political Economy of the United Nations Security Council: Money and Influence. New York: Cambridge University Press, 2014.

Walsh, Declan, and David D. Kirkpatrick. "U.A.E. Pulls Most Forces from Yemen in Blow to Saudi War Effort." New York Times, July 11, 2019.

Walsh, Declan, and Eric Schmitt. "Arms Sales to Saudis Leave American Fingerprints on Yemen's Carnage." *New York Times*, December 25, 2018.

Walter, Barbara F. "The Critical Barrier to Civil War Settlement." *International Organization* 51, no. 3 (1997): 335–364.

Ward, Alex. "The US May Still Be Helping Saudi Arabia in the Yemen War after All." *Vox*, April 27, 2021.

Ward, Alex. "Why the US Won't Break Up with Saudi Arabia over Jamal Khashoggi's Murder." *Vox*, November 20, 2018.

Warikoo, Niraj. "Yemeni-Americans Stuck in Yemen Say U.S. Failing to Help Them." *Detroit Free Press*, May 18, 2015.

Watchlist and Save the Children. "Every Day Things Are Getting Worse." April 2017.

Watling, Jack, and Namir Shabibi. "How the War on Terror Failed Yemen." *Foreign Policy*, May 18, 2016.

Weed, Matthew C. *The War Powers Resolution: Concepts and Practice*. Washington, DC: Congressional Research Service, 2019.

Wehrey, Frederic M. *The Burning Shores: Inside the Battle for the New Libya*. New York: Farrar, Straus and Giroux, 2018.

Weiss, Michael, and Hassan Hassan. *ISIS: Inside the Army of Terror*. New York: Regan Arts, 2015.

Westad, Odd Arne. *The Global Cold War: Third World Interventions and the Making of Our Times*. Cambridge: Cambridge University Press, 2007.

White House. "Letter from the President—War Powers Resolution: Text of a Letter from the President to the Speaker of the House of Representatives and the President Pro Tempore of the Senate." October 14, 2016.

White House. "On-the-Record Conference Call on the GCC Summit." Office of the Press Secretary, May 11, 2015.

White House. "President Trump Announces Iran Strategy." October 13, 2017.

White House. "Press Briefing by Press Secretary Josh Earnest, 9/26/2014." Office of the Press Secretary, September 26, 2014.

White House. "Press Briefing by Press Secretary Josh Earnest, 3/23/2015." Office of the Press Secretary, March 23, 2015.

White House. "Press Briefing by Press Secretary Josh Earnest and Ben Rhodes, 4/21/2016." Office of the Press Secretary, April 21, 2016.

White House. "Press Gaggle by Press Secretary Eric Schultz en Route Miami, FL 4/22/2015." Office of the Press Secretary, April 22, 2015.

White House. "Press Gaggle by Principal Deputy Press Secretary Eric Schultz en Route Pittsburgh, PA, 10/13/2016." Office of the Press Secretary, October 13, 2016.

White House. "Remarks by President Biden on America's Place in the World." Office of the Press Secretary, February 4, 2021.

White House. "Remarks by President Obama in Q&A with the Press—Riyadh, Saudi Arabia." Office of the Press Secretary, April 21, 2016.

White House. "Remarks by the President at Cairo University, 6-04-09." Office of the Press Secretary, June 4, 2009.

White House. "Remarks by the President on the Situation in Iraq." Office of the Press Secretary, June 19, 2014.

White House. "Statement by National Security Council Spokesperson Ned Price on Escalating Violence in Yemen." Office of the Press Secretary, January 24, 2016.

White House. "Statement by NSC Spokesperson Bernadette Meehan on the Situation in Yemen." Office of the Press Secretary, March 25, 2015.

White House. "Statement by NSC Spokesperson Ned Price on Additional U.S. Humanitarian Aid for Yemen." Office of the Press Secretary, September 16, 2015.

White House. "Statement by NSC Spokesperson Ned Price on Reports of Civilian Deaths in Yemen." Office of the Press Secretary, October 2, 2015.

White House. "Statement by NSC Spokesperson Ned Price on Yemen." Office of the Press Secretary, October 8, 2016.

White House. "Statement by the President on ISIL." Office of the Press Secretary, September 10, 2014.

White House. "Statement by the Press Secretary on Violence in Yemen." Office of the Press Secretary, April 5, 2011.

White House. "Weekly Address: President Obama Outlines Steps Taken to Protect the Safety and Security of the American People." Office of the Press Secretary, January 2, 2010.

Whitson, Sarah Leah. "Congress Must Halt Biden's Arms Sales to Saudi Arabia." *Foreign Policy*, December 6, 2021.

WHO (World Health Organization). "Yemeni Health System Crumbles as Millions Risk Malnutrition and Diseases." February 23, 2017.

Wolff, Michael. *Fire and Fury: Inside the Trump White House*. New York: Macmillan, 2018.

Wood, David, R. Joseph Huddleston, and Harshana Ghoorhoo. "The Best Way to Help Yemenis Survive Might Not Be What Aid Organizations Think." *Washington Post*, April 6, 2021.

World, The. "Why the 'Yemen Model' May Not Work in Iraq—or Yemen." *PRI*, June 25, 2014.

World Bank. "World Development Indicators 2016." Accessed December 30, 2016. https://databank.worldbank.org/source/world-development-indicators.

World Food Programme. "Four USAID-Funded Mobile Cranes Arrive at Yemen's Largest Red Sea Port." January 15, 2018.

World Food Programme. "WFP Demands Action after Uncovering Misuse of Food Relief Intended for Hungry People." December 31, 2018.

World Food Programme. "Yemen Facts and Figures: From April 2017 to 31 March 2018." June 2017.

Worth, Robert F. "The Man Who Danced on the Heads of Snakes." *New York Times*, December 7, 2017.

Worth, Robert F. "Mohammed bin Zayed's Dark Vision of the Middle East's Future." *New York Times*, January 9, 2020.

Yadav, Stacey Philbrick. "The 'Yemen Model' as a Failure of Political Imagination." *International Journal of Middle East Studies* 47, no. 1 (2015): 144–147.

Yemen Data Project. "Data." Accessed September 6, 2021. www.yemendata project.org.

Yemen Data Project. "5 Years of Data on the Saudi-Led Air War in Yemen." March 25, 2020. Accessed July 15, 2020. www.yemendataproject.org.

Yemen Data Project. "Monthly Update on Saudi Coalition Air Raids in Yemen." Accessed March 27, 2018. www.yemendataproject.org.

Yemen Peace Project. *America's Role in Yemen 2017 and Beyond*. Washington, DC: Yemen Peace Project, 2017.

Yom, Sean L., and F. Gregory Gause III. "Resilient Royals: How Arab Monarchies Hang On." *Journal of Democracy* 23, no. 4 (2012): 74–88.

Young, Todd. "Young Continues to Press Saudi Government on Yemen's Humanitarian Crisis." May 5, 2017. Todd Young's Senate website.

Zakaria, Tabassum. "Yemeni at U.S. Hearing Describes Drone Strike on His Village." *Reuters*, April 24, 2013.

Zimmerman, Katherine. "Yemen Model Won't Work in Iraq, Syria." *Washington Post*, July 17, 2014.

Zogby, James, Elizabeth Zogby, and Sarah Hope Zogby. *Middle East 2016: Current Conditions & the Road Ahead*. Washington, DC: Zogby Research Services, 2016.

Zornick, George. "Why Is the United States Risking Involvement in Possible War Crimes? This Congressman Wants to Know." *The Nation*, November 4, 2016.

Index

Maps and tables are indicated by italicized page numbers.

Abdullah (King of Saudi Arabia), 49, 63, 68

Abdulmutallab, Umar Farouk (underwear bomber), 33–34, 37, 196

Aboueldahab, Noha, 53, 57

Abraham Accords (2020), 170

accountability, 52, 56–58, 111, 176, 184–186, 196

ACLED (Armed Conflict Location & Event Data Project), 84, 99, 199

ACLU (American Civil Liberties Union), 36

Acquisition and Cross-Service Agreement (ACSA), 135

Aden Emergency (1963–1967), 15

advocacy coalition. *See* Yemen advocacy coalition

AECA (Arms Export Control Act of 1976), 141, 146, 147

aerial refueling, 7, 105, 108–109, 129, 135–137, 139, 161, 170, 172

Afghanistan: al-Qaeda in, 33; drone campaigns in, 187; Shia fighters from, 72; U.S. interventions in, 29, 170, 179

Ahmed, Ismail Ould Cheikh, 122

airstrikes: civilian casualties from, 1–3, 5, 33, 81, 83, 94, 111–122,

146, 154, 161–162, 168; counterterrorism, 29, 33–35, *35*, 38, 50, 129–130; deliberate, 114–115; double-tap, 119; dynamic, 114–115, 119, 122; by Houthi insurgency, 87–88, 92, 109, 174, 199; no-strike lists, 108, 113–115, 129, 136; by Saudi-led coalition, 1–3, 78–83, *82*, 93–94, 104, 109–123, 129, 146, 161–162; targeting process, 108–109, 113–117, 122, 130. *See also* drone strikes; *specific incidents*

al-Ahmar, Ali Mohsen, 48, 49

Al-Akhali, Rafat, 189

al-Asiri, Ibrahim, 37

al-Assad, Bashar, 62–63, 71–73, 103

al-Assiri, Ahmed, 116

al-Awlaki, Abdulrahman, 36, 37

al-Awlaki, Anwar, 34, 36–37, 39

al-Awlaki, Saleh Fareed Bin Mohsen, 87

al-Badawi, Jamal, 41

al-Badr, Imam, 12, 13

al-Banna, Ibrahim, 37

al-Beidh, Ali Salem, 18, 20, 21

Al-Dawsari, Nadwa, 56, 100, 172–173, 184

Al-Dhubhani, Mariam, 195
al-Ghasmi, Ahmad, 17
al-Hanshi, Sulaf, 183
al-Harethi, Qaed Salim, 32, 34
al-Hirak al-Janoubi. *See* Southern
   Movement
al-Houthi, Abd al-Malik, 24
al-Houthi, Abdul Karim, 98–99
al-Houthi, Badr al-Din, 24
al-Houthi, Hussein Badaraddin,
   23–24
al-Houthi, Mohammed Ali, 98–99
Ali, Salim Rubai, 17
Ali Nasir Muhammed, 18, 19, 21
Al-Iryani, Abdulghani, 46
al-Jubair, Adel, 104, 128–129, 166
al-Khayati, Abdulkareem, 47
Alley, April Longley, 20, 196, 197
al-Maliki, Turki, 1
al-Mowafak, Hadil, 53, 185
al-Muhandis, Abu Mahdi, 73
al-Muslimi, Farea, 37, 56, 184, 194
Al-Mutawakel, Radhya, 1, 154, 185
al-Mutawakkil, Yaha, 32
Al Otaiba, Yousef, 127, 128
al-Qaeda: USS *Cole* bombing (2000),
   27, 31, 32, 41, 196; recruitment
   by, 37, 101; resurgence of, 26, 32;
   September 11 attacks (2001), 31;
   U.S. embassy attack in Yemen
   (2008), 32; U.S. policy objectives
   toward, 179
al-Qaeda in the Arabian Peninsula
   (AQAP): containment of, 29,
   57; counterterrorism operations
   against, 29, 32–33, 36–39, 65,
   108–109, 129–130, 149; English-language propaganda, 36–37;
   formation and growth of, 30, 31,
   65; STC clashes with, 199; threat
   posed by, 28, 29, 31–34, 131; training camps, 33, 38, 41; U.S. policy
   objectives toward, 2, 5, 31–34; Yemen civil war of 2014 and, 79

al-Zindani, Abdul-Majid, 36
al-Zubaidi, Aidarous, 85, 87, 183
Amash, Justin, 158
American Civil Liberties Union
   (ACLU), 36
Amnesty International, 186
Ansar Allah. *See* Houthi insurgency
AQAP. *See* al-Qaeda in the Arabian
   Peninsula
Arab Cold War, 13
Arab League, 17, 62
Arab Spring, 44–58; calls for de-
   mocracy, 49–50, 58, 60, 71; Day
   of Rage protests, 47–48, 61; Gulf
   monarchies' response to, 61–63;
   Iranian response to, 60, 69–74; po-
   litical transition following, 3, 30,
   44–46, 51–58, 180, 196; Saleh regime and, 44, 46–51; U.S. response
   to, 48–51, 64, 106; violence against
   protesters, 48, 51, 56, 61–63
Armed Conflict Location & Event
   Data Project (ACLED), 84, 99, 199
Arms Export Control Act of 1976
   (AECA), 141, 146, 147
arms sales: Congress and, 1, 5, 7, 140,
   147–150, 157, 164–166; emergency measures for, 164–165; job
   creation and, 128, 147; legal issues,
   146; as leverage, 5, 14, 142, 148;
   policy debates regarding, 110,
   141; preconditions for, 129, 148;
   security partnerships and, 3, 16,
   107, 126, 127, 189; suspension
   of, 120–121, 170–171; timing for
   completion of, 109
Assabahi, Yousef, 194, 195
Austin, Lloyd, 105
Autesserre, Séverine, 182
authoritarian regimes, 124, 186–187

Baker, James, 21
Balam, Abbas Muhammad, 80–81
Balam, Alaallah Abbas, 81

Balam, Salem, 81
Baron, Adam, 47
Beasley, David, 97
Bekker, Peter, 186
Ben Ali, Zine al-Abidine, 46
Benomar, Jamal, 122
Biden, Joe: leverage utilization, 6,
    175; Middle East aid requests,
    189; Yemen civil war of 2014 and,
    7, 138, 140, 169–177, 197, 200
bin Breik, Hani, 85
bin Laden, Osama, 34
bin Nayef, Mohammed, 128
bin Shimlan, Faisal, 26
bin Zayed Al Nahyan, Abdullah, 66
Blinken, Antony, 50, 66
bombings. *See* airstrikes; *specific
    incidents*
Boston Marathon bombing (2013), 37
Boutton, Andrew, 186–187
Brand, Marieke, 65
Brehony, Noel, 18
Brennan, John, 34, 39, 50, 105
Brzezinski, Zbigniew, 17
Bunker, Ellsworth, 14
Burns, William, 106
bus bombing (2018), 1, 3, 83, 141,
    161–162
Bush, George W.: counterterrorism
    operations, 2, 28, 31–32, 34, 38;
    U.S.-Muslim relationships under,
    102
"by, with, and through" approach. *See*
    Yemen model of counterterrorism
Byman, Daniel, 71

Cairo Agreement (1972), 17
Carney, Jay, 48
Carter, Jimmy, 17, 193
Casey, William, 19
Cason, Jim, 166
cease-fire negotiations, 7, 95–96,
    122–123, 198–200

CENTCOM (United States Central
    Command), 32, 38, 105, 135–136,
    179
chaos states, 76, 99–100
Charles Koch Institute, 7, 141, 145,
    156
Charlie Hebdo shootings (2015), 37
chemical weapons, 13, 73, 103
children: as casualties, 1, 83, 116, 130,
    141, 154, 161; internal displace-
    ment of, 77; malnutrition and, 77,
    91, 140
China: Iran nuclear deal and, 107;
    South Yemen supported by, 16;
    UN Security Council and, 183
cholera, 77, 92, 129
civilian casualties: from airstrikes,
    1–3, 5, 33, 81, 83, 94, 111–122,
    146, 154, 161–162, 168; children
    as, 1, 83, 116, 130, 141, 154, 161;
    from counterterrorism operations,
    33, 35–37, 130; from drone strikes,
    2, 36–38, 118, 187; mitigation
    strategies, 113–118; in Saada wars,
    25; as war crimes, 112, 118, 146,
    149; wedding airstrikes (2015 &
    2018), 116, 146, 154; in Yemen
    civil war of 2014, 77, 81, 83, 92,
    94, 111–122, 146–147, 154, 161–
    162, 168
Clark, Victoria, 20
climate change, 179, 190–191
Clinton, Hillary, 42, 48, 50, 51, 102
Cold War, 4, 13, 17
USS *Cole* bombing (2000), 27, 31, 32,
    41, 196
communism, 17, 18, 196
Concerned Veterans for America, 145
conflict prevention strategies,
    180–181
Congress: arms sales and, 1, 5, 7, 140,
    147–150, 157, 164–166; on civil-
    ian casualties, 111, 145–147, 168;
    on Hodeidah blockade, 166–167;

Congress (*Continued*)
on humanitarian crisis, 111, 164;
Iraq intervention authorized by,
101; leverage utilization, 142, 148;
Saudi-led coalition, support for, 5,
7, 134–136, 140; War Powers Resolution and, 141, 157–164; Yemen
advocacy coalition and, 139–142,
145–168, *151–153*
corruption: anticorruption efforts, 41,
190; Arab Spring protests against,
46; of Hadi government, 97; of
Houthi insurgency, 97; of Saleh
government, 3, 22, 30, 42, 186.
See also patronage networks
counterterrorism operations, 27–43;
airstrikes, 29, 33–35, *35*, 38, 50,
129–130; against AQAP, 29, 32–33,
36–39, 65, 108–109, 129–130, 149;
Bush administration, 2, 28, 31–32,
34, 38; civilian casualties from,
33, 35–37, 130; drone strikes, 2,
28–29, 32–40, *35*, 125, 129–130,
149, 187; in Global War on Terror, 24, 28, 196; against ISIS,
28–29, 107–108; legal issues, 36,
37; moral hazard dynamic, 30;
Obama administration, 2, 27–40,
107–108; partnership challenges,
30, 32, 39–43, 186; public opinion
on, 33, 37–38; revising approach
to, 186–187; as shadow war,
38–39; targeting process, 34–37;
terrorist rehabilitation program,
41; Trump administration, 2, 125,
129, 130. *See also* Yemen model of
counterterrorism
COVID-19 pandemic, 77, 98, 170
Cronin, Audrey Kurth, 187

Day, Stephen, 22
Defense Priorities (think tank), 145,
156
deliberate airstrikes, 114–115

DeLozier, Elana, 87, 97
democracy: aid allocation to programs for, 189; Arab Spring calls
for, 49–50, 58, 60, 71; as foreign
policy tool, 6, 41, 177, 193–194; in
Yemen's post-unification period,
19–20
Dingell, Debbie, 146–147
diplomacy: domestic, 194; peace
processes and, 4; preventative,
181; sustainable, 189–191, 197;
traditional modes of, 69; Yemen
civil war of 2014 and, 132, 169,
172–177, 197, 200
Donilon, Tom, 50
double-tap airstrikes, 119
Dresch, Paul, 7, 11, 22
drone strikes: civilian casualties from,
2, 36–38, 118, 187; counterterrorism, 2, 28–29, 32–40, *35*, 125,
129–130, 149, 187; by Houthi
insurgency, 90, 91, 174, 199; targeting process, 34–37, 118
Dubowitz, Mark, 110
Duss, Matt, 132, 135, 154, 157, 161,
177
dynamic airstrikes, 114–115, 119, 122

Earnest, Joshua, 27, 34
Egypt: Arab Spring in, 49–50, 64,
106; Free Officers movement, 13;
Muslim Brotherhood in, 61, 106;
North Yemen civil war and, 12–15;
revolution in (1952), 15; Saudi
relations with, 12–14; sustainable
development programming for,
190. *See also specific leaders*
Eikenberry, Eric, 143
el Eryani, Moammar, 94
el-Sisi, Abdel Fattah, 126
El-Tayyab, Hassan, 171, 172
Engel, Eliot, 157, 165
Esfandiary, Dina, 74
Exum, Andrew, 38, 112

failed states, 99, 195
Faisal (King of Saudi Arabia), 14, 15, 67
famine, 77, 129, 133, 195
Farouk, Yasmine, 171
FCNL. *See* Friends Committee on National Legislation
Fearon, James, 175
Feierstein, Gerald, 42–43, 49, 56, 57
females. *See* women
Feminist Peace Roadmap (Peace Track Initiative), 182
FLOSY (Front for the Liberation of Occupied South Yemen), 15
Flynn, Michael, 125
Ford, Gerald, 160
Foreign Assistance Act of 1961, 146
foreign terrorist organizations (FTOs), 138, 170, 172–173
Fort Hood terrorist attack (2009), 36
France: Iran nuclear deal and, 107; Saudi-led coalition supported by, 78, 109, 136
Free Officers movement (Egypt), 13
Free Syrian Army (FSA), 63
Friedman, Thomas, 44, 45
Friends Committee on National Legislation (FCNL), 144, 145, 148, 150, 156, 166, 171, 172
Front for the Liberation of Occupied South Yemen (FLOSY), 15
FTOs (foreign terrorist organizations), 138, 170, 172–173
funeral hall strike (2016), 83, 118–120, 122, 142

Gates, Bob, 50, 102
Gause, Gregory, 68
GCC. *See* Gulf Cooperation Council
GEE (Group of Eminent Experts on Yemen), 185–186
General People's Congress (GPC), 20, 26, 32, 47, 51, 53–54, 57
Ghaddafi, Muammar, 50, 62, 102

Giants Brigades, 85, *86*
Global Fragility Act of 2019 (GFA), 181
Global War on Terror (GWoT), 24, 28, 196
Goldberg, Jeffrey, 101, 103
Goodman, Ryan, 162
Gorbachev, Mikhail, 18
Gould, Kate, 145, 148–149, 154, 159, 166–167
GPC. *See* General People's Congress
Graham, Lindsey, 110, 148, 165, 168
Grande, Lise, 94, 97–98
Green, Mark, 167
Green Movement protests (Iran), 70
Greenway, Robert, 131, 134
Griffiths, Martin, 94, 167
Group of Eminent Experts on Yemen (GEE), 185–186
Grundberg, Hans, 173, 183, 198, 199
Guardians of the Republic, 85, *86*
Gulf Cooperation Council (GCC): on Iran nuclear agreement, 2, 106, 107; National Dialogue Conference and, 44, 45, 196; Peninsula Shield Force, 62; transition initiative, 48–49, 51, 56; U.S. arms sales and, 3; Yemen civil war of 1994 and, 21, 90, 105. *See also specific member countries*
Gulf War (1990–1991), 20, 32
GWoT (Global War on Terror), 24, 28, 196

Hadi, Abdrabbuh Mansur: accession to presidency, 44, 50, 51; corruption and, 97; failure to implement NDC outcomes, 46, 52; in peace processes, 183; resignation as president, 57, 199; transition government led by, 51, 52, 54; U.S.-Yemen counterterrorism partnership and, 29, 50, 108; Yemen civil war of 2014 and, 76, 78–79, 84–88, *86*, 94, 105, 123, 196

Hadramawt Women for Peace, 182,
  183
Hadrami Elite Forces, *86*
Halliday, Fred, 17–18
Hamas, 71–73, 130
Hamid, Ahmed, 98–99
Hartung, William, 121
Hasan, Nidal, 36
Hassan, Hassan, 63
Hertog, Steffen, 67
Hezbollah, 70–75, 89–90, 125, 130
Hill, Ginny, 25, 51, 53, 57
Hodeidah blockade (2017), 92–93,
  132–133, 166–167
Hodeidah offensive (2018), 94–96,
  95, 134
Hook, Brian, 125–126
Houthi insurgency: airstrikes by,
  87–88, 92, 109, 174, 199; alliance
  with Saleh, 57, 85, 90, 98; cease-
  fire negotiations, 95–96, 122–123,
  198–200; corruption and, 97; coup
  by (2014), 10, 30, 46, 57–58, 66;
  diversion of humanitarian aid, 83,
  97–98; drone strikes by, 90, 91,
  174, 199; emergence and growth
  of, 23–24, 47; factionalization
  among, 98–99, 197; FTO designation for, 138, 170, 172–173;
  Iranian support for, 59–60, 65–66,
  74–75, 77, 89–91, 110, 131–132,
  196; leadership of, 23–24, 98–99;
  Marib offensive, 175, 199; National Dialogue Conference and,
  46, 53–55; Saada wars and, 24–25,
  40, 65; Saudi-led operations
  against, 78–80, 83–85, 93–94, 104,
  111–112; UN calls for surrender
  of, 183; U.S. engagement with,
  123; weapons acquisition, 74–75,
  90–91; Yemen advocacy coalition
  on, 155
Hoyer, Steny, 156–157
Hubbard, Ben, 65, 126, 137

humanitarian crises, 91–98; aid for,
  92–93, 95, 114, 119, 187–188,
  200; cholera outbreaks and, 77,
  92, 129; famine and, 77, 129, 133,
  195; Hodeidah blockade and,
  92–93, 132–133, 166–167; Houthi
  diversion of aid for, 83, 97–98;
  internally displaced persons and,
  77, 92, 175; malnutrition and, 77,
  91–92, 140; revising approach to,
  187–189; Yemen advocacy coalition on, 143–145, 167. *See also*
  civilian casualties
human rights: aid allocation for, 189,
  190; NDC's failure to address,
  184; UN High Commissioner for
  Human Rights, 115; UN Human
  Rights Council, 185–186; in U.S.
  foreign policy, 41, 171; violation
  of, 73, 136, 185–186, 195. *See also*
  Mwatana for Human Rights
Human Rights Watch, 33, 40, 98,
  116, 175
Hurlburt, Heather, 155
Hussein (King of Jordan), 14

imams, 11–13, 23, 24, 36
immigration ban on Muslim countries, 194
internally displaced persons, 77, 92,
  175
International Crisis Group, 90, 94,
  175, 182
International Red Cross, 116
Iran: Arab Spring response, 60, 69–
  74; axis of resistance, 71–74; dual
  track approach toward, 111, 174;
  engagement with Saudi Arabia,
  173–174; Green Movement protests, 70; Houthis supported by,
  59–60, 65–66, 74–75, 77, 89–91,
  110, 131–132, 196; proxy strategy,
  4, 60, 66, 70–74, 125–126, 131,
  155; revolution in (1979), 70, 71;

sanctions on, 64, 125; U.S. strategy review on, 130; Yemen advocacy coalition on, 155

Iran-Iraq War (1980–1988), 73

Iran nuclear agreement (2015): negotiation of, 106–107, 110–111; opposition to, 2, 64, 106, 107, 110; in prevention of regional instability, 123; talks regarding revival of, 173; U.S. withdrawal from, 125

Iraq: proxy wars in, 73, 74; U.S. intervention in, 70, 73, 101, 179. *See also* Islamic State in Iraq and Syria

IRGC. *See* Islamic Revolutionary Guard Corp

ISIS. *See* Islamic State in Iraq and Syria

Islah: in JMP alliance, 26, 46; leadership of, 84, *86*; Muslim Brotherhood and, 20, 66–67, 88; National Dialogue Conference and, 53; STC rivalry with, 87

Islam and Muslims: imams, 11–13, 23, 24, 36; Obama's Cairo speech and, 101–102; Shia, 23–25, 62, 72–73; Sunni, 23, 62, 72–73; Trump immigration ban, 194

Islamic Revolutionary Guard Corp (IRGC), 71–75, 89–90, 125, 199

Islamic State in Iraq and Syria (ISIS), 28–29, 73, 107–108, 110, 130–131, 179

Islamophobia, 194

Israel: Iran as threat to, 131; U.S. support for, 125, 163

Jacobsen, Corey, 158

Jamshidi, Maryam, 55

Janjaweed militia, 79

Johnsen, Gregory, 31, 197

Joint Comprehensive Plan of Action (JCPOA). *See* Iran nuclear agreement

Joint Incidents Assessment Team (JIAT), 81

Joint Meeting Parties (JMP), 26, 46–47, 54

Joint Unconventional Warfare Task Force Execute Order, 38

Jones, Walter, 159, 160

Jordan: North Yemen civil war and, 13–14; sustainable development programming for, 190; U.S. arms sales to, 14

Jumaan, Aisha, 144–145, 174–175

justice. *See* transitional justice

Kappes, Steven, 32–33

Karl, Jonathan, 27

Karman, Tawakkol, 41, 46, 47

Kataib Hizbullah (KH), 73, 125

Kennedy, John F., 14

Kerr, Malcolm, 13

Kerry, John, 112, 123

Khaled bin Salman (Prince of Saudi Arabia), 88, 137

Khamenei, Ayatollah, 65, 70

Khan, Azmat, 118

Khanna, Ro, 148, 155–156, 159, 160, 170, 177

Khartoum Conference (1967), 15

Khashoggi, Jamal, 5, 137, 141, 149–150, 191

Kilcullen, David, 38

Kirby, John, 170

Kizer, Kate, 135, 143, 145, 150, 157

Knights, Michael, 40, 78

Komer, Robert, 10

Konyndyk, Jeremy, 114, 134

Kushner, Jared, 127–128, 133

Kuwait Agreement (1979), 17

Kuwait's response to Arab Spring, 62, 63

Law of Armed Conflict (LOAC), 113, 146

Lee, Mike, 155, 160–161, 170

Leiter, Michael, 34, 37

Lenderking, Timothy, 126, 169, 171, 173, 175

leverage: arms sales as, 5, 14, 142, 148; effective usage of, 5–6, 181, 191–192; of Gulf monarchies, 64; in Iran proxy strategy, 72, 155; in peace negotiations, 100, 176; of U.S. over Saudi-led coalition, 92, 100, 121–122, 132–134, 175, 191

Lewis, Larry, 114–117

Libya: Arab Spring in, 45, 50, 61, 62; NATO-led intervention in, 50, 62, 102–104; proxy wars in, 4, 62, 63, 179

Lieu, Ted, 146, 148, 158

Linick, Steve, 165

LOAC (Law of Armed Conflict), 113, 146

Lockheed Martin, 1, 126

Luqman, Muna, 98

Mackintosh-Smith, Tim, 11

Malinowski, Tom, 117

Malley, Robert, 105, 108, 120

malnutrition, 77, 91–92, 140

Maloney, Suzanne, 72

Mansour, Renad, 173–174

Marib offensive (2020), 175, 199

Massie, Thomas, 159

Mattis, Jim, 128, 134, 167–168

MbS. *See* Mohammed bin Salman

MbZ. *See* Mohammed bin Zayed

MCC (Millennium Challenge Corporation), 42

McCain, John, 110

McConnell, Mitch, 163

Menendez, Bob, 164

mercenaries, 79, 84

Middle East and North Africa (MENA): balance of power in, 60, 61, 69; climate change effects in, 179, 190–191; during Cold War, 4, 13, 17; conflict pre-vention strategies in, 180–181; instability within, 3, 5, 60–61, 178–179, 181, 190–191; long-term approach to foreign policy in, 180; U.S. security objectives in, 4, 179, 189, 193; Western narratives of, 194–195. *See also* Arab Spring; *specific countries and regional organizations*

Millennium Challenge Corporation (MCC), 42

missile attacks. *See* airstrikes

Mohammed bin Salman (MbS): foreign policy views, 67–69; on Iranian threat to Saudi security, 65–66, 174; Khashoggi murder and, 5, 137; Kushner and, 127–128, 133; Saudi-led intervention and, 105, 118; U.S. trip (2018), 126, 127

Mohammed bin Zayed (MbZ), 61, 64, 67–69, 106, 134

moral hazards, 30

Morsi, Mohamed, 73

Mubarak, Hosni, 50, 64, 106

Murphy, Chris, 107, 111, 148, 149, 155, 160–161, 166

Muslim Brotherhood, 20, 61, 63, 66–67, 83–84, 88, 106

Muslims. *See* Islam and Muslims

Mwatana for Human Rights, 1, 80–81, 83, 154, 185–186

Napolitano, Janet, 34

Nasser, Gamal Abdel, 12, 13, 15

Nasser, Summer, 30, 188

National Dialogue Conference (NDC): failures of, 3, 45–46, 52, 53, 58, 180, 182, 184, 196; lessons learned from, 52–57; objectives of, 44–45, 51–52; representation at, 45, 52–55; short-term calculus of, 56–57; on southern issue, 52, 54–55; on transitional justice, 52, 55–57, 184, 196

National Liberation Front (NLF), 15, 16

National Resistance Forces, 93

NATO. *See* North Atlantic Treaty Organization

NDC. *See* National Dialogue Conference

New America, 34–35, *35*, 37

Newstead, Jennifer, 166

Niarchos, Nicholas, 109–110

Nixon, Richard, 157, 193

NLF (National Liberation Front), 15, 16

noncombatant casualties. *See* civilian casualties

North Africa. *See* Middle East and North Africa

North Atlantic Treaty Organization (NATO), 50, 62, 102, 104

North Yemen: civil war in (1962–1970), 12–15, 195–196; clashes with South Yemen, 16–18, 196; coups in, 12, 15; map (1990), *12*; Ottoman conquest of, 11; unification with South Yemen, 10, 11, 17–21, 54, 58

no-strike lists, 108, 113–115, 129, 136

Obama, Barack: on Arab Spring, 48–50, 64, 106; Cairo speech (2009), 101–102, 124; campaign promises, 1, 28, 29, 101, 178; counterterrorism operations, 2, 27–40, 107–108; criticisms of, 117, 124; Iran nuclear agreement, 2, 64, 106–107, 110–111, 123; on Iraq intervention, 101; leverage utilization, 6, 121–122, 142, 191; on Libya intervention, 102–104; on National Dialogue Conference, 45; Yemen civil war of 2014 and, 2–3, 103–123, 178

O'Brien, Paul, 144

October Revolution (1963–1967), 15

Office for the Coordination of Humanitarian Affairs (OCHA), 77

Open Society Foundations, 7, 141

Operation Decisive Storm (2015), 78–79

Operation Golden Victory (2018), 94–96, *95*

Operation Hard Surface (1963), 14–15

Operation Restoring Hope (2015), 79

Operation Scorched Earth (2009), 24–25

Orkaby, Asher, 188

Ostovar, Afshon, 70, 71, 74

Ottoman Empire, conquest of North Yemen by, 11

Oxfam, 91–92, 129, 143–145, 150

Pakistan, U.S. counterterrorism operations in, 38

Palimedio, Chayenne, 155

patronage networks: Saleh and, 16, 20, 25, 30, 32, 40, 45, 51; Saudi segmented clientelism and, 67–68

Paul, Rand, 155–156, 164

Paul, Scott, 129, 145

peace processes: diplomacy and, 4; failure of, 122–123; inclusivity of, 182–184; leverage in, 100, 176; UN-led, 132, 173, 176, 182–185, 200; women and, 182–183

Peace Track Initiative, 182

People's Democratic Republic of Yemen (PDRY). *See* South Yemen

Petraeus, David, 32–33, 38

Picard, Layla, 143

PLC (Presidential Leadership Council), 199–200

PMU (Popular Mobilization Units), 73

Pocan, Mark, 158–160

political parties. *See specific names of parties*

political transitions: accountability in, 184–186; inclusivity of, 111, 182–184; post–Arab Spring, 3, 30, 44–46, 51–58, 180

Pompeo, Mike, 124, 126, 131, 134, 138, 161–162, 165, 167

Pomper, Stephen, 105, 108

Popular Mobilization Units (PMU), 73

Power, Samantha, 50, 102–104

Presidential Leadership Council (PLC), 199–200

preventative diplomacy, 181

Price, Ned, 108–109, 120

Priest, Dana, 38–39

propaganda, 13, 36–37

Protectorates of South Arabia, 11

proxy wars: in post–Arab Spring period, 60–67, 70–74; prevention of, 181, 189–190; U.S. engagement with, 4, 155, 179; in Yemen, 13, 125–126, 131

Qatar: Arab Spring response, 62, 63; proxy strategy, 62

Rajaa, Jamila Ali, 182

Raytheon, 119, 154

refugee admissions, 194

remote warfare. *See* Yemen model of counterterrorism

Rhodes, Ben, 31, 50, 104, 107, 108, 110

Rice, Condoleezza, 31

Rice, Susan, 102, 134

Riedel, Bruce, 109, 128

Riyadh Agreement (2019), 88–89

Roosevelt, Franklin, 193

Rouhani, Hassan, 106–107

Ruffalo, Mark, 162–163

Russia: Iran nuclear deal and, 107; objections to GEE mandate, 186; UN Security Council and, 183. *See also* Soviet Union

Saada wars (2004–2010), 24–25, 40, 65

Saba, Geo, 156, 159, 160, 177

Saddam Hussein, 20, 70, 73

Saleh, Ali Abdullah: alliance with Houthis, 57, 85, 90, 98; Arab Spring and, 44, 46–51; consolidation of power, 19, 21, 25; corruption and, 3, 22, 30, 42, 186; death of, 85, 98; domestic challenges facing, 25–26, 40–41; Global War on Terror and, 24; immunity from prosecution, 45, 48, 51, 55–57, 184; North Yemen presidency, 15, 16; patronage networks, 16, 20, 25, 30, 32, 40, 45, 51; resignation as president, 30, 44, 49–51; U.S.-Yemen counterterrorism partnership and, 2, 27–33, 39–43, 179, 186

Saleh, Tareq, 84, 85

Salisbury, Peter, 76, 77, 99, 173, 183

Sallal, Abdullah, 12, 13

Salman (King of Saudi Arabia), 67, 68, 107, 109, 119, 126

Sana'a Agreement (1990), 19

Sanders, Bernie, 132, 154, 155, 160–161, 163, 177

Saud (King of Saudi Arabia), 67, 193

Saudi Arabia: Arab Spring response, 61–63; counterterrorism operations, 65; Egyptian relations with, 12–14; engagement with Iran, 173–174; foreign-policy-making authority in, 67–68; humanitarian assistance to Yemen, 98; on Iran nuclear agreement, 64, 107; Khashoggi murder and, 5, 137, 149, 191; North Yemen civil war and, 12–15, 196; North Yemen–South Yemen clashes and, 16; proxy strategy, 60, 63, 64, 67; Saada wars and, 24, 65; segmented clientelism in, 67–68; U.S. arms sales to, 107, 109–110, 120–121,

126–129, 146–150, 164–166, 171;
Vision 2030 initiative, 126, 174;
Yemen civil war of 1994 and, 21.
See also specific leaders
Saudi-led coalition: airstrikes, 1–3,
78–83, *82*, 93–94, 104, 109–123,
129, 146, 161–162; announcement of, 64, 104–105; cease-fire
negotiations, 7, 95–96, 122–123,
198–200; division of labor in, 78;
drawdown of forces, 59, 88, 142,
168, 191; Hodeidah blockade and
offensive, 92–96, *95*, 132–134,
166–167; mercenaries in, 79, 84;
motivations for, 64–69; Operation
Decisive Storm (2015), 78–79;
Operation Restoring Hope (2015),
79; strategic goal divergence, 63,
83–89, *86*; U.S. leverage over, 92,
100, 121–122, 132–134, 175, 191;
U.S. support for, 2–7, 78, 92–93,
103–122, 125–137, 140–143,
169–171, 178
Saudi-Yemeni War (1934), 65
SBB (Support and Backup Brigades),
86
Schenker, David, 131, 132, 138
Schmidt, Dana, 13
Schmitz, Charles, 54
Schumer, Chuck, 164
Schwartzstein, Peter, 190, 191
Seche, Stephen, 42, 75
Security Belt, 84, *86*, 88
Security Council (UN), 20–21, 183,
199
segmented clientelism, 67–68
September 11 terrorist attacks (2001),
31
Shabibi, Namir, 41
Shabwani Elite Forces, 84, *86*, 87
shadow war, 38–39
Shaheen, Jeanne, 161, 162
Shapiro, Daniel, 102
Shayea, Shelal, 85, 87

Shia Islam, 23–25, 62, 72–73
Shuail, Khlade, 92
Simon, Steve, 28–29
Six-Day War (1967), 15
Smith, Adam, 145, 156
Smith, Sarah, 156
SNC (Syrian National Council), 63
Soleimani, Qassim, 71, 73, 125
Somalia: Saudi-led coalition sup-
ported by, 78; U.S. counterterror-
ism operations in, 29, 35, 38
Soros, George, 141
Southern Movement (al-Hirak al-Ja-
noubi), 22–23, 47, 53–55, 57, 85
Southern Transition Council (STC):
AQAP clashes with, 199; Islah
rivalry with, 87; leadership of,
85–87, *86*; legitimization attempts,
100; militia groups and, 23, 79, 84,
197; Riyadh Agreement and, 88–
89; secessionism and, 85, 89, 185
South Yemen: British occupation
of, 11, 15–16; civil war in (1986),
18–19, 196; clashes with North
Yemen, 16–18, 196; coups in, 16,
17, 19; map of (1990), *12*; Oc-
tober Revolution in, 15; Soviet
support for, 16–19; unification
with North Yemen, 10, 11, 17–21,
54, 58
Soviet Union: Cold War and, 4, 13,
17; communism and, 17, 18, 196;
South Yemen supported by, 16–19.
See also Russia
Spindel, Jennifer, 166
STC. *See* Southern Transition
Council
Stephens, Michael, 69
Stockholm Agreement (2018), 95–96,
167–168, 182, 191
Sullivan, Jake, 106, 120, 167
Sunni Islam, 23, 62, 72–73
Support and Backup Brigades (SBB),
86

Supporters of God. *See* Houthi insurgency

sustainable diplomacy and development, 189–191, 197

Syria: Arab Spring in, 45, 61–63, 70–72; civil war in, 72, 103; proxy wars in, 4, 63, 72–74, 179. *See also* Islamic State in Iraq and Syria

Syrian National Council (SNC), 63

Tabatabai, Adnan, 174

Tabatabai, Ariane, 70, 74

Taliban, 130

Taub, Amanda, 30

terrorism: Boston Marathon bombing (2013), 37; *Charlie Hebdo* shootings (2015), 37; USS *Cole* bombing (2000), 27, 31, 32, 41, 196; Fort Hood attack (2009), 36; FTO designation, 138, 170, 172–173; Global War on Terror, 24, 28, 196; September 11 attacks (2001), 31; underwear bomber (2009), 33–34, 37, 196; U.S. embassy attack in Yemen (2008), 32. *See also* counterterrorism; *specific terrorist organizations*

Tihama Resistance Forces, 85

transitional justice, 52, 55–57, 176, 180, 184–186, 196

transpartisan coalitions, 155–156

truce. *See* cease-fire negotiations

Trump, Donald: counterterrorism operations, 2, 125, 129, 130; immigration ban on Muslim countries, 194; Iran nuclear agreement, withdrawal from, 125; Khashoggi murder and, 137, 149; leverage utilization, 6, 132–134, 142, 191; Saudi Arabia trip (2017), 126; on War Powers Resolution, 159–160, 163; Yemen civil war of 2014 and, 3, 7, 93, 98, 125–138, 166–168

Tunisia: Arab Spring in, 46; Muslim Brotherhood in, 61

UAE. *See* United Arab Emirates

UAV (unmanned aerial vehicle) strikes. *See* drone strikes

Ulrichsen, Kristian, 174

UN. *See* United Nations

underwear bomber (Umar Farouk Abdulmutallab), 33–34, 37, 196

UNICEF (United Nations Children's Fund), 77

United Arab Emirates (UAE): Arab Spring response, 61–63; drawdown of forces in Yemen, 59, 88, 142, 168, 191; foreign-policy-making authority in, 68–69; humanitarian assistance to Yemen, 98; militia groups supported by, 84; on Muslim Brotherhood, 67, 83–84, 88; proxy strategy, 60, 62–64, 67; U.S. arms sales to, 109, 128, 148, 164, 166, 170–171. *See also* Saudi-led coalition

United Kingdom: counterterrorism operations, 41; Iran nuclear deal and, 107; North Yemen civil war and, 13; North Yemen–South Yemen clashes and, 16; Saudi-led coalition supported by, 78, 109, 136; South Yemen occupation, 11, 15–16

United Nations (UN): on civilian casualties, 92, 116; credibility as mediator, 96; on FTO designation for Houthis, 138; on funeral hall strike, 119; Group of Eminent Experts on Yemen, 185–186; High Commissioner for Human Rights, 115; Human Rights Council, 185–186; on National Dialogue Conference, 53; North Yemen civil war and, 14; Office for the Coordination of Humanitarian Affairs, 77; peace processes led by, 132, 173, 176, 182–185, 200; Security Council, 20–21, 183, 199; terrorist

designations, 36; World Food Programme, 91, 97, 133; Yemen Panel of Experts, 90–91, 97
United Nations Children's Fund (UNICEF), 77
United Nations Verification & Inspection Mechanism for Yemen (UNVIM), 90–91
United States: Afghanistan intervention, 29, 170, 179; Arab Spring response, 48–51, 64, 106; Cold War and, 4, 13, 17; credibility as mediator, 174–175; embassy attack in Yemen (2008), 32; foreign policy recommendations, 180–195; Global War on Terror, 24, 28, 196; humanitarian assistance to Yemen, 98, 187–188; Iraq intervention, 70, 73, 101, 179; Islamophobia in, 194; Libya intervention, 50, 102–104; Middle East security objectives, 4, 179, 189, 193; on National Dialogue Conference, 55, 196; North Yemen civil war and, 14–15, 195–196; North Yemen–South Yemen clashes and, 16–18, 196; proxy wars, engagement with, 4, 155, 179; refugee admissions, 194; Saudi-led coalition supported by, 2–7, 78, 92–93, 103–122, 125–137, 140–143, 169–171, 178; September 11 attacks (2001), 31; South Yemen civil war and, 19; Strategy to Prevent Conflict and Promote Stability, 181; withdrawal from Iran nuclear agreement, 125. *See also* arms sales; Congress; counterterrorism; Iran nuclear agreement; *specific presidential administrations*
United States Agency for International Development (USAID), 93, 113–114, 133, 167, 191

United States Central Command (CENTCOM), 32, 38, 105, 135–136, 179
unmanned aerial vehicle (UAV) strikes. *See* drone strikes
UNVIM (United Nations Verification & Inspection Mechanism for Yemen), 90–91

Vakil, Sanam, 174
Votel, Joseph, 136, 179

Walter, Barbara, 175–176
war crimes, 73, 79, 112, 118, 146, 149, 186
War Powers Resolution of 1973 (WPR), 141, 157–164
Warren, Elizabeth, 136
Wasser, Becca, 109, 113
Watling, Jack, 41
weapons: chemical, 13, 73, 103; Houthi acquisition of, 74–75, 90–91; smuggling, 81, 90, 91, 93, 133. *See also* airstrikes; arms sales; drone strikes
Westad, Odd Arne, 18
WFP (World Food Programme), 91, 97, 133
Whitson, Sarah Leah, 171
Win Without War, 144, 145, 150, 156
Wolff, Michael, 125
Wolfowitz, Paul, 32
women: internal displacement of, 77; at National Dialogue Conference, 45, 52–53; peace processes and, 182–183; political participation quotas, 53
World Bank, 190
World Food Programme (WFP), 91, 97, 133
World Health Organization, 92, 98
World Peace Foundation, 116
WPR (War Powers Resolution of 1973), 141, 157–164

Yadav, Stacey Philbrick, 53
Yahya, Imam, 11–12
YAR (Yemen Arab Republic). *See* North Yemen
Yemen: as chaos state, 76, 99–100; climate change effects in, 190; COVID-19 pandemic in, 77, 98; democratic experiment in, 19–20; development aid for, 21, 31–32, 41–42, 189; military assistance for, 30, 38–41; proxy wars in, 13, 125–126, 131; Saada wars in, 24–25, 40, 65; socioeconomic crisis in, 25–26; unification of, 10, 11, 17–21, 54, 58. *See also* Arab Spring; North Yemen; South Yemen; *specific leaders*
Yemen advocacy coalition, 139–168; Congress and, 139–142, 145–168, *151–153*; on humanitarian crisis, 143–145, 167; lessons learned from, 142–143, 193–194; lobbying efforts, 139, 153–155; media engagement, 139–140, 149, 162; momentum building, 149–150, 153–157, 162; origins and growth of, 143–145
Yemen Arab Republic (YAR). *See* North Yemen
Yemen civil war (1994), 10, 21–22, 25, 54, 58, 196
Yemen civil war (2014–present): Biden administration and, 7, 138, 140, 169–177, 197, 200; cease-fire negotiations, 7, 95–96, 122–123, 198–200; civilian casualties, 77, 81, 83, 92, 94, 111–122, 146–147, 154, 161–162, 168; diplomacy and, 132, 169, 172–177, 197, 200; economy during, 77, 97, 188; internally displaced persons during, 77, 92, 175; methodology for study of, 8–9; Obama administration and, 2–3, 103–123, 178; peace talks, 122–123; Trump administration and, 3, 7, 93, 98, 125–138, 166–168; Western media coverage, 76–77, 195, 197; zones of control and conflict, *80*, *96*. *See also* airstrikes; Houthi insurgency; humanitarian crisis; Saudi-led coalition; weapons
Yemeni National Resistance, 85, *86*
Yemen model of counterterrorism: drone strikes and, 2, 28–29, 187; failures of, 3, 4, 30–31, 196; lessons learned from, 4–7; objectives of, 2, 28–29; successes of, 29–30, 34
Yemen Peace Project (YPP), 135, 143, 144, 150
Yemen Relief and Reconstruction Organization, 145
Yemen Socialist Party (YSP), 16, 18–20, 26, 53
Young, Todd, 142, 161, 162, 166

Zakani, Ali Reza, 66
Zaydis, 13, 23–25. *See also* Houthi insurgency
Zimmerman, Katherine, 30